WALS

'Hic Niger Est.'

Samuel Crowther, D.D.,

Who began life as a Slave, but, through the grace of God working upon a simple and docile nature, has acquired the honoured reputation of being one of the earliest explorers of a great River, the revealer of several previously unknown Languages, the first Negro Bishop, and the first proof that Equatorial Africa can produce able, enlightened, honest, courteous, and God-fearing men.

Koelle   Schön   Barth

(Portraits and text from R. N. Cust, *A sketch of the modern languages of Africa*, 1883)

WEST AFRICAN LANGUAGE MONOGRAPH SERIES

EDITED BY JOSEPH H. GREENBERG AND JOHN SPENCER

7

THE EARLY STUDY OF NIGERIAN LANGUAGES: ESSAYS AND BIBLIOGRAPHIES

This series of monograph supplements
is issued in connection with The Journal
of West African Languages

THE EARLY STUDY
OF NIGERIAN LANGUAGES:
ESSAYS
AND BIBLIOGRAPHIES

BY

P. E. H. HAIR

CAMBRIDGE

AT THE UNIVERSITY PRESS

IN ASSOCIATION WITH

THE WEST AFRICAN LANGUAGES SURVEY AND THE

INSTITUTE OF AFRICAN STUDIES, IBADAN

1967

PUBLISHED BY

THE SYNDICS OF THE CAMBRIDGE UNIVERSITY PRESS

IN ASSOCIATION WITH THE WEST AFRICAN LANGUAGES SURVEY

AND THE INSTITUTE OF AFRICAN STUDIES, IBADAN

Bentley House, 200 Euston Road, London, N.W.1
American Branch: 32 East 57th Street, New York, N.Y.10022
West African Office: P.O. Box 33, Ibadan, Nigeria

LIBRARY OF CONGRESS CATALOGUE CARD NUMBER

Printed in Great Britain by
Percy Lund, Humphries & Co. Ltd. London and Bradford

I am always sorry when any language is lost, because languages are the pedigree of nations.

> Samuel Johnson in J. Boswell,
> *Journal of a tour to the Hebrides* (1786)

No class of mankind is so narrow-minded and opiniated as the Missionary, except the Linguist: quot homines, tot sententiae.

> R. N. Cust, *A sketch of the modern languages of Africa* (1883)

In a bibliography no judgement of value is to be made. Some of the books and articles here entered may be worthless. However, to the bibliographer every title is important, and to the linguistic student even a bad piece of work may be of use.

> B. Struck, *A linguistic bibliography of Northern Nigeria* (1911–1912)

CONTENTS

PREFACE

The present work has been honoured by publication in the *West African Language Monograph Series*, but it is only fair to the reader to point out, at the start, that it differs from previous publications in the *Series* in one important respect. Earlier publications were written by authors who are linguistic specialists, and were directed to readers who are also linguistic specialists. The present work is written by a historian with no formal linguistic training, and the prose part of the work is intended for the general reader of West African history as much as for the specialist linguist or historian. In particular it is hoped that the essays in this work will be of interest to the African student of West African history, and will, if necessary, introduce him to those fields of study where African history overlaps with African linguistics. One of the fields is the history of the study of West African languages (a field in which as yet only a little work has been done). In this field of study, much attention is paid to the earliest documented material on West African languages: hence, this field serves as a natural approach to another field, that of the history of the distribution and development of West African languages – and this latter field (also as yet little studied) represents probably the most profitable area of research today for the investigation of the earlier history of the West African peoples. If the reader in West Africa is encouraged to look on African linguistics as a study of fundamental importance for African history – apart from its importance in terms of other practical and academic considerations – then one aim of this work will have been fulfilled; and it may be claimed that in encouraging within West Africa further consideration of the value of African linguistics, the work is also fulfilling one of the aims of the West African Languages Survey, the parent of the *Monograph Series*.

The monograph is in the form of three long essays, with accompanying bibliographies. The latter are undeniably directed to specialists and the general reader is invited to skip them. For the linguistic specialist, however, it is hoped that the bibliographies will provide evidence of the modest wealth of earlier material, wealth at least in quantitative terms. If the linguist is induced by both bibliographies and essays to look again at the earlier material, in order to assess it qualitatively in detail, another aim will have been fulfilled. To date, much of the earlier material has been summarily dismissed as 'unsound' or even 'worthless'. This has made the task of the historian of the study of the languages concerned more difficult, not least if he combines no linguistic training with no command of any of the languages. In the essays, judgements on the linguistic value of individual early studies have therefore been kept to a minimum, and there is room for eventual further comment by a specialist who has scrutinised the early works for detailed faults, and insights. Meanwhile, the generalisations offered on the development of West African language studies are merely an attempt to suggest preliminary hypotheses from common sense and general knowledge, with conceivably a trace of coat-trailing here and there. If linguists are persuaded or provoked to turn to the early works and produce judgements controverting these essays, among the edified will be the present author. He would, however, remind linguists that early works may be 'worthless' from the point of view of sound linguistic analysis of contemporary speech forms, and yet may contribute to literary and cultural progress. Many of the pseudo-medieval words coined by Elizabethan poets are still to be found in a modern

English dictionary: their unsoundness as Middle English has not rendered them worthless in modern usage. In the development of written literatures in Africa, uncolloquial, unidiomatic and perhaps even ungrammatical elements in early translations – especially if sanctified in Bible translations – may have affected the growth of the literary dialect. Even a bad, a hopelessly unreadable translation may yet, when it is the first work in a language, provide not only a stimulus to better productions, but a cultural turning point – if the implications for a people of their accession to literacy are immediately realised.

Each of the essays is complete in itself, but as each deals with a language or several languages in Nigeria and each covers in part the same period, the essays are connected through leading characters and episodes. The triple form was adopted in order to clarify the history of individual languages, partly for the benefit of readers particularly interested in a single language, partly because it was felt that the story would be too complicated and diffuse if all the languages were dealt with simultaneously. Some repetition of reference to certain episodes is unavoidable in this form, but an attempt has been made to present the episodes from different angles in the different essays.

Turning to the bibliographies, it is a sad fact that the bibliography of African languages which contains most detail about individual items – detail to an extent comparable with that accepted as standard in scholarly bibliographies of European languages – was produced over a century ago. The great Dr Bleek's catalogue of the splendid collection of Africana at Cape Town belonging to Sir George Grey was printed in 1858. Since that time, the accumulation of material (but seldom in a single library, or even in the libraries of a single continent), the economies prescribed by rising printing costs, and possibly a certain disdain even among learned Africanists for early and ephemeral publications in African languages, have together led to the production of bibliographies in which functional considerations – the practical needs of the missionary or the academic linguist, in the main – have overridden pure bibliographical scholarship. The number of African languages in which all works on or in the language – translations as well as texts, tracts as well as scholarly studies – have been listed is presently well under a dozen.

While the bibliographies in the present work are a move towards the fullness and completeness of Bleek's work, the author is aware that at many points they fall short of these high standards. A single excuse will be offered. Bleek sat in one library and checked and rechecked at will. The present writer has listed items in a dozen libraries, in six cities (two in Africa and four in Britain), during a period of eight years in which opportunity only allowed visits of a few days at a time, at most: and with the best will in the world, it has not always proved possible to return to check items. Nor was it possible to visit Nigeria, although information about certain items was kindly supplied by staff of the University of Ibadan Institute of African Studies, and Library. Professor Ajayi has told the writer that much early Yoruba material is to be found in private libraries at Abeokuta; and no doubt some early Ibo and Ijaw material is similarly to be found in Delta households and churches. One result of the bibliographical investigation has been to show that a surprisingly large amount of early material is not available in the important libraries named; and yet another aim of the monograph is to invite scholars, in Nigeria and outside, to hunt for copies of the untraced early material.

The author remembers with affection his friends, including former colleagues and pupils, in Nigeria and Sierra Leone, among whom his interest in African languages was first aroused. He gratefully acknowledges the access to bibliographical material afforded by the following libraries: British Museum, Cambridge University, Edinburgh University, Liverpool University, School of Oriental and African Studies (London), Fourah Bay College (Freetown), Khartoum University, Scottish National Library, Friends' House Library (London), Liverpool Public Library, Library of the British and Foreign Bible Society: and the information sent to him by the South African Public Library and the University of Ibadan Library. He also acknowledges the access to manuscript material in the Archives of the Church Missionary Society generously permitted by the authorities of the Society and the Archivist: the permission to inspect accessible manuscript material at the British and Foreign Bible Society headquarters: and the kindness of Miss R. Keen, Archivist of C.M.S., and Miss G. E. Coldham, Deputy Librarian of B.F.B.S., in answering inquiries. He is further grateful to linguist friends who at various periods have lent encouragement and assisted in collecting references, especially Professor Robert G. Armstrong and Dr David Dalby: to an understanding editor, John Spencer: and to Margaret Hair for sundry clerking and overall care.

KEY TO THE BIBLIOGRAPHIES

The Yoruba bibliography is in four parts, (a) Early vocabularies, (b) Studies, (c) Translations and other literature, (d) Earlier bibliographies. The other bibliographies are briefer and are therefore not divided into parts, and the section on 'Earlier bibliographies' (on p. 106) applies to all the languages other than Yoruba.

All items have been examined personally, except those starred. All items unstarred, other than Bible translations, are in the British Museum, unless another library is indicated. All Bible translations are in the Library of B.F.B.S., unless another library is indicated.

Items within a bibliography or part of a bibliography are arranged in chronological order by date of publication.

*	An asterisk (after the date) indicates that it has not been possible to trace and examine a copy of the work, and particulars of it are merely copied from another source.
[ ]	Square brackets indicate particulars not supplied on the title-page. Hence:
[date]	no publication date supplied.
[author, or, ?]	anonymous (when anonymous works become common in the later decades, those of unknown authorship are indicated simply by omitting the authorship slot).
[publisher]	no name of publisher supplied.
[place]	no place of publication supplied.
[title]	summary title where full title not known.
C.M.S.	Church Missionary Society.
B.F.B.S.	British and Foreign Bible Society.
S.P.C.K.	Society for the Promotion of Christian Knowledge (a Church of England publishing house).
Author's name	is given first, in full (if known) on its first appearance in the particular bibliography.
Title	is next given, in full as on the title-page for (almost all) works which deal solely with the language concerned (but not for general works), with lines of type shown by strokes (/). But when titles are largely repeated in a series of items, sections of the title are omitted with references back in the form [etc, as previous item]: if the omitted section does not reach to the end of the title, the number of lines omitted is indicated by that number of strokes (////). Further, within a title abbreviation to initials is employed for two terms, Church Missionary Society, and the author's name.

Publisher's name and place of publication are normally given in abbreviated form, and are introduced, if after a full title, by a comma after the last stroke (/,). Commonest abbreviations are – C.M.S., London, which in full is usually, Church Missionary Society (or House), Salisbury Square, London, or, London: Printed for the Church Missionary Society. – B.F.B.S., London, which in full is usually, London: Printed for the British and Foreign Bible Society. Printer's name, even if supplied on the title-page, is normally omitted.

Number of pages is given in the description of contents for all works which deal solely with the language concerned, apart from Bible translations. [pp] indicates that the pages are unnumbered.

Capital letters in titles are employed minimally, at the beginning of words apart from normal English usage and other than first words of a sentence or title only when specifically distinguished in the title: in vernacular titles, capitals have been supplied for personal and divine names when recognised, but not for words meaning 'Holy', 'Gospel', etc., unless specifically distinguished in the title. In the description of contents, a capital letter beginning the first word after a page-reference indicates that the wording is taken from the text (in which case further comment supplied is given in square brackets), but if the description has been supplied by the compiler, the first word begins with a small letter.

Size of format is supplied only for a few very large or very small items.

Vernacular titles, if no full or summary translation was supplied on the title-page, are given a summary in English in the description of contents. In the case of Bible translations, this summary often appears in the work on a page other than the title-page. It is regretted that it has not been possible to provide a full translation of most of the vernacular titles.

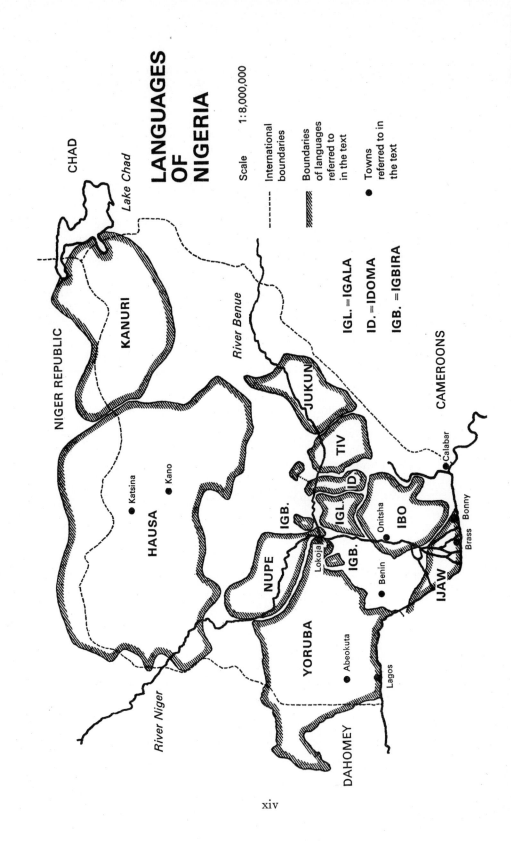

LANGUAGES OF NIGERIA

Scale   1:8,000,000

International boundaries

Boundaries of languages referred to in the text

● Towns referred to in the text

IGL. = IGALA

ID. = IDOMA

IGB. = IGBIRA

CHAD

Lake Chad

NIGER REPUBLIC

KANURI

River Benue

HAUSA

● Katsina

● Kano

NUPE

IGB.

YORUBA

● Abeokuta

● Lagos

DAHOMEY

Lokoja

IGL.

ID.

IGB.

● Benin

JUKUN

TIV

IBO

● Onitsha

IJAW

Bonny

Brass

Calabar

CAMEROONS

River Niger

xiv

INTRODUCTION

Scientific study of the languages of Nigeria – whose number is well over one hundred – only began in the nineteenth century. Though these languages appear to have been spoken, in developing forms, for hundreds and perhaps in some cases thousands of years, in or near the territory where they are spoken today, the vast majority had not been put into writing, and none had been analysed in writing, before 1800.

The study of Nigerian languages since 1800 has had four main results. (a) The outside world has been shown that these languages, like all other human languages, are comprehensive and expressive, while their structures are regular and subtle. (b) Comparison of the languages each to each, and with outside languages, has thrown much light on their history, and hence on the history of the peoples who today speak them. (c) The languages have been put into writing (or in a few cases, given more efficient orthographies), and have acquired written (that is, printed) literatures, most of them very brief but a few fairly extensive. (d) Publication of studies of the languages has enabled persons who do not speak a particular language as their mother-tongue to gain a knowledge of that language more easily than otherwise, occasionally for academic purposes but more often in order to speak the language, and to prepare written material in it, more correctly.

Today, when a great many Nigerians can and do prepare written material in their own mother-tongue, the last result – in general, enabling foreigners to learn and write a Nigerian language – may not seem as important as the other results. But the study of Nigerian languages began with the last result principally in mind. The greater part of the early study was carried out by missionaries from Europe, who studied the languages primarily in order to translate religious material into them, particularly of course the Christian Scriptures. The history of the early study of Nigerian languages is thus closely connected with the history of Christian missions in Nigeria.

From the 1840s, important work on the Efik (Ibibio) language was carried out by the Scottish Presbyterian mission at Calabar. Later in the century, useful material in Yoruba and Ibo was prepared by the Methodist and Roman Catholic missions. But the earliest, most thorough, most extensive, and most effective linguistic research was that, covering a dozen or so languages, undertaken by agents of the Church Missionary Society, a society founded and supported by Evangelical members of the established Church of England. As it happens, the records of this society and its missions are more easily available than those of other societies and missions, and a section of the C.M.S. Archives in London has been examined by the present writer. This monograph therefore concentrates upon the early study of about a dozen Nigerian languages, all of which received their main study from agents of C.M.S. The sound and detailed study of Efik by the Scottish mission is not included in this monograph: it requires and deserves separate attention.[1] Apart from this, all formal study of Nigerian languages up to about 1890 is covered.[2]

---

[1] Though it could perhaps be conveniently studied together with the early study of languages on the coast to the east and south east of Calabar, i.e. with the work of the missionaries Clarke, Merrick and Saker on Bubi and Duala, and of Wilson and other American missionaries on Mpongwe and other languages of Gabon.

[2] Except the study of Fula, a language extending far outside Nigeria, whose early study began with the dialects spoken in Senegal and in the Futa Jallon, north of Sierra Leone.

The Church Missionary Society operated in West, East and North Nigeria, and studied languages of all these parts. Up to the 1850s, however, the West African base of the society was not in Nigeria, but at Freetown, in Sierra Leone. The first C.M.S. missionaries to Nigeria came there from Freetown, and the earliest work on several Nigerian languages was carried out at Freetown. As is well known, in the early nineteenth century the population of Freetown consisted largely of liberated slaves, and a large proportion of these slaves had come from the territory that is now Nigeria. Thus, in early nineteenth century Freetown, many inhabitants spoke a Nigerian language as their mother-tongue, and missionaries who decided to study a particular Nigerian language had no difficulty in finding informants in Freetown (or in the neighbouring villages of the Sierra Leone peninsula).

The scientific study of a language may be divided, on the simplest analysis, into two parts; first, the collection of words to form a vocabulary or a dictionary; second, the investigation of the ways in which words are shaped, transformed, and grouped to indicate particular thoughts, to form a grammar of the language. Early work on a language generally terminated in the production of a dictionary and a grammar. But the earliest students of Nigerian languages faced a preliminary problem before they could begin any detailed study. They had to discover what languages existed; and further – because so many were found and their research capacity was limited – how extensive geographically, and important socially, each language was. Only when they had acquired at least some idea on these points, could they decide to study a particular language. The very earliest work done on Nigerian languages was therefore the attempt to discover what languages existed within this area of Africa. Occasionally information about the existence and distribution of languages could be obtained from Africans who had travelled within the area or who were otherwise knowledgeable, but information obtained in this way was usually of limited reliability. In general, therefore, the discovery of a Nigerian language by outside students began with the collection of a very brief vocabulary – often only the numerals – which could be compared with words in other languages, in order to determine, even if only very roughly, whether the language of the vocabulary was the same as any previously known language, or an addition to the list of African languages.

The earliest information about Nigerian languages to reach Europe was gathered around 1500: a handful of words in languages of South Nigeria was collected by Portuguese visitors to the coast, while a little information about some of the peoples of North Nigeria appeared in Leo Africanus' printed account of the Northern parts of West Africa. But no systematic interest in Nigerian languages was shown by Europeans during the early centuries of European contact – just as none was shown by North Africans or Arabs during a millenium of contact – and the scraps of information that became available were not put together until around 1800. The first detailed study of all known African languages was published in 1812, and in this work brief vocabularies of six Nigerian languages were printed.[3] The languages were Hausa, Kanuri, Fula, Ibo, Ijaw and Ibibio, but so little was known about them that most of them were referred to under misleading or incorrect names. It was the task of the missionaries to identify fully these and other Nigerian languages, and to study them in detail.

The first essay in this monograph deals with the study of the Yoruba language up to the 1850s, when the study moved from Freetown to Yorubaland itself. Within the last

---

[3] J. C. Adelung and J. S. Vater, *Mithridates oder allgemeine Sprachenkunde*, Berlin, vol. 3, 1812.

few years, the first generation of Yoruban professional historians and linguists has begun to research into all aspects of the history of the Yoruba people and language. The detailed history of Yoruba studies in Yorubaland after the 1850s may be appropriately left to these sons of the language, but the accompanying bibliography provides a framework for research by listing Yoruba material up to 1890. The second essay deals with the early study of two main languages of North Nigeria, Hausa and Kanuri, beginning with the discovery of the languages by academic linguists, and continuing with the careers of two Freetown missionaries, Schön and Koelle, who were respectively the founders of Hausa and Kanuri studies. The third essay turns to the languages of the lower Niger and Benue, of which the most widely spoken and intensively studied language is Ibo. In this essay, attention is especially paid to the linguistic work of the controversial Niger Mission, whose agents were mainly Sierra Leoneans. Their work represented the final link between Freetown and the early study of Nigerian languages.

1

THE EARLY STUDY OF YORUBA, 1825–1850

The Yoruba language possesses today one of the most prolific vernacular literatures of that part of Africa – the southern and western two-thirds – where languages traditionally of African origin are still spoken. Yet a century and a half ago, the Yoruba language was not only unwritten (as, indeed, were the vast majority of African languages at that date), but was not even known to the language scholars of the world. Whereas most other widely-spoken African languages had had substantial vocabularies collected and put into print during the seventeenth and eighteenth centuries,[1] the earliest collection of Yoruba words in print dates only from 1819: collected in Ashanti by the English diplomatic agent, Bowdich, in 1817 and printed in his account of this mission, the vocabulary consists only of the numerals. The name of the language is here given as 'Hio', but in the course of the account, mention is made of a state immediately neighbouring the kingdom of Hio, the kingdom of 'Yariba'.[2] This was almost the earliest appearance in print[3] of the term which later came to be used, by speakers of the language as well as by foreigners, to describe all dialects of the language.[4]

One reason for the late appearance of the Yoruba language in print is that Yorubaland was not regularly or extensively visited by Europeans until the nineteenth century. The Portuguese, who dominated Afro-European contacts in West Africa during the period 1450–1630, concentrated their efforts on neighbouring territories, Gold Coast to the west, Benin to the east, and had little to do with even coastal Yorubaland. Though Ijebu town was occasionally visited, trade was slight there; and for information about

---

[1] To give West African examples only: Akan in 1602, Ewe in 1658, Duala in 1665, Jolof in 1732, Malinke in 1732, Fula in 1732, Ibo in 1777, Hausa in 1790.

[2] T. E. Bowdich, *Mission . . . to Ashantee*, 1819, pp. 209, 505.

[3] Bowdich wrote – 'a large kingdom called Yariba by the Moors, but Yarba more generally by the natives'. Bowdich's 'Moors' were Hausa, who today call the Yoruba Yarabāwā/Yarbāwā (R. C. Abraham, *Dictionary of the Hausa language*, 1946). Bowdich added that 'Yariba must certainly be the Yarba of Imhammed', i.e., the place-name mentioned by an Arabic-speaking North African trader who supplied information about Hausaland and neighbouring territories to an agent of the African Association in 1789. If the identification is correct, then the earliest appearance in print of the term was in 1790, when the agent's report was printed (*Proceedings of the Association for promoting the discovery of the interior parts of Africa*, London, 1790, p. 224). But there is some slight doubt about the identification, since the location of 'Yarba' was given as 18–20 days to the north-west of Gonja, whereas Yorubaland lies due east (and hence, on maps produced between 1790 and 1819, 'Yarba' was not given the position of Yorubaland).

[4] 'The Missionaries . . . ought to search after the proper national name of the whole Aku country. For the last few years they have very erroneously made use of the name 'Yórùbá' in reference to the whole nation . . . [But] if you call an Ijebuan or a Yagban a Yoruban, he will always tell you, "Don't call me by that name, I am not a Yoruban", just as the Wurtembergians or Bavarians would never suffer themselves to be called Prussians (S. W. Koelle, *Polyglotta Africana*, 1854, p. 5; Koelle was a Wurtemberger). Apparently the Oyo (i.e. Eyo, Hio) by 1850 accepted the name Yoruba, while other sections accepted it in colonial times. It is possible that 'Yoruba' was originally a stranger's name (like the now-accepted names for many African peoples), and that this helped it to be accepted, eventually, by the various sections of the Yoruba as an overall name. Since it was first applied to a section near the Niger, it was perhaps first used among the northern neighbours of the Yoruba. It would be of interest to know if the name appeared in any Sudano-Arabic source before the much quoted reference in Mohammed Bello, *c.* 1820 (see T. Hodgkin, *Nigerian Perspectives*, 1960, p. 58).

the further interior, the Portuguese relied on inquiries made at Benin.[5] The Dutch and British who followed the Portuguese to the Guinea coast developed the Niger Delta trade, particularly at New Calabar and Bonny, and the trade at (Old) Calabar on the Cross River. The French in the later seventeenth century developed trade on the Eweland coast, at Whydah and the Popos, and in the later eighteenth century attempted to resuscitate the Benin River trade. Only towards 1800 did white traders, Portuguese, Spanish, British and North-American in the main, begin direct and extensive activities on the Yoruba coast. But these activities soon produced drastic results: the Yoruba coast came to be, between 1800 and 1850, one of the major centres for the export of slaves from Western Africa. And Yorubaland, which had previously exported only a trickle of slaves through Benin and Eweland ports, now provided a large proportion of the human cargo in the whole Atlantic trade.[6]

Because there was no Yoruba vocabulary in print, the language was not mentioned in the earliest book to discuss African languages in detail, a study by two German scholars of all the known languages of the world, whose volume on African languages appeared in 1812.[7] From the little that was then known of Yorubaland, the existence of a single widely-spoken language between Ewe ('Popo') and Benin could hardly be guessed at. Kingdoms of Ijebu, of 'Oedobo' (? Oyo), of 'the Ogane' (? the Oghene, or Oni of Ife), were named in Portuguese and Dutch accounts between 1500 and 1700, but with few details and none regarding language.[8] Slaves from Yorubaland were known on the other side of the Atlantic first as 'Locumi' (the earliest use of this term in print appears to be in 1627), and then in the eighteenth century as 'Nago'.[9] Accounts of Dahomey in English in the later eighteenth century referred to the neighbouring kingdom of Hio or Eyo (i.e. Oyo).[10] Confusion over these various names obscured Yoruba unity.

Yoruba-speaking slaves were to be met with in the Americas from at least the seventeenth century. Though their numbers were relatively small before 1800, it is still curious that the first general collection of West African vocabularies, which was collected from slaves in the West Indies in the 1760s, while it contained vocabularies of Akan, Ewe, Ibo, and Ibibio, had no Yoruba.[11] It is just possible that a vocabulary of

---

[5] Around 1505, the coast east of the Lagos River was described as 'difficult to know', and the coast west as 'without trade and profit', and both as 'hot and unhealthy', though some trade at Ijebu was noted (Duarte Pacheco Pereira, *Esmeraldo de situ orbis*, book 2, chapter 7, Bissau edition 1956, pp. 130, 132). In the next century, a Dutch work of 1625 describing the Guinea coast simply stated that from River Lagos to the Benin River there was 'no trade' (D. Ruiters, *Toortse der Zeevaert*, 1913 edition, p. 77).

[6] P. D. Curtin and J. Vansina, 'Sources of the nineteenth century Atlantic slave trade', *Journal of African History*, 5, 1964, pp. 185–208, especially p. 190.

[7] J. C. Adelung and J. S. Vater, *Mithridates oder allgemeine Sprachenkunde . . .*, vol. 2/1, Berlin, 1812.

[8] Pacheco Pereira, *op. cit.*, book 2, chapter 7; J. de Barros, *Asia*, Decade 1, book 3, quoted in Hodgkin, *op. cit.*, pp. 96–7; O. Dapper, *Naukeurige Beschrijvinge der Afrikaensche Gewesten . . .*, 1668, p. 125.

[9] Alonso de Sandoval, *Naturaleza . . . de todos Etiopes*, Sevilla, 1627, lib. 1, cap. 1, f 7r; cap. 16, f. 59v, 66r; G. Aguirre Beltran, *La poblacion negra de Mexico 1519–1810*, 1946, p. 132 ('Locumi'); P. F. X. de Charlevoix, *Histoire de l'Isle Espagnole . . .*, 1733, vol. 4, p. 362 ('Nagos, les plus humains'); Moreau de Saint Mery, *Description de la partie francaise de l'Île de Saint-Domingue* (1797), 1958 edition, vol. 1, p. 50 ('Nagos'). Unfortunately, Sandoval's work was not known to later seventeenth and eighteenth century writers on Guinea; it could have been deduced from his list of Guinea coast peoples, that the 'Locumi' were the only people between Popo and Benin.

[10] E.g. A. Dalzel, *The History of Dahomey*, 1793, pp. xv ff.

[11] G. C. A. Oldendorp, *Geschichte der Mission der Evangelischen Brüder auf den Caraibischen Inseln . . .*, Barby, 1777, pp. 271–91 and table opposite p. 346.

Yoruba pre-dating Bowdich's may yet be discovered among unpublished manuscript sources, and the most likely location would be in the Caribbean or Brazilian archives. As we have noted, from the 1790s Yoruba slaves began to be exported in large numbers. Hence, when the British Navy after 1807 endeavoured to suppress the Atlantic trade by capturing slave-ships, and when a large number of the slaves thus liberated were re-settled at Freetown, the African language most widely spoken among these liberated slaves was Yoruba – or 'Aku' as it was called at Freetown.[12] It was at Freetown, a thousand miles away from Yorubaland, but using members of the Aku community as informants, that Yoruba studies began.

*   *   *

After the Bowdich numerals of 1819 which introduced linguists to the language, the next vocabularies of Yoruba to appear in print were collected by Mrs Kilham (published 1828), by Clapperton (1829) and by Raban (1830–1832). Of these three, only Clapperton collected his material in Yorubaland: he appears to have been the first person to write down Yoruba within its homeland, and he called the language, perhaps decisively, 'Yourriba'. However, Clapperton's material was neither as full nor as analytical as the material produced by Mrs Kilham and Raban, both of whom worked in Freetown.

Mrs Hannah Kilham was a Quaker educationalist and one of the first Europeans to recommend the education of Africans in their vernaculars.[13] A woman of outstanding courage, vision and humanity, she published in 1828 a collection of vocabularies of thirty African languages which she had assembled while living in Sierra Leone in 1827–8. In the introduction to this volume, Mrs Kilham noted that, as regards the vocabulary of 'Aku, the writer had the kind assistance of two of the Missionaries who furnished most of the words and sentences . . . having taken them down chiefly from the dictation of one of the young men educated in the Mission schools.' 'The Missionaries' referred to were the agents of the Church Missionary Society in Freetown and district, with whom, despite conflicting denominational loyalties,[14] Mrs Kilham enjoyed

---

[12] 'Aku, or rather 'Oku, is a mode of salutation among all the [Yoruba-speaking] tribes' (Koelle, *op. cit.*, p. 5); but cf. 'They were called Akus because of the way they greeted, which also shows that up till then [the 1820s] the majority of them were Oyo, since it is the Oyo-Yoruba who greet in this way' (J. F. A. Ajayi, *Christian missions in Nigeria 1841–1891*, 1965, p. 21). Aku appears to have been normally pronounced a ku, but occasionally e ku. According to Abraham, *op. cit.*, p. 367, the greeting given by a younger to an older person in Yoruba is ọọ ku or ẹẹ ku, either of which might have given rise to 'Aku'. But there are other greetings which begin e ku, and which might give rise to the second pronunciation of 'Aku'. The term may therefore represent a general impression of all these greetings.

[13] On Mrs Kilham (born 1774 and therefore in her fifties when visiting Freetown), see *Dictionary of National Biography*; [S. Biller], *Memoir of the late Hannah Kilham . . .* , London, 1837; P. E. H. Hair, 'A bibliographical note on Hannah Kilham's linguistic work', *Journal of the Friends' Historical Society*, 49, 1960, pp. 165–8; O. Greenwood, 'Hannah Kilham's plan', *Sierra Leone Bulletin of Religion*, 4, 1962, pp. 9–22, 61–71. Mrs Kilham's most notable proposal was for a linguistic institute in England, where selected Africans could study their languages, in order to put them into writing and to prepare translations of religious material; she proposed this in 1819 and again in 1829.

[14] However, Mrs Kilham's African schemes failed to win support from the generality of Quakers who disapproved of 'missionary' religious enterprises. In 1830, she travelled out to Freetown with four returning C.M.S. missionaries, but with no Quaker colleague.

excellent relations, as the published selections from her diary show:[15] one of the two missionaries interested in Yoruba was almost certainly the Reverend John Raban (Mrs Kilham's 'esteemed friend', according to her step-daughter),[16] author of the first book on Yoruba: and the young Yoruba-speaking informant may well have been Samuel (Ajai) Crowther,[17] who was to become the founding father of Yoruba written literature.

When Raban was sent to Freetown in 1825, he was instructed by the C.M.S. authorities to collect linguistic information.[18] His letters and reports during the years 1825–36, preserved in the C.M.S. Archives,[19] frequently refer to the collection of vocabularies, though no linguistic material appears to have been sent to the mission headquarters. A manuscript collection of vocabularies of nine West African languages, now in the South African Public Library, which includes a vocabulary of 'Ackoo', was probably collected during these years, at least in part by Raban.[20] In 1827, the Christian Institution – the forerunner of Fourah Bay College – was moved from an outlying village to a site nearer Freetown, and thereafter Raban made use of the students as informants. He lived in the Institution for a period, and in 1831–2 acted as principal. One of the students during 1827–8 was Samuel Crowther,[21] whom Raban had baptised in 1825:[22] on leaving the

[15] Unfortunately, the manuscript of Mrs Kilham's diary has not yet been traced, and few of her letters are extant, while the published *Memoir* gives only extracts from the diary on occasional dates. This makes it difficult to study her activities in Freetown in detail. The journals of the missionaries in Freetown at the appropriate dates would no doubt help to fill some of the gaps, but the present writer has had the opportunity to examine only a sample of these rather extensive records.

[16] 'An Anglican missionary to whom she was much attached' (Greenwood, *op. cit.*, p. 65). The other missionary was John Weeks, at whose home in Regent village she lived during this visit, and who took her to other villages in search of informants (Biller, *op. cit.*, p. 327). Weeks suggested the arrangement of her book, whereby all the languages were represented on each page, and she returned to England with him and his wife. While Weeks is named in the diary extracts relating to this visit, Raban is not.

[17] After his arrival in Sierra Leone as a liberated slave, Crowther lived for a time with the Weeks (see previous footnote), learning carpentry. He was therefore known to both of Mrs Kilham's missionary friends, a circumstance which makes it likely that he was the Yoruba-speaking informant.

[18] Apart from his Freetown experience, little is known about Raban. An Englishman (not a German, as stated by J. F. A. Ajayi, 'How Yoruba was reduced to writing', *Odu: journal of Yoruba studies*, 1961, pp. 49–58, on p. 49), he seems not to have been a university graduate. His letters give the impression that he was a man of independent means. His later career is not known, but he was still alive in 1846 (according to a letter from J. F. Schön in the C.M.S. Archives, CA 1/o 195, letter of 21.12.1846).

[19] C.M.S. Archives, section CA 1/o 180.

[20] For a description of this manuscript, see W. H. I. Bleek, *Catalogue of the Library of Sir George Grey*, vol. 1, London and Leipzig, 1858, p. 205, item 410. The manuscript was given to Bleek at Freetown in 1854 by C. F. Schlenker, and it has been previously assumed that the vocabularies were collected by Schlenker in the 1840s. But the orthography (e.g. Ackoo, Hebo) suggests that the vocabularies were collected by a linguist less sophisticated than Schlenker, probably at a much earlier date than the 1840s. I have compared a photostat of part of a page of the manuscript with material in the C.M.S. Archives written by Schlenker, Raban and other Freetown linguists. But the manuscript is written in a conventional copying hand which neither the Archivist (whose cooperation and assistance in this exercise is gratefully acknowledged) nor myself could decisively identify. It is unlike Schlenker's letter-writing hand. It is not unlike Raban's, but not sufficiently alike to rule out the possibility that the manuscript was copied by a clerk or an unidentified colleague. The spelling 'Ackoo' may provide a clue: in 1830, Raban publicised the spelling 'Aku', and it is difficult to believe that at a later date any Freetown collector would have introduced the unnecessary consonant. Perhaps, therefore, this is a collection of the late 1820s, putting together material collected by Raban and by his assistants. Close study of the orthography of the African terms throughout the manuscript might clear up the matter.

[21] Crowther was one of the first year of students at the Institution; that his was the first name on the roll is perhaps only a pious legend.

[22] Ajayi, *op. cit.* (1965), p. 26.

Institute, Crowther worked as a teacher in the mission schools, and in 1831 he was transferred to a district over which Raban had pastoral supervision. It is certain that Raban knew Crowther well, and likely that Crowther soon became one of Raban's Yoruba informants.

Since the 1790s, missionaries at Freetown had worked on individual African languages, especially Temne, Bullom and Susu, languages of the Freetown hinterland;[23] but Raban was the first missionary to be entrusted with the general task of collecting information about the many languages spoken, in and about Freetown, not only by the original inhabitants but also by the liberated slaves. In missionary correspondance, Raban was described as 'charged with the study of Native Languages',[24] and though he never went very far with this general study, we know that vocabularies of Temne and Hausa he collected (or compiled, for he sometimes put together vocabularies collected by colleagues or assistants) were found to be useful by later students of these languages. However, by 1830, Raban was wearying of this labour, and he wrote to England – 'I have come to the conclusion that it will be better to confine myself to *one* or *two* languages. . . . The two which have been pointed out to me as particularly important . . . are the A-ku and the I-bo'.[25] In naming the two most widely-spoken languages of Southern Nigeria, Raban was unconsciously forecasting a connection between Freetown and the study of Nigerian languages which was to last for the rest of the century. But when he began his intensive study, Raban chose to study only one of the two, 'Aku' or Yoruba.

We have seen that a large proportion of the liberated Africans at Freetown were Yoruba, and Raban believed that it was not only in numbers that the Yoruba excelled. 'Another reason', he wrote, 'for cultivating the A-ku (or E-yoh) is that the people who speak it are thought to be superior in intellect to most of the other tribes located in Sierra Leone.'[26] Perhaps another reason for selecting Yoruba was that Mrs Kilham had already developed a special interest in the language, as shown by the fact that she added to her 1828 collection of vocabularies, brief grammatical examples in two languages, Bassa (Liberia) and 'Aku'. In 1831, she started a school for girls at Charlotte village, and planned to carry out the revolutionary educational experiment of conducting instruction partly in African vernaculars. The languages she selected for use in instruction were 'Kossa' (i.e. Mende, a language of the Sierra Leone hinterland) and 'Aku'. It was in 'Aku' that the first vernacular lessons were given, and on the 29th of August, 1831, Mrs Kilham wrote in her diary: 'I would not close this day without acknowledging Thy goodness, O my heavenly Father, in permitting me to see the desire of my heart in the instruction of dear African children through their own languages. The trial was not made until the Aku girls were brought last week; yet, even now, the success exceeds my hopes.'[27]

Raban's choice of Yoruba may therefore have been made on the advice of Mrs Kilham, and perhaps in the expectation that she would collaborate with him in the work. In 1830, they travelled out to Freetown on the same ship, and in 1831 he referred to 'a list of words obtained in the Colony by Mrs Kilham and myself'.[28] Several of

---

[23] P. E. H. Hair, 'The Sierra Leone settlement – the earliest attempts to study African languages', *Sierra Leone Language Review*, 2, 1963, pp. 5–10.

[24] C.M.S. Archives, CA 1/o 180, letter of 10.3.1830.

[25] *ibid.* It may be significant that at this stage Raban adopted Mrs Kilham's spelling, A-ku (and I-bo).

[26] *ibid.*

[27] Biller, *op. cit.*, p. 423.

[28] C.M.S. Archives, CA 1/o 50, report of 22.3.1831.

Raban's mission colleagues, however, also helped him with the collecting of words.[29] Raban suffered from recurrent ill-health, and returned to England for months at a time almost annually: while in England, he arranged the publication of his Yoruba material, and three booklets appeared in print, in 1830, 1831, and 1832. The prefaces do not indicate that Mrs Kilham gave any assistance,[30] and Raban's orthography differed from hers. On the other hand, in his 1831 volume Raban expressed the hope that he would soon be able to begin the translation of the Scriptures into Yoruba, and we may deduce that Mrs Kilham had been pressing him since she disappointedly noted in her diary, at the very end of the same year, that 'the only stationary member of the mission appointed to the work [of African language study and translation] does not see the means of it being at present carried forward to the extent necessary, on account of the deficiency of agents.'[31] It would seem therefore that Raban had been encouraged in his Yoruba studies, if not assisted, by Mrs Kilham: and it may be more than a coincidence that after 1832, the year in which Mrs Kilham died (at sea, off Liberia), Raban published nothing further.

Raban's tiny books (they add up to just over one hundred pages, and are of vest-pocket size) were the first volumes on any single Nigerian language, as well as the first volumes on Yoruba. They basically consist of a series of vocabularies, as their title indicates, supplemented by a few grammatical remarks. The slight attempts to grasp the structure of the language are groping and rather feeble,[32] though they do show some awareness of the complexity of the investigation and the need for a systematic approach. Raban himself modestly but correctly entitled one section of one book, 'Gleanings for Grammar'. The work is more to be commended as 'a pioneering attempt at evolving a system of orthography' for Yoruba, as Professor Ajayi has suggested.[33] And further, the contents of the books were perhaps not Raban's greatest contribution to Yoruba studies: this lay rather in the effect his activities, including the publication of the books, had on the young Yoruba schoolteacher, Samuel Crowther.

We do not know if Raban continued his Yoruba studies between 1832 and 1836 when he finally left Freetown. But we hear of a slowly spreading circle of interest in Yoruba studies in Freetown in the later 1830s and early 1840s. At the lowliest level of interest, a young English clerk collected a short vocabulary of 'Akoo' and inserted it in an account of Freetown he published in 1836.[34] At a higher level, several German and English missionaries attempted to learn the language and to translate religious material into it. But these attempts probably did not begin before 1840: after Raban left, a committee of Freetown missionaries reported to London that 'the fixing of the Akoo

---

[29] *ibid.* A colleague, W. K. Betts, collected 'some Eyo', and more came from pupils at the Christian Institute. A mission schoolteacher, Henry Graham, who during 1830 worked under Raban collecting vocabularies, obtained 200 words. C.M.S. Archives, CA 1/o 180, letter of 27.1.1831.

[30] She may, however, have asked for her name not to be mentioned: all her African language books were published anonymously.

[31] Biller, *op. cit.*, p. 462. By 'agents', Mrs Kilham presumably meant informants who were capable of helping with translational activity.

[32] It has been said that Raban commented on the need for tonal accents (Ajayi, *op. cit.* (1961), p. 49). On my reading, Raban looked only for stress (as in European languages) and, like other students of African languages at this date, had no realisation of the function of tonality.

[33] Ajayi, *op. cit.*, (1961), p. 49.

[34] F. H. Rankin, *The White Man's Grave* ..., London, 1836, pp. 232, 316–8. Vocabulary collecting appears to have been a popular hobby in Freetown in the 1830s; a visitor met 'Mr Pratt, in charge of the stores for liberated Africans, from whom I procured vocabularies of many of the languages of Western Africa' (J. A. Alexander, *Narrative of a voyage* ..., 1837, vol. 1, p. 115).

language in which Brother Raban had been engaged, appeared to be not so desirable'
as had been formerly thought, since the liberated Africans were rapidly learning
English.[35] Instead, attention was directed to the language of the tribespeople around
Freetown, Temne, and a mission station was set up at Port Loko in Temneland. Spasmodic attempts to study the Temne language had been made since the 1790s, and in
the early 1830s Raban had given some assistance to the principal of the Christian
Institution, C. F. Haensel, a notable student of Temne.[36] We know that at some time
in his early life, Samuel Crowther attempted to learn Temne,[37] and this may have been
another result of his acquaintance with Raban. In any case, Crowther's attention to
Temne, however brief and superficial, probably marked the beginning of his scholarly
interest in African languages; for while he may have acted earlier as an informant in his
native language, this would not necessarily be as intellectually stimulating an activity as
that of endeavouring to acquire a strange, unstudied language. The decision to transfer
the weight of linguistic effort from Yoruba to Temne was a reasonable one when it was
taken in 1838: time was to show that the missionaries were right in supposing that the
Freetown community of liberated slaves was acquiring English and forgetting its
ancestral African languages. For a moment, therefore, it seemed that Freetown language
studies would serve mainly the Sierra Leone hinterland, and not further Africa.

Around 1840, however, the situation radically changed. The British government's
decision to send an expedition to the Niger, together with appeals from Christian converts who had returned from Freetown to their original homes in Yorubaland, drew the
attention of the C.M.S. to the lands around the lower Niger, and it was decided to send
missionaries from Freetown both on the Niger expedition and to Yorubaland.[38]
J. F. Schön, a German missionary in the Sierra Leone peninsula who had recently
resumed the study of the neighbouring Bullom language begun thirty years earlier by
his father-in-law, G. R. Nyländer, was ordered to drop his Bullom studies and to learn
instead two Niger languages, Ibo and Hausa. (Schön's subsequent study of these
languages will be a central theme of the other essays in this monograph.) Another
German missionary, J. U. Graf, in 1841 was reported to be learning Yoruba, though he
apparently never went far with the study.[39] More lasting were the Yoruba studies of an
English missionary, Henry Townsend, who began them (it seems) before he left
Freetown for Yorubaland in 1842. To a work written in 1842, Townsend contributed
an amount of material on 'Akoo': a brief vocabulary and a list of personal names with
their meanings, three proverbs, two texts of about six sentences each, and a song with
the words and tune supplied.[40] The last item is the most interesting as it represents the

---

[35] C.M.S. Archives, CA 1/o 3, report of 10.1.1838.

[36] Hair, op. cit. (1963), p. 8: C.M.S. Archives, CA 1/o 108, journal of Haensel, entry for 11.12.33 (also
printed in Missionary Register, 1834, p. 338) – this refers to Raban's orthography for Temne.

[37] Ajayi, op. cit. (1961), p. 51.

[38] Described in detail in two recent works: Ajayi, op. cit. (1965), chapters 1–2; J. H. Kopytoff, A
preface to modern Nigeria: the Sierra Leonians in Yoruba 1830–90, 1965, chapter 3.

[39] Church Missionary Record, 1842, p. 229. Up to the 1840s, a large proportion of the missionary
clergy of the C.M.S. in West Africa were men of German birth and nationality; the requirement of
learning and working in a second language, together with their share of the contemporary German
respect for diligent, exotic scholarship, no doubt goes some way to explain why the Germans produced
not only more but better works on West African languages than their English colleagues.

[40] Robert Clarke, Sierra Leone . . . , London, n.d. (Preface dated 1843: from internal evidence, the
text was completed during 1842), pp.154–61. How original this material is, it is difficult to say.
Townsend may well have borrowed some of it from manuscripts circulating in Freetown. The song
presumably also came from Townsend, though Clarke omitted to say so.

earliest attempt to record Yoruba music in print.[41] A third European who began work on Yoruba was another German, C. A. Gollmer: probably he began only in early 1844, but before he left Freetown for Yorubaland at the end of the same year, he announced that he had translated the Lord's Prayer, the Decalogue and the first two chapters of the Gospel of Matthew.[42]

The resumption of Yoruba studies at Freetown in the early 1840s particularly affected the handful of educated Africans there who were Yoruba-speaking. Ten years earlier, Raban had blamed the slowness of progress on 'the deficiency of agents', meaning – we suppose – a lack of Africans capable of, or interested in, undertaking Yoruba studies. The extent to which Yoruba-speaking members of the Freetown community took pride in their tribal traditions or language before the 1840s is not known;[43] though a reference in 1836 to a 'Liberated African at Macaulay Island [in Gambia] instructing his countrymen in Accou'[44] might indicate a growing awareness among dispersed Yoruba that their language was capable of being employed to modern ends in the civilised world. By the 1840s at least, among the growing class of educated Africans in Freetown, there was a small group of Yoruba-speakers eager to study the language and produce literature in it. One of these men was Thomas King, who later joined Crowther in Yorubaland:[45] but the most distinguished was of course Crowther himself. Unfortunately we do not know exactly when Crowther decided to undertake a full study of his mother-tongue,[46] but it was most probably in 1840, when he was selected to accompany Schön on the Niger Expedition. Together with Schön, he was expected to learn Hausa for use on the expedition; and we may guess that it was in the course of his daily contact with the better-educated and linguistically more experienced German, in Freetown and during the expedition, that he was inspired to prepare the grammar and vocabulary of Yoruba which, after the failure of the expedition and his return to Freetown, was published in 1843.[47] Schön and Crowther remained friends and collaborators

---

[41] D'Avezac wrote down some Yoruba tunes in 1839–40, but his essay which included these did no reach print until 1845. Bowdich recorded Akan tunes in his work of 1819.

[42] [C. H. V. Gollmer], *Charles Andrew Gollmer: his life and missionary labours in West Africa, by his eldest son*, 1889, p. 12; *C. M. Record*, 1845, p. 36.

[43] There is no doubt that the 'Aku' regarded themselves as to some extent a separate group, since they had leaders ('chiefs', later a 'king') who were recognised by government. In 1834, 'a regular war' broke out between Aku villagers in part of the peninsula and their Ibo neighbours. But in 1830 it was reported that the Aku were handing over their 'idols' to the missionaries, evidence that interest in traditional religion was fading. Further, it has to be remembered that the very idea of the unity of the Yoruba-speaking peoples was a novelty; 'only in Sierra Leone were all the children of Oduduwa, the Yoruba ancestor-god, united' (C. Fyfe, *History of Sierra Leone*, 1962, pp. 120, 172, 186, 233, 292).

[44] *Missionary Register*, 1836, p. 17.

[45] *C. M. Record*, 1847, p. 197.

[46] The long awaited biography of Crowther by Professor Ajayi, based on an unrivalled knowledge of the C.M.S. Archives and the Crowther family papers, will doubtless clear up this point, as well as those other points in Crowther's career where knowledge is at present lacking. The semi-official life of Crowther, Jesse Page, *The Black Bishop*, London, 1910, is naturally of limited value, and the fullest study to date of at least the later part of Crowther's career is to be found in Ajayi, *op. cit.* (1965). The earlier life, especially the years in Freetown, have as yet had little attention in published works. Crowther was born *c*.1806, and was therefore a man of middle age, by African standards, when he transferred his activities from Sierra Leone to Nigeria.

[47] As late as 1841, Crowther was content to use the accepted but crude spelling 'Yarriba' ('A second narrative of Samuel Ajayi Crowther's early life', *Bulletin of the Society for African Church History*, 2, 1965, pp. 5–14); but his 1843 work introduced the form 'Yoruba'. This may be taken as an indication of the way his linguistic interest ripened in these years. In connection with Crowther's first

—Continued on following page

for nearly fifty years, a period during which each worked persistently on African language studies, even in extreme old age. Schön had a hand in most of Crowther's publications, sometimes advising on linguistic points and amending texts, often arranging material for publication, almost always proof-reading; and this assistance was given, probably on his wish, without acknowledgement in print.

Schön and Crowther joined the Niger Expedition when its ships reached Freetown. Between Freetown and Cape Coast, Schön translated into Hausa an 'Address to the Chiefs and People of Africa': the same address, in a Yoruba translation, appeared in Crowther's 1843 volume, and no doubt this too was prepared aboard ship: it was probably Crowther's first long piece of translation into Yoruba. However, when the linguists reached the Niger, it was discovered that, though dialects of Yoruba were spoken at one point (on the west bank, near the confluence with the Benue, where the station of Lokoja was later established), Yoruba was not an important language on the river.

Meanwhile, Henry Townsend, travelling with a Yoruba-speaking Sierra Leonean, Andrew Wilhelm,[48] during early 1843 made a missionary reconnaissance of Abeokuta, one of the largest interior towns of Yorubaland and capital of the Egba section. He was so well received that the C.M.S. resolved to establish a mission in Yorubaland. Samuel Crowther, on his return from the Niger, was summoned to England and, after training, ordained as a priest; and in 1843 he was able to see his book on Yoruba through the press. Thus the C.M.S. now had available both a Yoruba-speaking priest, and a printed study of the language to enable European agents to learn it more easily and effectively. In 1844, the C.M.S. Yoruba Mission was inaugurated.[49] Once this mission was under way, Yoruba studies moved from Freetown to Yorubaland.

*   *   *

Before 1844, only one important piece of work on Yoruba had been done outside the Freetown circle of linguists. Two brief vocabularies of the language, collected in Brazil in 1833 and 1839, were of interest only in that they were collected from Yoruba-speaking slaves.[50] But another Yoruba slave in Brazil was carried by his master to Paris where he attracted the attention of a French savant, d'Avezac; in 1839, this Yoruba, Osifekunde (or Osifekode) supplied information about the customs and language of his

---

Continued from previous page—

publication, it may be noted that on this and on all subsequent publications his name appeared as simply 'Samuel Crowther'. Whatever justification there may be for referring to him in accounts of his public activities by his family name, Ajai (Ajayi), there is none for listing the author of books as 'S. A. Crowther'. The only recognition of his African name in a scholarly work during his lifetime was a friendly reference by Lepsius to 'S. Crowther (Adža ' ye)' in the *Standard Alphabet*, 2nd edition, 1863, p. 277.

[48] The surname borrowed from that of a German missionary-linguist who had worked in the 1810s at Freetown and on the Rio Pongas, studying the Susu language.

[49] The Methodists established a mission in Yorubaland a few months earlier. But this mission failed to produce any linguistic work before the 1870s.

[50] They may therefore be regarded as the earliest material on Yoruba survivals in Brazil, a subject which has recently produced a vast literature. Yoruba culture would seem to have had a high survival value in the New World, but this may only be the result of the fact that the Yoruba were the last African people to cross the Atlantic in large numbers.

homeland which enabled d'Avezac to prepare a lengthy article on these subjects.[51] D'Avezac complained that Osifekunde was an inadequate linguistic informant (partly because he had only a smattering of either Portuguese or French), nevertheless he obtained from him a vocabulary of 800 words and was able to produce forty-five pages of comment on the grammar of the language. In 1839–40, this would have been a definite contribution to academic knowledge of Yoruba; but d'Avezac did not publish till 1845, by which time his work had been rendered virtually valueless by the publication in 1843 of Crowther's fuller and more accurate study.[52]

The middle and later 1840s saw the transference of Yoruba studies from Freetown to Yorubaland. When Crowther returned to Freetown from England, he began pastoral activities in Yoruba. He started work on a translation of the New Testament, and on January 9th, 1844, preached his first sermon in his mother tongue.[53] Later in the year, he, Townsend and Gollmer (together with their wives, and a dozen Sierra Leonean assistants) made their way to Yorubaland, to begin the mission.[54] In 1846, the party reached Abeokuta, where Andrew Wilhelm had been installed since Townsend's reconnaissance in 1842. The 'Saro'[55] community in Abeokuta had been reminded of its Christian experience in Freetown not only by Wilhelm's presence, but by the active evangelism of some of its own members: it was reported in 1845 that 'one particularly, William Savage, keeps regular prayers at his house; at which time he explains the Holy Scriptures, to about thirty of his relatives, in the Yoruba language'.[56] Meanwhile, in Freetown the Aku community was collecting funds to support the missionaries in Yorubaland.[57]

By 1850, Crowther and his European colleagues were firmly established at Abeokuta, and Yoruba studies were centred there. Naturally the major part of the translational work was done by Crowther. In 1847, he began work again on the Gospels, and between 1850 and 1856 published annually at least one book of the Old or New Testament in Yoruba. But his very first book written wholly in Yoruba was a school primer, printed

---

[51] See P. C. Lloyd, 'Osifakorede [sic] of Ijebu', *Odu: journal of Yoruba studies*, 1961, pp. 59–64; P. E. H. Hair, 'An Ijebu man [Osifekunde] in Paris 1839', *Nigeria*, 68, March 1961, pp. 79–82 (with photographs of a bust of Osifekunde in the Musée de l'Homme, Paris). According to Ajayi, *op. cit.* (1961), p. 48, the modern form of the name is Osìfèkòdé. D'Avezac made use of earlier material on Yoruba as well as the information from Osifekunde.

[52] Some of d'Avezac's vocabulary appeared in print earlier, however, in [E. Norris], *Outline of a Vocabulary . . .* , 1841; d'Avezac's contribution was acknowledged in the introduction. No doubt Crowther saw this work while on the expedition, and conceivably some of the terms given by Osifekunde may have inspired entries in Crowther's own vocabulary, then in process of preparation.

[53] Ajayi, *op. cit.* (1961), p. 49.

[54] In 1952, while organising (on behalf of the Nigerian Record Survey) the survey of mission records which brought the papers of the C.M.S. Yoruba Mission into the Nigerian National Archives, I was allowed to see the manuscript Minute Book of the early years of the Yoruba Mission, which was then in private hands in Lagos. It showed that, aboard ship in 1844, en route from Freetown to Badagry, the three missionaries, German, English, and Yoruba, held weekly meetings to discuss administrative problems, e.g. the purchase of cowries at Cape Coast, and that each took it in turn to be Chairman, Secretary and Treasurer – Victorian respect for the formalities of the committee system which has had a major cultural impact on Middle Africa and blossomed into a formidable mystique.

[55] Sàro ', the Yoruba term for Sierra Leone (Abraham, *op. cit.*), and derived from the common Freetown pronunciation, S'a L'one: the Saro community was the community of Yoruba-speaking ex-slaves returned from Sierra Leone and making their homes permanently in Yorubaland.

[56] Kopytoff, *op. cit.*, p. 316, n. 49, citing C.M.S. Archives, CA 2/o 67.

[57] *ibid.*, p. 53 (1841, support to Methodists at Badagry); Fyfe, *op. cit.*, pp. 236 (1843, ' Freetown Church' in Abeokuta), 292 (1850s).

in 1849 (and reprinted in 1852 and 1853), and in 1850 he also published a translation of part of the Anglican Prayer Book. He was increasingly helped in his translations by a number of Yoruba-speaking Sierra Leoneans who joined the mission after 1850,[58] especially by Thomas King, who also published Scriptural translations under his own name between 1857 and 1862 (when he died at Igbein). After 1854, Crowther's main attention was directed more and more to the Niger and to languages other than Yoruba, but he continued to supervise and check the translation of the Yoruba Bible; and in the mid-1880s, some years before his death, the work was completed and the whole Bible appeared in print. Crowther also worked for many years on an enlarged version of his vocabulary. In 1862, he reported that a fire at his house had destroyed his – 'collection of words and proverbs in Yoruba, of eleven years' constant observations. . . . The loss of these is greater to me than anything else, in as much as it cannot be recovered with money nor can I easily recall to memory all the collections I had made during my travels at Rabba and through the Yoruba country, in which places I kept my ears open to every word to catch what I had not then secured, with which I had expected to enrich and enlarge my Yoruba vocabulary this year. Now all are gone like a dream.'[59] Despite this blow, Crowther resumed work and published the enlarged vocabulary in 1870.

Whereas the home authorities of the mission allowed – and probably encouraged – the Africans, Crowther and King, to publish their translations under their names, the Europeans, Gollmer and Townsend, published anonymously; and in Townsend's case, it is particularly difficult to establish which publications were wholly or largely his work.[60] Both men had begun to study Yoruba in Freetown, but undoubtedly became proficient in the spoken language only during their long years in Yorubaland. Each carried out minor translational work. Gollmer translated a large number of religious tracts, which were published between the 1850s and the 1870s; and in the 1860s he revised, or supervised the revision, of the parts of the Bible already translated.[61] As for Townsend, it is likely that the early collections of hymns in Yoruba were at least partly his work, and one hymnal was printed on the press he established and supervised at Abeokuta. Translation of English verse into a tonal African language in such a way that the product is meaningful when sung to European tunes is an almost impossible task. But one of these collections was notable in that the hymns were not translations but compositions in traditional style, intended to be sung to traditional tunes; they were composed and employed in services by a congregation at Otta, which had as its pastor the Sierra Leonean, James White, but the collection and printing, at Abeokuta in 1861, was probably Townsend's work.[62] Townsend was not a wholehearted admirer of his Sierra Leonean colleagues, not even of Crowther,[63] largely because of his interest in, and emotional commitment to, Abeokuta society (which resented the non-Abeokuta origins of the leading Sierra Leoneans), but his views on missionary tactics appear to have been often original and intelligent. His major contribution to Yoruba literature was less textual

---

[58] E.g. James White, Thomas B. Macaulay, William Morgan, on whom see the biographical notes in Kopytoff, *op. cit.* Note that, unlike Crowther and King, these men were born in Sierra Leone, their parents being liberated Yoruba slaves.

[59] Ajayi, *op. cit.* (1965), p. 128, citing C.M.S. Archives, CA 3/0 4.

[60] Again we may hope that Professor Ajayi's combing of the C.M.S. Archives will clear up this point.

[61] Gollmer, *op. cit.*, pp. 165–84, which includes on p. 181 a reproduction of a page of the Yoruba New Testament with manuscript revisions in Gollmer's hand.

[62] Cf. Ajayi, *op. cit.* (1965), p. 225, n. 4.

[63] And hence, for those who see Crowther merely as a racial standard-bearer, Townsend appears as the evil genius of the Yoruba mission.

than administrative: he edited, contributed to, and printed at Abeokuta from 1859 to 1867, the periodical *Iwe Irohin*, the earliest vernacular periodical to be produced entirely in West Africa.[64]

By 1890, as the bibliography that follows shows, Yoruba printed literature was assuming the form it bore for the next sixty years. A steady flow of religious and educational literature, mainly translations, produced by or under the direction of European missionaries and printed in Europe, was supplemented by a growing stream – intermittently, a flood – of more spontaneous, home-grown material, pamphlets and booklets written by Yorubans, dealing with local social or historical themes, and printed on local presses. Together the two sources built up a culturally vigorous vernacular literature, a prolific one by African standards. Elements in this literature could be traced back to the pioneers; to Crowther's example of Yoruban authorship; to Gollmer's cheap, popular tracts; to Townsend's encouragement of traditional themes, and of local printing. The Yoruba studies that began in Freetown thus bore substantial fruit.

* * *

The number of books and booklets printed in Yoruba since Crowther's primer of 1849 is between eight hundred and one thousand. This represents one of the largest printed vernacular literatures in any African language, and is the proof of the success of those early workers who devised ways of putting Yoruba into writing – Raban who showed what some of the problems were, and Crowther, Gollmer and Townsend, who between them had worked out many adequate practical solutions by the 1850s. How this was done in the field of orthography has been described in some detail by a modern Yoruban scholar, in a paper which is itself a pioneering contribution to the history of African language studies,[65] and which we shall now briefly summarise. Raban's orthography was reasonably systematic:[66] Crowther adopted part of it, but his greater knowledge of the language raised fresh problems. In 1847, he asked his Abeokuta colleagues for comments on the orthography of his revised translation of Luke, and the subsequent discussion centred around such fundamental practical points as the use (or misuse) of diacriticals, and the necessity (or otherwise) of tone-marking. As regards diacriticals, Crowther in his 1843 work had been very sparing, using them only to distinguish vowels, and apparently in 1847 he proposed to use spare diacriticals for distinguishing tone.[67] Gollmer criticised Crowther's employment of combinations of consonants (e.g. kp, bh, ng, hr) to indicate sounds not heard in European languages, and suggested

---

[64] According to a note in *Africa*, 3, 1930, p. 537, 'the first periodical in Twi was edited by J. G. Christaller . . . [and] existed for six years'. Christaller was in Gold Coast 1852–8 and 1862–8, but the list of publications in his *Grammar*, 1875, does not include any vernacular periodical. Apart from this Twi periodical, which may or may not have been earlier, I know of no vernacular periodical earlier than *Iwe Irohin* in any West African language, though there were much earlier vernacular periodicals in South Africa. Since all the publications in Christaller's list were printed in Basel, it is highly unlikely that his Twi periodical was printed in West Africa.

[65] Ajayi, *op. cit.* (1961).

[66] Over the whole field of African languages, Mrs Kilham had persistently called for a systematic orthography.

[67] In 1843, Crowther distinguished certain tones by using 'spare' consonants; on the significance of this, see P. E. H. Hair, 'A nineteenth century link between Chinese and African language studies', *Bulletin of S.O.A.S.*, 29, 1966, pp. 143–5.

instead the use of additional diacriticals (thus, ṗ, ḅ, ṅ, ṙ,), but he also accepted Crowther's suggestion of tone-marking with diacriticals. Townsend, as a good printer no doubt,[68] was appalled by the multiplicity of diacriticals proposed, and he further disputed a number of minor points, for instance, whether it was necessary to write kp, since there is no p in Yoruba. All this was sensible informed discussion on a set of extremely difficult technical problems:[69] 'if these problems are, in one way or another, still with us, this merely emphasises their massive intractability'.[70] The discussion was carried from Abeokuta to London, in correspondence, and was continued when Gollmer and Townsend visited England in 1848–9 and Crowther spent some time there in 1851. Henry Venn, the brilliant and forward-looking Secretary of the C.M.S., finding that orthography was a vexed matter in many of his mission fields,[71] not only discussed the problems with his field workers, but also sought the views of the most distinguished language scholars of the day. As a result, in 1848 Professor Samuel Lee of Cambridge, a Semiticist, and J. F. Schön, Crowther's colleague on the Niger Expedition and a Hausa scholar, produced a set of rules for writing African languages; and in 1854 C. R. Lepsius, the German Egyptologist and philologist, published a Standard Alphabet for all the languages of the world. Yoruba orthography was changed accordingly:[72] in 1851, Crowther worked with Schön to revise his current translations before they went to the press, and his 1852 grammar 'drastically modified'[73] his 1843 orthography. In the new style, Townsend gained his plain p (not kp): Gollmer gained many of his suggested diacriticals: Crowther gained a few tone-marking diacriticals. None of the three was fully satisfied, and the revised Yoruba orthography has been justly criticised on many points by others in the period since its inception; yet, with only slight modifications,[74] it has continued to be used, and the literature written in it to be widely read, right up to the present day, and it must therefore be, in a measure at least, adequate for its purpose. While it is reasonably certain that a new orthography could

---

[68] Diacriticals are disliked by printers; the type breaks easily and wears quickly (hence the printing of diacriticals is often defective), and proof-reading requires added care. From the point of view of the person paying for the printing, diacriticals may be expensive if the type has to be replaced relatively frequently. From the point of view of the reader, diacriticals may be difficult to see (particularly if they are the small under-dots used in nineteenth century Yoruba) and this may slow up reading. A fast writing hand is of course impossible if many diacriticals have to be inserted, while if the writer leaves out the diacriticals to save time, the communication may be unreadable on receipt.

[69] The account in Ajayi, op. cit. (1961), is here at fault in tending to underestimate the seriousness of the problems discussed and to overestimate the influence of petty national feelings (e.g. German orthography versus English) on the suggestions made.

[70] John Spencer, 'S. W. Koelle and the problem of notation for African languages, 1847–1855', Sierra Leone Language Review, 5, 1966, pp. 83–105, on p. 101.

[71] 'Though he had no special love for philology and phonology, when it became necessary to construct a scientific alphabet to record languages hitherto unwritten . . . [especially when] there seemed to be a fair opening into Yoruba country, then he threw himself, heart and soul for the time, into the question of phonetics . . . ' (W. Knight, The missionary secretariat of Henry Venn, London, 1880, p. 377). In Venn's diary, we find the following entry – 'Jan. 28th [1850] – From 9 till 1 engaged without intermission in the investigation of the Yoruba language and the translation of the Prayer-book' (E. Stock, History of the C.M.S., vol. 2, 1899, p. 646).

[72] Spencer, op. cit., passim but especially footnote 11. Ajayi's assertion that Yoruba orthography 'sought not uniformity with other systems, but [conformed only to] the demands of its own genius' (Ajayi, op. cit. (1961), p. 54) must be judged in the light of Spencer's evidence; this may affect Ajayi's conclusion that today Yoruba 'is not to be reformed to suit the body of foreign linguists, phoneticians, ethnographers and even printers' (p. 56).

[73] Spencer, op.cit., p. 84.

[74] Ajayi, op. cit., (1961), pp. 54–5.

be designed which would improve the readability of Yoruba,[75] the fact remains that the orthography designed by an 'international cooperative effort' (as Professor Ajayi calls it) of missionaries in Freetown and Abeokuta and linguistic experts in Europe, around 1850, has enabled the Yoruba to write down their thoughts in their own language, and to read in the same a variety of instructive and stimulating works, for over a century.[76]

If Crowther's personal responsibility for the orthography employed in Yoruba writings from the 1850s was less than has been sometimes supposed, nevertheless his total contribution to the founding of a written literature in the language was very great. His choice of a dialect and his selection of idioms and expressions in this dialect, sanctified for the Yoruba reader through his Bible translations and for the linguist through his grammar and dictionary, created standard Yoruba, which has now even affected the spoken language and become so widespread that other dialect forms are rapidly disappearing.[77] As regards the written language, 'Yoruba writing still today bears Crowther's stamp'.[78] His translations – unlike those first translations in almost every other African language which were executed by foreigners – were idiomatic and readable; they not only represented the language correctly but had literary style. Afro-European contacts in Yorubaland in the half-century before colonial rule were dominated by the missionary and his converts: in this mission atmosphere, the Bible influenced thought and action: therefore Yoruba literature was extremely fortunate in that, though its early decades lay in a period in which the first literature to be produced was necessarily a translation of the Bible, that translation was of a literary order comparable with that of Luther's German translation or the English Authorised Version. Crowther's influence on subsequent Yoruba literature – though it remains to be examined in detail by Yoruban scholars – without doubt was overwhelming.

* * *

Yoruba studies began at Freetown; after 1845, publications originated elsewhere, but interest in Yoruba at Freetown declined only slowly. The first bishop of Sierra Leone, O. E. Vidal, was also episcopally responsible for Yorubaland. He had been selected as a man with linguistic interests (he had studied several Asian languages[79]), and in Freetown he began to learn Yoruba. When he visited Yorubaland, at his first service – 'to the surprise of many, the Bishop commenced reading [from the Bible] intelligibly in

---

[75] It would seem that, on the whole, bilingual Yorubans read Yoruba more slowly, i.e. with more difficulty, than they read English: this is presumably the fault of the orthography – though it has to be noted that the same problem, in some degree, has been noted with many other African languages which employ more up-to-date orthographies.

[76] Yoruba is almost uniquely conservative among African languages in retaining an orthography with so many diacriticals. The less happy aspects of the Yoruba experience with diacriticals have helped to encourage other languages to accept orthographies of a different style.

[77] E. C. Rowlands, 'Some features of nasalised vowels in Yoruba', *Akten des 24en Internationalen Orientalisten Kongresses*, 1959, pp. 719–21, on p. 720; E. C. Rowlands, 'Yoruba dialects in the Polyglotta Africana', *Sierra Leone Language Review*, 4, 1965, pp. 103–8.

[78] D. Westermann, in a review in *Africa*, 23, 1953, pp. 260–1.

[79] 'Vidal had previously learned Tamil that he might correspond with the Native Christians in Tinnevelly: when the Borneo Mission was started, he edited for it a Malay grammar: and he was at this time studying the East African languages [sic!] in correspondence with Krapf.' (E. Stock, *History of the C.M.S.*, vol. 2, 1899, p. 121). Allowing for the hagiographical element in this passage the linguistic activity was still remarkable, considering that Vidal conducted it all from a Sussex vicarage.

Yoruba'.[80] Vidal contributed a most useful and perceptive introduction to Crowther's 1852 grammar and vocabulary, in which he discussed the structure of Yoruba and its relationship with other languages, the social significance of Yoruba proverbs, and other general matters.[81] He also advised Crowther on the arrangement of the grammar, as Schön had done for the 1843 work.[82] Vidal's death in 1853 ended Yoruba studies in Freetown, but the Aku community continued to take an interest in the missionaries in Yorubaland and their linguistic activities.

In 1858, Townsend and Crowther revisited Freetown, and the bishop of the time reported that a congregation was 'much gratified when [they] preached in Akoo'. The next year, it was the turn of the missionary at Ibadan in Yorubaland (David Hinderer) to visit Freetown, and the bishop jubilantly wrote to his sister – 'You should have seen the Moslems in Fourah Bay Road listening to Hinderer preaching in Ako yesterday evening'.[83] As late as 1888, a speech in Yoruba from a missionary was welcomed.[84] But gradually the Aku community was assimilated to English-speaking Freetown and the descendants of Oduduwa forgot their ancestral language. By the early twentieth century, only a hard core of Aku Moslems, who declined to dissolve into Christian Freetown, remained separate, and since then the name Aku has come to be used only for this small group of Moslems of Yoruba descent. While they have retained some Yoruba traditions up to the present day, and have the reputation of speaking Yoruba, it is doubtful whether even the more conservative families use Yoruba as a first language.[85]

---

[80] Gollmer, *op. cit.*, p. 150.

[81] In the course of discussing language relationships in Africa, Vidal pointed out that Temne resembled the languages of South Africa; on the significance of this, see P. E. H. Hair, 'Temne and African language classification before 1864', *Journal of African Languages*, 4, 1965, pp. 46–56, on pp. 48–9. Vidal noted that Yoruba did not possess the 'alliteral concord' which Krapf had told him was common among the languages of Southern Africa. Vidal was attacked for this observation by Burton, who also seized the opportunity to criticise Crowther's Yoruba grammar which, he said, was too much like Lindley Murray (the then standard grammar of English) – a comment typically both sour and shrewd. (R. F. Burton, *Abeokuta and the Camaroons Mountains*, 1863, 1, p. 307).

[82] When Baikie travelled with Vidal in 1853, he was impressed by the way the bishop spent his time 'inspecting and revising translations' (W. B. Baikie, *Narrative of a voyage . . .*, 1856, p. 362). The following anecdote about Vidal's ability was included in Crowther's own account of an audience he had with Queen Victoria and the Prince Consort at Windsor in 1851: 'Lord W. Russell mentioned my translations in the Yoruba language. He told the Queen the proverb about the Agiliti, which he requested me to repeat to Her Majesty, that she might hear the sound of the language, which I did. I repeated the Lord's Prayer in addition that she might hear it better. She said it was soft and melodious, and asked with what language it was classified. I replied 'Mr Vidal has not as yet been able to classify it with any of the languages, on account of its peculiarity.' Lord Wriothesley mentioned Mr Vidal as an extraordinary linguist. I told them he was very clever indeed, that even now the proofs of my translations are sent to him to revise before they pass through the press, which quite astonished the Queen and the Prince. Lord Wriothesley then said to the Prince, 'It is not the Germans alone who have the talent for languages, but Englishmen also'. The Prince did not reply much to him' (E. Stock, *op. cit.*, 2, 1899, p. 113).

[83] *Memorials of John Bowen, by his sister*, 1862, pp. 526, 587.

[84] C.M.S. Archives, CA 1/o 122, letter of 9.12.1869: *The Artisan* (newspaper), 4.8.1888.

[85] O. Bassir, 'Marriage rites among the Aku (Yoruba) of Freetown', *Africa*, 24, 1954, pp. 251–6: some of the statements in this interesting paper must however be received with caution; a fuller study of this community is urgently needed. There is evidence that the community has been supplemented in recent decades by new arrivals from Yorubaland, mainly Moslem traders, and that therefore some of the Yoruba traits are not century-old survivals. Cf. 'Aku has survived in the Freetown area for over 150 years, but it appears to have been kept alive by constant contact with Nigeria' (T. D. P. Dalby, 'Language distribution in Sierra Leone 1961–2', *Sierra Leone Language Review*, 1, 1962, pp. 62–7 on p. 66).

Henry Johnson, who was born at Hastings village in the Sierra Leone peninsula around 1840, and as an agent of the C.M.S. in 1876 transferred to Yorubaland, was one of the last Yoruba-speaking missionaries from Sierra Leone. In the early 1870s, he and the ubiquitous Schön worked together on Bible translations into the Mende language of Sierra Leone (Mrs Kilham's 'Kossa', chosen with 'Aku' for instruction in the Charlotte school); and Johnson stated that when he was trying to produce idiomatic Mende, he found that it helped if he worked from the Yoruba translation.[86]

The English-speaking inhabitants of Freetown came in the later nineteenth century to be known as 'Creoles', and in the mid-twentieth century the patois of the Creoles, christened the 'Krio language', began to be studied, and to be employed in serious written literature. The lexical content of this language includes an element derived from African languages, and there is little doubt that the largest contribution comes from Yoruba. A recent article lists two hundred words of Yoruba origin.[87] Apart from the Yoruba contribution to Krio, there are other Yoruba-language survivals in Freetown and district – in the speech of the Aku community, in Creole personal names, in traditional songs.[88] Yoruban linguists might still find much to interest them in the first home of Yoruba studies.

---

[86] C.M.S. Archives, CA 1/o 122, letter of 28.2.1872.
[87] A. T. von S. Bradshaw, 'A list of Yoruba words in Krio', *Sierra Leone Language Review*, 5, 1966, pp. 61–71.
[88] In 1961, Dr David Dalby recorded a song in Yoruba, sung, without their knowing the meaning of the words, by Creole fishermen at the peninsula village of Kent.

A. Early vocabularies

1819   Thomas Edward Bowdich, Mission from Cape Coast Castle to Ashantee
. . . . , London

On pp. 209, 505, numerals of 'Hio', presumably collected at Kumasi.

1828   [Hannah Kilham], Specimens of African languages spoken in the Colony
of Sierra Leone, London

On pp. 2–47, 140 terms in 'A-ku': bound in the same volume, but separately paginated,
'Lessons in Aku, (or Eio) and English', pp. 2–10, Part I, vocabulary of 350 terms,
pp. 10–12, Part II, 'A few examples in the leading parts of speech'. Note footnote 23
to the essay on Hausa and Kanuri.

1829   [Hugh] Clapperton, Journal of a second expedition into the interior of
West Africa . . . , London

On pp. 341–2, ' a vocabulary of the Yourriba tongue', numerals and 150 terms.

1830   John Raban, A / vocabulary / of the / Eyò, or Aku / a dialect of Western
Africa./ Compiled by / the Rev. J. R.,/ one of the missionaries of the C.M.S./
in Sierra Leone/, C.M.S., London

pp. iii–v Preface; 4–7 Alphabet; 8 Contents; 9–15 Vocabulary; 16–17 Verbs; 18–19
Numerals; 20–32 Short sentences, Phrases, etc; 32–4 Gleanings for grammar. Small
size, 9 × 12 cm. Copy in B.F.B.S. Library.

1831   J. Raban, A / vocabulary [etc, as previous item]/ / / / / / / in Sierra Leone /
Part II /, C.M.S., London

pp. 2–3 Advertisement; 4–5 Alphabet; 6–20 words, phrases; 20–1 Sentences analysed;
22 Psalm 127.1; 23–6 Sketch of an English–Eyò vocabulary. Size as previous. Copy in
B.F.B.S. Library.

1832   J. Raban, The Eyò vocabulary: / compiled [etc, as previous items]/ / / / / / / /
Part III / including a few / Dialogues and Lessons /, C.M.S., London

pp. 4–5 Advertisement; 6–7 Alphabet; 9 Additional words; 10–11 Names of places and
relatives; 11–15 Phrases, Prepositions, Verbs; 18–20 Short sentences and Dialogues;
31–6 Sentences from [Robert] Simpson's Sunday-School Primer. Size as previous.

[?]   Manuscript, 'Copy. African vocabulary', South African Public Library

pp. 114: parallel vocabularies of 9 languages, including 'Ackoo'; described in Bleek
[see Earlier bibliographies], p. 206, item 410: see footnote 20 of the essay on Yoruba,
which suggests that the 'Ackoo' may have been collected before Raban's publications.

1833*   J. B. Douville, manuscript, 'un vocabulaire nogo ou inongo de 5 pages
d'écriture, receuilli à Bahia au mois de juillet 1833'

About 50 terms from this manuscript were included in item 1845.

1841   [Edwin Norris], Outline of a vocabulary of a few of the principal languages
of Western and Central Africa compiled for the use of the Niger Expedition, London

Includes about 800 words in 'Ako, Eyo, Yabu or Yorriba', said to be taken mainly from
Raban or contributed by d'Avezac [see item 1845]: also reprints Mrs Kilham's
vocabulary.

[1843]   Robert Clarke, Sierra Leone. A description of the . . . Liberated Africans
. . . . , London

On pp. 154–61, proverbs, vocabulary, texts, a song in 'Akoo', supplied (probably all)
by H. Townsend. Copy in Royal Commonwealth Society Library.

1845   M. A. D'Avezac-Macaya, 'Notice sur le pays et le peuple des Yébous en Afrique', *Mémoires de la Société Ethnologique* [Paris], 2, 1845, Part 2, pp. 1–196

> On pp. 151–96, a vocabulary of 1500 terms, 800 collected from an informant in Paris, the remainder compiled from items 1819–1832 and 1833 above.

1846   H. Hale, Ethnography and philology: United States Exploring Expedition during the years 1838–42, Philadelphia

> On pp. 657–66, numerals and 50 terms in 'Eyo', collected at Rio de Janeiro.

1848/9   John Clarke, Specimens of dialects . . . in Africa, Berwick on Tweed/London

> Vocabularies under the following names and numbers: (a) numerals – Uu Ogalli 104, Iao 115, Kotshi 116, Neiri 124, Ufruda 182, 338, Aya 183, Egarra 218, Nago 296, 346, Yagba 339, Oyo 377,? Tshamba 160, 350; (b) ten nouns – Ako 43, Kotshi 45, Okkiri 46, Yarriba 47, Popo Akoko 48, Nago 49, 261, 281, Uu 51, Ueiri 52, Ufruda 53, 239, Eya/Oyo 54, 290, Yagba 240; (c) twenty terms – Yoruba on p. 59. Other vocabularies are not original, and are copied from item 1841, etc.

1851   John Leighton Wilson, 'Comparative vocabularies of some of the principal Negro dialects of Africa', *Journal of the American Oriental Society*, 1, pp. 337–381

> The 'Yebu' vocabulary opposite p. 350 is from item 1841.

1854   Sigismund Wilhelm Koelle, Polyglotta Africana, London

> Includes vocabularies of 12 'Aku' dialects: see E. C. Rowlands, 'Yoruba dialects in the Polyglotta Africana', *Sierra Leone Language Review*, 4, 1965, pp. 103–08.

1855   Samuel Crowther, Journal of an expedition up the Niger and Tshadda Rivers . . . , London

> On pp. 208–27, in Appendix 2, comparative vocabularies of 'Igarra', 'Doma' and Yoruba, 100 terms.

B. Studies

1828   Kilham [see Early vocabularies]

> Lessons, Part II, 'A few examples in the leading parts of speech'.

1830–1–2   Raban [see Early vocabularies]

> E.g., 1830, pp. 32–4, 'Gleanings for grammar'.

1843   S. Crowther, Vocabulary / of the / Yoruba language./ Part I – English and Yoruba./ Part II – Yoruba and English. / To which are prefixed, / the grammatical elements / of the / Yoruba language./ By S. C.,/ native teacher,/ in the service of the C.M.S. . /, C.M.S., London

> Pp. i–vii Introductory remarks; 1–48 On the grammatical construction of the Yoruba language; (1)–(83) A vocabulary of the Yoruba language Part I; (84)–(176) Part II; (177)–(196) Specimens of translations [Lord's Prayer, Decalogue, Scripture verses, A treaty with the chiefs, Address to the chiefs and people of Africa – last two with English].

1845   D'Avezac [see Early vocabularies]

> On pp. 106–51, 'Esquisse grammaticale de la langue Yéboue'.

1851   Wilson [see Early vocabularies]

> On p. 379, a brief note by 'E.E.S.'

1852   S. Crowther, A / vocabulary / of the / Yoruba language / compiled by the / Rev. S. C.,/ native missionary of the C.M.S./ together with / Introductory Remarks,/ by the / Rev. O. E. Vidal, M.A. / Bishop Designate of Sierra Leone./ Seeleys, London

Pp. i–v Advertisement; 1–38 Introductory remarks; unnumbered page, A vocabulary of the Yoruba language, and verso, sounds of the language; 1–291 Yoruba vocabulary [i.e. Yoruba–English].

1852   S. Crowther, A / grammar / of the / Yoruba language / by the Rev. S. C.,/ native missionary of the C.M.S. / Seeleys, London

Unnumbered page, introduction by W[illiam]. K[night]., and verso, sounds of the language; pp. i–vii Introductory Remarks; 1–44 On the grammatical construction of the Yoruba language; 45–52 On the formation of words in Yoruba [signed O. E. V[idal].] Both 1852 works were revised versions of the relevant sections in the 1843 work. According to Hintze [see Earlier bibliographies], the two works were also issued in one volume, 'A grammar and vocabulary of the Yoruba language . . .', 1852, pp. (38), vii, 52, 291.

1854   A. F. Pott, 'Sprachen aus Afrika's Innerem und Westen', *Zeitschrift der Deutschen Morgenländischen Gesellschaft*, 8, pp. 412–442

Reviews Crowther's works on Yoruba, together with works on other languages.

1858   Thomas J. Bowen, Smithsonian contributions to knowledge / Grammar and dictionary / of the / Yoruba language / with an / introductory description / of / the country and people of Yoruba. / By the / Rev. T. J. B. / missionary of the Southern Baptist Convention. / Accepted for publication / by the / Smithsonian Institute / May, 1858 [bound as part of] Smithsonian contributions to knowledge, vol. x, 1858

Pp. [iii] Advertisement; [v] Preface; [vii]–viii Contents; ix–xxi Introduction; [xxiii] List of Yoruba publications; 1–55 Yoruba grammar; 56–71 Specimens of composition, proverbs, translations; 1–134 Dictionary of the Yoruba language [Yoruba–English, English–Yoruba]; 135–6 Errata. Folio size. The inclusion of the work in this series effectively prevented it becoming a contribution to knowledge.

[1870] [S. Crowther], [no title page, half page reads –] A / vocabulary / of the / Yoruba language / etc, etc./

Verso of half page, sounds of the language; pp. 1–254 Vocabulary of the Yoruba language [English–Yoruba, Yoruba–English]. The date is that usually given, but according to Mann [see Earlier bibliographies] it was 1867.

1877   Friedrich Müller, Grundriss der Sprachwissenschaft, Wien, 1/2, pp. 126–134

'Die Sprachen Ewe, Gã (Akra), Odschi (Otšui) und Yoruba', an analysis based on earlier sources.

1878   C. H. Toy, 'On the Yoruban language', *Transactions of the American Philological Association*, pp. 19–38

1879   Jonathan L. Buckland Wood, Notes / on the / construction / of the Yoruba language; / by the / Rev. J. B. W.,/ missionary of the C.M.S. / Exeter /
Pp. 47.

1880   Karl R. Lepsius, Nubische grammatik, Berlin

On p. xxxvii, a note.

1880   Pierre Bouche, Extraits des Études Catholiques / Étude sur la langue Nago / par l'Abbé P. B. / ancien missionaire à la Côte des Esclaves / Archives des Pères Missionaires / No 1 / Bar-le-Duc
Pp. 51.

1883   P. Bouche, Oeuvre de Saint-Jérome / pour la publication des / travaux philologiques des missionnaires / Premier fascicule / Les / Noirs peints par eux-mêmes / par / M. l'Abbé B. / ancien missionnaire apostolique à la Côte des Esclaves / Paris

Pp. 144: includes Yoruba proverbs, from Crowther; an Italian translation 1884–6 is cited in Streit/Dindinger [see Earlier bibliographies].

1884   [Noel Baudin], Essai / de / grammaire / en / langue Yoruba / Séminaire / des missions africaines / Lyon

Pp. 117: lithographed from manuscript.

[?1885]   N. Baudin, Dictionnaire / Francais–Yoruba / par le R. P. B. / [bound together with –] Dictionnaire / Yoruba–Francais

Pp. 560, 612: lithographed from manuscript; no date, no place of publication.

1885*   S. A. Allen, Iwe owe, General Printing Press, Lagos

595 Yoruba proverbs: title from Mann [see Earlier bibliographies]

1885*   D. B. Vincent, Iwe alo, Lagos

200 Yoruba proverbs and riddles: title from Mann [see Earlier bibliographies].

1886   Henry Johnson and Johann G. Christaller, Vocabularies of the Niger and Gold Coast, S.P.C.K.

On pp. 1–4, English–Yoruba, 250 words.

1888–9   Adolphus C. Mann, 'Eine geschichtliche Sage aus der Zeit der ersten Niederlassungen der Egba, ein Stamm der Yoruba-Nation, West Afrika', *Zeitschrift für afrikanische Sprachen*, Berlin, 2, 1888–9, pp. 209–219

C. Translations and other literature

1849*,   [S. Crowther], The / Yoruba primer. / Iwe ekinni. / On ni fu awọn ara Egba
1852,   ati awọn ara Yoruba /, C.M.S., London
1853*

Pp. 3–4 spelling and reading lessons; 14–20 Scripture verses, prayers. Above title and contents from 1852 edition: according to Bleek [see Earlier bibliographies], other editions are identical, except that 1853 has added, in a fifth line of title, 'Third edition'. For a later version, see 1868.

1850,   S. Crowther, Iwe adua Yoruba. / A / selection / from the / Book of Common
1853*,   Prayer, / according to the use of the / United Church of England and Ire-
1862*   land. / Translated into Yoruba, / for the use of / the native Christians of that nation, / by the / Rev. S. C., / native missionary./, C.M.S., London [bound together with –] The administration / of the / Sacraments, / and a selection of / other rites and ceremonies of the church, / according to the use of the / United Church of England and Ireland. / Translated into Yoruba, / by the Rev. S. C., / native missionary.

Pp. 37, 82: according to Bleek [see Earlier bibliographies], 1853 edition is identical with 1850, except that the former has added on the title page 'Second edition': the 1862 edition is listed in Hinze [see Earlier bibliographies].

1850   S. Crowther, The / Epistle of Paul the Apostle / to / the Romans. / Translated into Yoruba / for the use of / the native Christians of that nation, / by the Rev. S. C., / native missionary. /, C.M.S., London

Printed at the expense of B.F.B.S., in 500 copies.

[?1850]* [no title page] Katekismu ti Wattu, I

Pp. 20: Watts' Catechism, part 1: information from Bleek [see Earlier bibliographies]. Later editions or versions, 1857, 1862.

1851 S. Crowther, The Gospel according to St Luke, / the Acts of the Apostles; / with the / Epistles of St James and St Peter. / Translated [etc, as 1850 items], C.M.S., London

Printed at the expense of B.F.B.S.

1853 S. Crowther, The first book of Moses, / commonly called Genesis / translated [etc, as previous item], B.F.B.S., London

1853 S. Crowther, The Gospel / according to / St Matthew. / Translated [etc, as previous items], B.F.B.S., London

1853* [hymnbook]

30 hymns, part translations, part compositions: information from Mann [see Earlier bibliographies].

1854 S. Crowther, The second book of Moses, / commonly called Ẹksodus / translated [etc, as 1850 items], B.F.B.S., London

1854 S. Crowther, The / Psalms of David./ Translated [etc, as previous item], B.F.B.S., London

1856 S. Crowther, Iwe owẹ, / ati / iwe oniwasu. / li ede Yoruba,/ fu awọn Kristian ti ilu nan, / nipa / Rev. S. C., / alufa ti ilu nan. / London: / a ti kọ fu awọn ẹgbẹ Bibeli ti a npe ni Britiṣe on ilu ni / London: / Printed for the B.F.B.S.

Proverbs and Ecclesiastes.

1856 S. Crowther, Ihin rere ti St Luku; / ati / iṣe awọn apostoli; / ati / episteli to St Paulu apostoli si awọn ara / Romu; / pẹlu / awọn episteli ti St Yakobu on St Peteru. / li ede [etc, as previous item], B.F.B.S., London

Luke, Acts, Romans, James, Peter 1–2: a revision of the 1850 and 1851 items.

1856 [Charles Andrew Gollmer], Ẹrun ọrun / tabi / mẹrindilogun iwasu kukuru./ London: awọn ẹgbẹ ti nkọ iwe kekere to daradara / ti a npe ni Religious Trakt Sosiety /

'Crumbs from Heaven, or fourteen short sermons', actually 16 tracts, and 4 hymns, each paginated separately, totalling 50 pp. Copy in Cambridge U.L. Later edition, 1874.

1856* [?Henry Townsend], Iwe orin mimọ, C.M.S. Press, Abeokuta

Hymns, unnumbered pages 48, perhaps incomplete: information from Bleek [see Earlier bibliographies].

[?1856] [Itan Abramu], [?Abeokuta]

Unnumbered pages 4, no title page: information from Bleek [see Earlier bibliographies]

1857 Thomas King, The Gospel according to / St John: / translated into Yoruba/ by the / Rev. T. K., / native missionary. / ihin rere nipa ti / St Jọhannẹ: / li ede Yoruba / nipa / Rev. T. K./, B.F.B.S., London

1857 Iwe orin mimọ /, C.M.S., London

12°, pp. 84: 90 hymns. Copy in Cambridge U. L.

1857* T. King, Katekismu itan, ti Dr Watts, Testamenti lailar on testamenti titun
-Watts' catechism of the Old and New Testament. Translated into Yoruba,
by the Rev. T. K., native missionary, London
Title as given in Bowen [see Earlier bibliographies].

1859* [C. A. Gollmer], Itan inu Bibeli, Dr Barth's Bible stories, Stuttgart
Title as given in Mann [see Earlier bibliographies].

1859   T. King, The book / of / Daniel. / Translated into Yoruba / for the use of /
the native Christians of that nation, / by the Rev. T. K., / native missionary./,
B.F.B.S., London

1859   T. King, The Gospel / according to / St Mark. / Translated [etc, as previous
item], B.F.B.S., London

1859–67* [H. Townsend, editor, and others?], Iwe irohin for [?fu] awọn ara Egba ati
Yoruba, Abeokuta
Fortnightly news-sheet, in Yoruba and English. 190 issues between November 1859
and October 1867. A set in University Library, Ibadan, has missing nos. 1–5, 12, 32,
36, 41–2, 53–60, 62–75, 186, 188. Normally 4 pp.

?1859* [C. A. Gollmer], [The sinner's friend], Religious Tract Society, London
Reference in 'Life of Gollmer, by his son', p. 165. Later edition, 1874.

[?1860] [David Hinderer], Ilọ-siwaju ero-mimọ / lati / aiyé yi si eyi ti mbọ. / ni ifiwe
alá. / nipa John Bunyan, / ẹniti abi 1628, ti osi ku 1688
Pp. 417, illustrated: no date or place of publication: translation of 'Pilgrim's Progress'.

1861   T. King, The Gospel according to / St John: / translated [etc, as the 1857
item, except for 'Johanni'], B.F.B.S., London
Revision of 1857.

1861   T. King, Awọn epistili ti Paulu Apostoli / si awọn / ara Korinti, ati Galatia,/
ati Efesi: / ti ede Yoruba. / The Epistles of St Paul / to the / Corinthians,
Galatians, / and / Ephesians./ Translated into Yoruba / by / the Rev. T. K.,/
native missionary at Abeokuta. / , B.F.B.S., London

1861* Orin mimọ, Abeokuta
Hymns, in traditional style, composed for the Christians at Otta: information from
Mann [see Earlier bibliographies].

1862   S. Crowther and T. King, The Epistles of St Paul / to the / Phillippians
[sic], Colossians, / Thessalonians, Timothy, Titus, / Philemon and the
Hebrews; / the General Epistles of / St John; / the General Epistle of St
Jude; / and the Revelation of St John. / Translated into Yoruba / by the /
Rev. S. C. and the Rev. T. K. / native missionaries. / , B.F.B.S., London
Completing the translation of the New Testament.

1862* [Watts' first and second catechisms]
Earlier editions, perhaps of parts, ?1850 and 1857: reference from Mann [see Earlier
bibliographies].

1863   Iwe orin mimọ / , C.M.S., London
Pp. 108: 120 hymns.

1865   Testamenti titọn / ti / Jesu Kristi / oluwa ati olugbala wa. / London / a kọ fu
awọn ẹgbẹ Bibeli ti a npè ni Britiṣe ati / ti ilu omiran /, B.F.B.S., London
New Testament – revision of previous parts, edited by C. A. Gollmer.

1865   Iwe orin. / [Scriptural text in Yoruba] / , C.M.S., London
Pp. 113: 106 hymns, not the same as the 1863 item.

1867   Bibeli mimọ́ / eyi ni / ọ̀rọ ọlọrun / ti / testamenti lailai ati ti titọn. / apa ekini ti / testamenti lailai. / iwe ti Mose marun. / iwe ti Joṣua. / iwe ti awọn onidajọ / iwe ti Rutu./, B.F.B.S., London
Genesis–Ruth. Translated or revised 'apparently' by S. Crowther and C. A. Gollmer, according to Darlow/Moule [see Earlier bibliographies].

1868   Iwe / ti / awọn Psalmu. / tabi / awọn orin mimọ́ / , C.M.S., London
Psalms. Revision of 1854.

1868   Iwe ekini / ti / ède Yoruba. / itanlọwọ fu kíko ède na ti a npè ni primeri. /, C.M.S., London
Pp. 20: primer.

1871   Testamenti titọn / [etc, as 1865 item with same title]/, B.F.B.S., London / (Yoruba New Testament)
Revision of 1865, edited by C. A. Gollmer.

1871   Ihin rere / ti / Mateu / London: / a ko [etc, as first 1865 item] / , B.F.B.S., London / (Yoruba Gospel)
Matthew, revised.

1871   [J. A. Maser], Iwe ẹkọ́ / tabi / onirûru ọ̀rọ ọlọrun on adura. / fu ikọni / ni ile iwi ti awọn agba ati ọmọ / Scripture class book in Yoruba. / , C.M.S., London
Pp. 119: authorship from Mann [see Earlier bibliographies].

1872*   Iwe ekini ti ede Yoruba (First book of the Yoruba language), with English translation, Wesleyan Missionary Society
Listed in East, perhaps the same as 'First reading book, 1872' in Mann [both sources in Earlier bibliographies].

1872   [Mark, Luke and John, exactly as Matthew 1871, but substituting 'Marku', 'Luku', 'Johanu']

1872   [C. A. Gollmer], Kutukutu owurọ̀ ọjọ. / tabi / ẹkọ́ ti inọ iwe mimọ́ ọlọrun. / ti a fi lelẹ lẹsẹsẹ li ède to oyé / awọn ọmọde / "The Peep of Day" in Yoruba./ [five lines giving three texts in Yoruba] / Oxford; / Printed at the University Press, / for the Religious Tract Society.
Pp. 136: moral tales. Copy in Cambridge U. L.

1872   The / first catechism / of the / Wesleyan Methodists. / Katekismu ẹkini / ti awọn / Wesleyan Methodist. / London: for the W.M.S.
Pp. 16. Copy in S.O.A.S. Library.

[?1872]   The order of / confirmation; / Or, Ilana i mokanle. /
Pp. 4: portion of Anglican Prayer Book.

1873   Awọn katikismu / ti awọn / Wesleyan Methodist. / No II / , London: for the W.M.S.
Pp. 68. Copy in S.O.A.S. Library.

1874*   Ẹrún ọrun, tabi, mẹrindilogun iwasu kukura; 'Heavenly Crumbs', in Yoruba, or, sixteen short sermons, Religious Tract Society
Pp. 67: presumably enlarged version of 1856 edition. The B.M. copy is missing.

1874*   Ọna si alafia ni iwe kekere mẹrinla, 'Way to Peace' in Yoruba, Religious
         Tract Society
         Listed in East and Mann [see Earlier bibliographies].

1874*   Ọre ẹlẹsẹ, The Sinner's Friend, Religious Tract Society
         Listed in Mann [see Earlier bibliographies]. Earlier edition, ?1859.

1874*   Irohin ti Egbẹ ijo ẹnia ọlọrun l'Eko, Annual Report of the Lagos Native
         Church, Lagos
         Yoruba and English: thereafter annually?: listed in Mann [see Earlier bibliographies].

1874*   Iwe ekini, Yoruba primer
         Listed in East [see Earlier bibliographies]: another edition of 1868?

1874   Katekism / ti / ijọ enia ọlọrun / fun awọn àgba ti ako ti / baptisi / Oxford: /
         Printed at the University Press, / for the C.M.S. /
         Pp. 11: catechism. Copy in S.O.A.S. Library.

1876   Orin mimọ́ / ti awọn / Methodist / ni ède / Yoruba. / [on cover –] Wesley's
         hymns in Yoruba, new edition
         Pp. 158: 150 hymns: earlier edition not traced. Copy in S.O.A.S. Library.

1877   Iwe keji / ti o ni / ẹkọ́ / kika, kikọ, ati isiro ninu, / fun / ìlo ile-ẹkọ, / ati fun /
         awọn ti nkọ́ ẹkọ́ ni ile /, C.M.S., London
         Pp. 52: '2nd reading book', reading and arithmetic lessons: probably follows the 'Iwe
         ekini' of 1868/1874. Copy in S.O.A.S. Library.

1877*   [2nd, 3rd, 4th Reading Book]
         Pp. 256: probably includes last item: listed in Mann [see Earlier bibliographies].

1877*   Iwe kini ti o ni kika (primer), C.M.S.
         Listed in East [see Earlier bibliographies]: presumably the first part of the series in
         the last item, and another edition of 1868/1874.

1878*   [Samuel 1–2], Lagos
         According to Darlow/Moule [see Earlier bibliographies], a tentative edition of the
         translation, supervised by S. Crowther, 'seems' to have been published at Lagos.

1878–80* [further parts of the Old Testament], Lagos
         According to Darlow/Moule [see Earlier bibliographies], tentative editions of some
         books of the completed translation of the Old Testament, edited by A. C. Mann, were
         published 'but exact details are lacking'.

1879   Testamenti titún / [etc, as 1865 New Testament] / , B.F.B.S., London
         New Testament, revision of 1871 by D. Hinderer.

1879*   Annual Report of the Lagos Auxiliary Association of the B.F.B.S., Lagos
         Yoruba and English: presumably thereafter annually: listed in Mann [see Earlier
         bibliographies].

1879*   [enlarged hymnal]
         206 hymns: information from Mann [see Earlier bibliographies].

[1879]   [S. Crowther], Iwe / adura Yoruba, / ati ti isẹ-iranṣẹ / awọn sacramenti, / ti
         o sì ni / ilana mǐ ati isìn-ilana, / pẹlu / awọn Psalmu ti Dafidi. / , S.P.C.K.,
         London
         Pp. 485: Book of Common Prayer, with Psalms and 39 Articles.

1880*   [2 small hymnals for Sunday schools]
         Listed in Mann [see Earlier bibliographies].

[?1880]   Iṣiṣe si otitọ. / Fun ile-ẹkọ ọjọ-isimi. ti / Eugene Stock ati Geraldine Stock / kọ / ti a si yi si / ede Yoruba /, Townend, Exeter

Pp. 80: 'Steps to truth, a first course of teaching for Sunday schools', translation of a work by E. and G. Stock, probably by J. B. Wood. Copy in S.O.A.S. Library.

1881   Iwe / ti / Samueli / ekini & ekeji / ati ti / Jobu / London: / a kọ fun ẹgbẹ Bibeli ti a npe ni Britiṣe ati ti ilu miran. /, [B.F.B.S., London]

Samuel 1–2, Job: the Old Testament translations (largely revisions), of which parts appeared 1881–4, singly and in sets, were the work of a committee in Lagos under S. Crowther and A. C. Mann, according to Darlow/Moule [see Earlier bibliographies].

1881   Iwe / ti / woli Isaiah / ati ti Ezekieli. / London: / [etc, as previous item] /, [B.F.B.S., London]

Isaiah, Ezekiel.

1881   Iwe / ti / awọn woli / okẹhin mejila / ani lati / Hosea / lọ de / Malaki. / London: / [etc, as previous items] /, [B.F.B.S., London]

Hosea to Malachi. Copy in Cambridge U. L.

1882*   Annual Report of Abeokuta National Church

Yoruba and English: hereafter annually?: listed in Mann [see Earlier bibliographies].

1882*   Annual Report of Lagos Church Missions

Yoruba and English: hereafter annually?: listed in Mann [see Earlier bibliographies],

1882*   Prières du Matin et du Soir, Résumé du Catéchisme, Chant Yoruba, Société des Missions Africaines de Lyon

Listed in East, but as not in Streit/Dindinger, a dubious item [both sources in Earlier bibliographies].

1882*   Manuel de chants religieux en langue Yoruba, S.M.A. de Lyon

As previous item.

1883   Awọn iwe / lati / awọn oba / lo de / Esteri. / London: / [etc, as 1881 items] /, [B.F.B.S., London]

'Kings to Esther in Yoruba' on verso.

1883   Iwe / awọn woli, / Jeremiah / ati / Danieli. / London: / [etc, as previous item] /. B.F.B.S., London

'The prophets Jeremiah and Daniel in Yoruba' on verso, but also includes Lamentations.

1884   N. Baudin, Oeuvre de Saint Jérome pour la publication des / travaux philologiques des missionnaires / No 1 / Katekismu / L'Ede / Yoruba / traduit du catéchisme de Cambrai / par / le R.P.B. / des Missions Africaines de Lyon / Paris / Librairie Poussielgue Frères /

Pp. i–x Introduction in French; 1–95 Catechism in Yoruba; 95–8 Mass in Latin.

1884   Iwe mimọ́ / lati / orin Dafidi / lo de orin Solomoni / London: / [etc, as 1883 items] /, B.F.B.S., London

'From the Book of Psalms to Song of Solomon' on verso.

1884   Iwe mimọ / lati / I Samueli / lọ de / orin Solomoni / London: / [etc, as previous item] /, [B.F.B.S., London]

'I Samuel to Song of Solomon' on verso: six parts, each paginated separately. Reprinted 1886.

1884 Iwe mimọ / lati / Isaiah woli / lọ de / Malaki. / London: / [etc, as previous items] / , [B.F.B.S., London]

'Isaiah to Malachi' on verso: five parts, each paginated separately. Completing printed translation of Bible.

1884* Iwe irohin ati ile isura ẹkọ ti ẹgbẹ awọn olufẹ ìlẹ ibi wọn li Abeokuta, [?Abeokuta]

Pp. 48: treasure house of stories for Abeokuta patriots, historical and biographical, from a longer description in Mann [see Earlier bibliographies]. Another issue in 1885*.

1886* E. M. Lijadu editor, Kekere iwe orin Aribilọso, [?Lagos]

Verses by Aribilọso, a renowned wit and poet: information from Mann [see Earlier bibliographies].

1887–* The Yoruba and Niger Church Missionary Gleaner

Printed in English in London, but three pages, left blank, were printed in English and Yoruba in Lagos: information from Mann [see Earlier bibliographies].

1888* Ipari ero t'awon olobirin pipo, S.P.C.K., London

Listed in Mann [see Earlier bibliographies].

[1889] Testamenti titún / ti / Jesu Kristi / oluwa ati Olugbala wa /, B.F.B.S., London / 1887

New Testament, further revised by a committee under J. B. Wood: date of publication wrongly given on title page, according to Darlow/Moule [see Earlier bibliographies].

1889 Iwe mimọ / testamenti lailai: / Genesisi / titi o fi de / Rutu, / li ede Yoruba./, [B.F.B.S., London]

Genesis to Ruth, a revision of 1867, edited by J. B. Wood.

D. Earlier bibliographies

1845–6 R. G. Latham, 'Upon the philological ethnography of the countries around the Bight of Biafra', *Edinburgh New Philosophical Journal*, 40, pp. 327–9.

Repeated in *Journal of the Ethnological Society of London*, 1, 1848, pp. 224–7.

1847 J. S. Vater, revised B. Jülg, Litteratur der Grammatik, Lexika und Wörtersammlungen aller Sprachen der Erde, Berlin, p. 116

1848 R. G. Latham, 'On the present state and recent progress of ethnographical philology, Part 1, Africa', *Report of the 17th meeting of the British Association, 1847*, pp. 154–229

1858 W. H. I. Bleek, The Library of Sir George Grey: Philology, vol.1, part 2, London and Leipzig, pp. 213–18.

More detailed descriptions of the items listed than any later bibliography. Most of the items now in the South African Public Library.

1858 Bowen, [see Studies], p. xxiii

1883 R. N. Cust, A sketch of the modern languages of Africa, London, vol. 1, pp. 205–7; vol. 2, p. 483

1888–9 Mann, [see Studies], pp. 216–219

1911 T. H. Darlow and H. F. Moule, Historical catalogue of the printed editions of the Holy Scriptures in the Library of B.F.B.S., vol. 4, London, pp. 1707–1710

1911–12   B. Struck, 'Linguistic bibliography of Northern Nigeria', *Journal of the African Society*, 11, pp. 47–61, 213–230, on p. 229

1927   D.Westermann, Die Westlichen Sudansprachen . . . , Berlin, pp. 66–82

1941   R. M. East, A vernacular bibliography for the languages of Nigeria, Literature Bureau, Zaria

The Yoruba references appear to be copied from unnamed sources: despite the remark on p. 83, the rarer works were not seen at the International African Institute Library. Because of its lack of detail, a disappointing work.

1952   D. Westermann and M. A. Bryan, Handbook of African languages Part 2 / Languages of West Africa, International African Institute, London, pp. 192–3

1953   M. de Lavergne de Tressan, Inventaire linguistique de l'A.O.F. et du Togo, Mémoires de l'IFAN, no. 30, Dakar, pp. 55–58

1953–4   R. Streit and J. Dindinger, Bibliotheca Missionum, Freiburg, vols. 18–19

1958   R. Jones, Africa bibliography series / West Africa, International African Institute, London

1959   U. Hintze, Bibliographie der Kwa-Sprachen und der Sprachen der Togo-Restvölker, Deutsche Akademie der Wissenschaften zu Berlin Institut für Orientforschung, Veröffentlichung 42, Berlin, pp. 66–76

1963   F. Adetowun Ogunsheye, A preliminary bibliography of the Yoruba language, Ibadan

Duplicated, pp. 38, issued from the Institute of Librarianship, University Library, Ibadan.

1966   G. E. Coldham, A bibliography of Scriptures in African languages, B.F.B.S. London, vol. 2, pp. 758–764

Revising and updating the relevant section in Darlow/Moule. Privately circulated (to date).

2

THE EARLY STUDY OF
HAUSA AND KANURI, 1840–1890

The Hausa states and the kingdom of Bornu were the major political units in the central part of the Sudanic zone of Africa – that is, in the district west of Lake Chad and north east of the lower section of the middle Niger – for some hundreds of years before the disruptive nineteenth century. Around 1500, the district was visited by a North African youth, who described it in the account of Africa he wrote in later life, when a captive in Italy. This account was almost immediately published in several European languages, under the author's adopted name of Leo Africanus, and it gave Europeans their earliest knowledge of the Central Sudan.[1] Leo Africanus provided the name 'Borno', but he described the Hausa states under their separate names (Gubir, Cano, Casena, Zegzeg,[2] etc), and the account does not include the term 'Hausa'. On the languages of the Sudanic zone, Leo Africanus gave a clear statement: in the Eastern Sudan, Nubian was spoken, and in the Western Sudan, Songai; between these two, in the Central Sudan, Bornu had its own language, while the other states used the language of Gubir (i.e. Hausa).[3]

Leo Africanus's accurate but limited account of the Hausa states and Bornu was for nearly three centuries almost all that Europeans knew about the Central Sudan. The long continuance of this relative lack of information requires some explanation. To the south, the Europeans during this period were in regular contact with the Guinea coast; but from there they were unable either to travel inland, through the politically-fragmentated pagan peoples of the coast, or to learn much about the interior states. To the north, the Central Sudan was in regular contact with the Moslem shores of the Mediterranean. (Merchants and notables from Bornu frequently visited Tripoli: Sudanese pilgrims passed through Cairo: slaves from the pagan fringes of the Islamic states of the Central Sudan were sold throughout the Western Moslem world; at the end of the period, possibly earlier, colonies of Hausa traders began to settle in the major towns between Morocco and Asia Minor: throughout the period, North African merchants took occasional business trips to the Sudan.) But Christian Europe had only limited and spasmodic contact with Moslem North Africa: North Africans were unwilling to supply information to Europeans about the Sudan, or to allow them to travel there. As a result of these obstacles, in 1800 no Christian European had yet

---

[1] R. Hallett, *The Exploration of Africa*, vol. 1, 1965, pp. 53–9. While other Arabic-speaking scholars had written about the Central Sudan much earlier than Leo Africanus (for earlier references to the Hausa people and the name 'Hausa', see D. Westermann in G. P. Bargery, *A Hausa–English dictionary*, 1934, pp. ix–xii), their accounts were not available in European languages before 1800. However, al-Idrisi, available in Latin from 1619, referred to Kanem, the fore-runner of Bornu, situated to the north-east of Lake Chad.

[2] Gubir, or Gobir, was the Hausa state in which the Fulani jihad originated: the others are the modern Kano, Katsina, Zaria.

[3] A. Epaulard *et al.* (translator and editors), *Jean-Léon l'Africain: Description de l'Afrique*, 1956, pp. 16, 472–83. Leo Africanus added that the language of Gaoga (or Kanem) resembled that of Bornu: Kanuri and Kanembu are in fact closely related languages.

visited and returned from any part of the Central Sudan.[4] It is clear that European ignorance about the Central Sudan before 1800 was due more to religious, political, and commercial barriers than to the geographical remoteness of the region.[5]

We know of only one attempt by Christian Europeans to penetrate to the Central Sudan before 1800. In 1710–11, two Roman Catholic missionaries travelled from Tripoli, via Murzuk and Agades, to Katsina, where they died from disease and ill-treatment. They were hoping to reach 'Borno' and the neighbouring kingdom of 'Corurfa' (Kwararafa), the latter having been reported, almost certainly incorrectly, to be Christian. The missionaries spoke Arabic: the fragmentary sources apparently do not state whether they endeavoured to learn an African language – 'Borno', Hausa, or 'Corurfa' (?Jukun) – before or in the course of their journey.[6]

This unsuccessful expedition was not made public by the mission authorities, and was not known to the persons in Europe who, towards the end of the eighteenth century, began systematic attempts to obtain new information about the Central Sudan. The first attempts were in the form of contacts made with natives of the Central Sudan who were living in, or were visiting, other parts of the world. As we shall see, contacts were made in places as far apart as Copenhagen and Brazil, Cairo and Kumasi. When these contacts were discovered to be only moderately informative, attempts were then made to obtain information more directly, by sending Europeans to the area.[7]

The earliest contact was made in 1773, in Copenhagen. A few years earlier, the Danish king had sent the first scientific expedition to Arabia: its surviving member, Carsten Niebuhr, on his return wrote a classic description of the Yemen. In 1773, Copenhagen was visited by 'Abderrahman', an envoy of the ruler of Tunis, who was touring the courts of Northern Europe,[8] and Niebuhr, as an Arabic-speaker, was called on to talk to him. Abderrahman had been a trader before he became a diplomat, and had traded with, though not himself visited, the Central Sudan. Moreover, among his

---

[4] There is evidence which suggests that a few European merchants visited Timbuktu and the Western Sudan before 1500, and may conceivably have reached the Central Sudan; and that Christian slaves were taken to both the Western and the Central Sudan in later centuries (R. Mauny, *Tableau géographique de l'Ouest Africain au Moyen Age*, Mémoires de l'IFAN, 61, 1961, pp. 462–4; Hallett, *op. cit.*, p. 101 – Christian slaves said to be sent from Tripoli to Bornu in the seventeenth century). Further, European renegades, often holding important posts in Islamic states, are known to have travelled through the Sahara and Western Sudan, and it is likely that some of these men were in fact the first natives of Europe to reach the Central Sudan. But no European, merchant, slave or renegade, is known to have returned to Europe from the Central Sudan.

[5] 'The inland geography of this vast continent presents an obscure scene . . . less invisible to the Arabian Moors than to any other nation of the ancient or modern world' (Gibbon: quoted in Hallett, *op. cit.*, p. 51).

[6] Richard Gray, 'Christian traces and a Franciscan mission in the Central Sudan, 1700–1711': I am most grateful to Dr Gray for allowing me to see this seminar paper, a version of which will shortly appear in the *Journal of African History*. It is curious that this episode in West African history has until recently been overlooked by historians; the reference to it in the *Quarterly Review* for 1818, in a footnote, was certainly a slight one, but it was also the subject of a lengthy note in a German periodical at the time of Barth's expedition (T. E. Gumprecht, 'Eine Entdeckungsreise nach Fezzan, Aghadez und Kaschna in den Jahren 1710 und 1711', *Zeitschrift für allgemeine Erdkunde*, 2, 1854, pp. 245–8).

[7] The reasons why it became possible after 1800 for Europeans to penetrate the Sahara and the Sudan, with a fair degree of cooperation from Moslem powers, are discussed, at least tentatively, in A. A. Boahen, *Britain, the Sahara, and the Western Sudan*, 1964.

[8] Although the name Abdel Rahman is a very common one in Islamic countries, it is possible that this 'Abderrahman' was the same man who was later minister of foreign affairs in Tunis and was then described as 'a most enlightened man, having been repeatedly at the chief courts of Europe' (see R. Hallett, *Records of the African Association*, 1964, p. 63, n. 2).

attendants was a slave who had been brought from Bornu and was apparently Hausa-speaking. From discussions with the envoy and his slave, Niebuhr obtained information about 'Inner Africa', and thus stimulated, he proposed to follow up his exploits in Arabia with a journey across the Sahara to Bornu. But the savant married a wife, and the journey was postponed indefinitely, while the material he had collected on 'Inner Africa' was not published until 1790–1.[9] The material included the numerals in 'Bernu' and in 'Afnu'[10] (i.e. Hausa), and a score of nouns in the latter language.[11] Published in a German periodical, this linguistic information appears to have escaped the attention of the African Association, and was not mentioned in English writings until it was referred to in the linguistic encyclopedia, *Mithridates*, in 1812. These are the earliest-collected formal vocabularies of Hausa and Kanuri at present known to exist.[12]

---

[9] On Niebuhr, see the Danish and German biographical dictionaries and B. G. Niebuhr, *Life of C. Niebuhr* (English translation of the original), 1836, especially p. 36. In the preface to the second volume of his *Reisebeschreibung nach Arabien und andern umgeliegenden Ländern*, 1778, Niebuhr promised to publish some material on Africa, but none was included in this volume, or in the third volume which appeared very posthumously in 1837 (see p. xx of the third volume). Instead Niebuhr published two articles, as follows: 'Das Innere von Afrika', *Neues Deutsches Museum*, Leipzig, October 1790, pp. 963–1004, April 1791, pp. 419–30.

[10] 'Afnu', from the Kanuri name for the Hausa, 'Afūno' (S. W. Koelle, *Polyglotta Africana*, 1854, p. 17). A misreading of a manuscript, or a misprint, occurred in the African Association's published report of 1802 which gave the first detailed map of the Central Sudan (on information from Hornemann), where the name is given as 'Asna' instead of 'Afna' or perhaps 'Afno': the relevant section of the report in Hallett, *op. cit.* (1964), p. 301.

[11] The Afnu nouns (with equivalents in modern Hausa) are as follows:

ghaui = Dorf (garī = town, etc.)
dudsji = Berg (dūtse = hill)
koroma = Fluss (kōrama = large stream)
dsjenari = Gold (zīnārīyā = gold)
dolma = Silber (dalma = lead, tin)
ghurassa = Brod (sic) (gurāsa = wheaten food)
crua = Wasser (řūwā = water)
daua = durra, kleiner Mais (dāwa = guinea-corn)
sinkaffer = Reis (shiŋkāfā = rice)
sirki = Sultan (sarki = emir)
motün = Mann (mutum/mutuŋ = man)
bavia = Frau (?baiwā = female slave)
ja = Mädgen (sic) ('yā = daughter)
schensali = Teufel (shaitsāni = Satan)
Allah = Gott
berni = Stadt, mit einer Mauer umgebene (birni = walled town)

The modern forms are taken from R. C. Abraham, *Dictionary of the Hausa language*, 1946. I am indebted to Dr D. Dalby and Mr A. H. M. Kirk-Greene for advice on some of these identifications.

[12] Odd words, however, appeared in earlier Arabic sources, especially titles and toponyms, e.g. the Kanuri title mai, explained correctly by the Turkish geographer Çelebi, *c.*1680 as being the equivalent of 'sultan'. Even Sudano-Arabic writers displayed the traditional contempt of the Arabic-speaker for other languages, above all pre-literate ones, and they clearly endeavoured not to sully the purity of their prose by including too many barbarian terms. The extracts from Arabic sources in T. Hodgkin, *Nigerian perspectives*, 1960, provide only a handful of vernacular terms, e.g. wendi, a kind of cloth at Kanem (p. 77, al-Maqrizi, *c.*1420): Jamshish, a title meaning 'buffalo' in Kanuri (p. 80, a diplomatic document, *c.*1450); gagara, a drinking-trough for animals, hence a canoe, in Kanuri [? magara = canoe, in modern Kanuri] (p. 115, ibn Fartua, *c.*1600). None of the Arabic sources mentioning the Central Sudan and covering about eight hundred years, shows any scientific interest in, or even pre-scientific curiosity about, the vernacular languages; none provides a formal collection of vocabulary.

Between 1773 and the 1850s, when the travels and writings of Heinrich Barth finally provided a sound and detailed description of the Central Sudan, over a score of travellers and savants published original material on the area. Most of them provided information about the Hausa and Kanuri languages, but none provided more than very limited details. The briefest way to record this period of extensive but superficial inquiry into the languages, will be simply to list the persons involved, together with a summary of their activity, in chronological order by the date of collection of the information.

(1) Simon Lucas, on behalf of the African Association, in 1789 travelled from Tripoli a little way towards Fezzan, and from a Fezzan merchant who accompanied him and who had traded to Bornu, he collected the numerals of 'Bornou' and 'Cashna' (i.e. Katsina Hausa): published London 1790.[13]

(2) El Haj Abd Salam Shabeni, a Moroccan merchant passing through England, supplied the Secretary of the African Association with an account of a town called 'Houssa' in the Central Sudan, the earliest knowledge in Europe of this name: published London 1792.[14]

(3) Friedrich Hornemann, on behalf of the African Association, in 1800 travelled from Murzuk, across the desert, into the Central Sudan; he learnt some Kanuri (being perhaps the first European to do this) and passed through Bornu and part of Hausaland, but died in Nupe country, where all his trans-Saharan papers were destroyed.[15]

(4) J. L. Burckhardt, on behalf of the African Association, travelled in Nubia, and at Cairo in 1816–17 collected from pilgrims from Bornu, a 'Bornu' vocabulary: published London 1819.[16]

(5) T. E. Bowdich, on behalf of the African Company, travelled in 1816–18 from the Gold Coast into Ashanti, and at Kumasi collected the numerals and a few words of Hausa (under the names 'Houssa', 'Mallowa', and 'Quolla-liffa') and the same of Kanuri ('Bornou' and 'Maiha'): published London 1819.[17]

(6) An unknown person collected, 'a few years' before 1821, at an unstated place, possibly even in England, from 'a native of Gubir' a short vocabulary of 'the language of Guberi and Kachenah' (i.e. Hausa): published London 1821.[18]

(7) J. B. de Andrade y Silva, a Brazilian scientist and politician, questioned African slaves in Brazil in 1819, and collected a 'Haussah' vocabulary: published Paris 1826.[19]

---

[13] *Proceedings of the Association for promoting the discovery of the interior parts of Africa*, London, 1790, p. 166. On Lucas, see Boahen, *op. cit.*, p. 15; Hallett, *op. cit.* (1964), chapter 2; Hallett, *op. cit.* (1965), pp. 204–9.

[14] *Proceedings of the Association . . .*, London, 1792, p. 12; Hallett, *op. cit.* (1964), chapter 6; Hallett, *op. cit.* (1965), pp. 217–19. Shabeni affirmed that literacy was common in Houssa, in an alphabet not Arabic or Hebrew (perhaps a misplaced recollection of the Tuareg script?).

[15] *Journal of F. Hornemann's travels . . .*, London, 1802. On Hornemann, see Boahen, *op. cit.*, pp. 24–6; Hallett, *op. cit.* (1964), chapter 10; Hallett, *op. cit.* (1965), pp. 250–63; E. W. Bovill, *Missions to the Niger*, vol. 1, 1964, pp. 8–41.

[16] John Lewis Burckhardt, *Travels in Nubia . . .*, London, 1819, pp. 491–2 (140 words in Kanuri). On Burckhardt, see *Neue Deutsche Biographie*; C. Burckhardt-Sarasin and H. Schwabe-Burckhardt, *Scheik Ibrahim (J. L. Burckhardt): Briefe an Eltern und Geschwister*, Basel, 1956; Hallett, *op. cit.* (1964), chapter 13; Hallett, *op. cit.* (1965), pp. 366–77.

[17] T. E. Bowdich, *Mission from Cape Coast to Ashantee . . .*, London, 1819, pp. 196–8, 213–14, 505–12 (numerals and 20 words in each). On Bowdich, see *D.N.B.*

[18] *Annals of Oriental Literature*, London, [1820], pp.549–52 (numerals and 60 words).

[19] *Journal des Voyages*, Paris, 32, 1826, pp. 322–4 (60 words).

(8) G. F. Lyon, on behalf of the British government, travelled in 1819–20 from Tripoli to Murzuk, and from Bornu traders collected 'Bornu' and 'Haoussa' vocabularies: published London 1821.[20]

(9) Sheikh Mohammed ibn-Omar El-Tounsy, while living and trading in Wadai, apparently around 1820, collected a brief vocabulary of 'Barnaoui': published Paris 1851.[21]

(10) D. Denham and H. Clapperton, on behalf of the British government, travelled 1822–5 from Tripoli to Bornu and Sokoto, and collected a fairly extensive 'Bornou' vocabulary, and their account included a little Hausa: published London 1826.[22]

(11) Hannah Kilham, on behalf of a Quaker 'Committee for African Instruction', in 1824 and 1827 collected in Sierra Leone from ex-slaves 'Houssa' and 'Borno' vocabularies: published London 1828.[23]

(12) H. Clapperton and his servant R. Lander travelled in 1825–7, on behalf of the British government, from the Guinea coast to Sokoto, and one of them collected a 'Houssa' vocabulary: published London 1830.[24]

(13) M. Laird and R. A. K. Oldfield, on a private expedition, travelled in 1832–4 up the River Niger to the confluence with the Benue, and collected a fairly lengthy 'Houssa' vocabulary: published London 1837.[25]

(14) E. Koenig, a French scientist and a traveller in Nubia, collected there a 'Barnaoui' vocabulary: published Paris 1839.[26]

(15) W. B. Hodgson, an American consul, in the 1830s collected from slaves at Algiers, vocabularies of 'Bornu' and 'Haoussa': published New York 1844.[27]

---

[20] G. F. Lyon, *Narrative of travels in Northern Africa* . . . , London, 1821, pp. 122–3, 149–51 (50 words in Kanuri, 100 in Hausa). On Lyon, see *D.N.B.*; Boahen, *op. cit.*, pp. 49–53.

[21] Cheykh Mohammed ibn-Omar el-Tounsy, *Voyage au Ouaday*, Paris, 1851, pp. 726–7 (a dozen words and phrases). We noted (in footnote 12) that Arabic writers tried to ignore African languages. Nevertheless, it is likely that Arabic-speaking traders, for their own convenience, sometimes collected vocabularies of useful terms in vernaculars, since some of the printed collections were obtained from Arabic-speakers who can hardly have carried so many vernacular terms in their heads. If so, it would be extremely interesting to see their manuscripts (if any are extant), to compare their recording of vernacular terms in Arabic sounds and Arabic script, with comparable recordings by Europeans.

[22] Dixon Denham, Hugh Clapperton, [Walter] Oudney, *Narrative of travels and discoveries in Northern and Central Africa* . . . , London, 1826, Appendix 17, second pagination pp. 175–9 (600 Kanuri words and phrases, Hausa terms scattered through Clapperton's contribution). On these men, see Boahen, *op. cit.*, pp. 53–8; E. W. Bovill, *Missions to the Niger*, 2, 1966, pp. 3–108 (note that in this edition, the linguistic appendices are omitted; but in vol. 3, p. 625, a Hausa song).

[23] [H. Kilham], *Specimens of African languages spoken in the Colony of Sierra Leone*, London, 1828. A version of the Specimens, in loose, untitled, undated handsheets, contains lengthier vocabularies; it is sometimes bound with and dated from [H. Kilham], *African school tracts*, 1827. For more details, see P. E. H. Hair, 'An introduction to John Clarke's "Specimens of Dialects . . . " 1848/9', *Sierra Leone Language Review*, 5, 1966, pp. 72–82, on p. 80, n. 5.

[24] R. Lander, *Records of Captain Clapperton's last expedition* . . . , London, 1830, vol. 2, pp. 289–93 (60 phrases). On Clapperton and Lander, see Boahen, *op. cit.*, pp. 75–82. A manuscript vocabulary of Hausa by Clapperton was referred to in W. B. Cooley, *The Negroland of the Arabs* . . . , London, 1841, p. 142.

[25] M. Laird and R. A. K. Oldfield, *Narrative of an expedition* . . . , London, 1837, 2, pp. 421–41 (700 words). On Laird and Oldfield, see K. O. Dike, *Trade and politics in the Niger Delta*, 1956, pp. 61–2; Boahen, *op. cit.*, pp. 95–6. Another member of the expedition, William Allen, also collected a Hausa vocabulary which he contributed to the 1841 *Outline of a Vocabulary* referred to below. Another member, Dr Briggs, began to learn Hausa, but died.

[26] –. Koenig, 'Vocabulaires appartenant à diverses contrées ou tribus de l'Afrique', *Receuil de voyages et de mémoires publié par la Société de Géographie*, 4, 1839, pp. 181–9 (200 words).

[27] W. B. Hodgson, *Notes on Northern Africa, the Sahara and the Soudan* . . . , New York, 1844, pp. 109–10 (numerals, 15 Kanuri words, 100 Hausa).

(16) John Clarke, a British missionary, in the 1840s collected, in the West Indies or on Fernando Po Island, several short vocabularies of Hausa and Kanuri, under various names: published Berwick on Tweed/London 1848/9.[28]

(17) F. de Castelnau, a French scientist, in the late 1840s collected from slaves in Brazil a 'Haoussa' vocabulary: published Paris 1851.[29]

(18) S. W. Koelle, a German missionary, around 1850 collected from ex-slaves in Freetown accurate vocabularies of Hausa and Kanuri: published London 1854.[30]

To sum up this long list of vocabulary collectings. Most of these attempts to obtain information about the Hausa and Kanuri languages were either made by British subjects or were backed by British interests, and the decisive contacts of the 1850s similarly originated in Britain. These latter contacts were necessary because the sum of linguistic knowledge obtained after all the attempts listed above was disappointingly meagre. Most of the vocabularies were very short and very inaccurate. In all, allowing for duplication of terms, they added up to about 1,000 words in each language, with only a small proportion in phrases from which grammar could be deduced. No texts were collected.

The earliest attempt to compare vocabularies was in 1812, when the German scholar, J. S. Vater, in the third volume of the linguistic encyclopedia, *Mithridates*, examined two Hausa and two Kanuri vocabularies, and correctly showed that the language which Niebuhr called 'Afnu' was the same as the one which Lucas called 'Cashna'.[31] J. C. Prichard, an English ethnographer, listed the material on the languages available in 1826, and again, when there was rather more, in 1837, but made no attempt at analysis.[32] Edwin Norris, an English amateur Orientalist, prepared vocabularies of Hausa and Kanuri from earlier sources, and had them printed in 1841 in a handbook entitled 'Outline of a vocabulary of a few of the principal languages of Western and Central Africa, compiled for the use of the Niger Expedition'.[33]

Before the 1840s, the only published material on Hausa or Kanuri which was more than a mere vocabulary, or a simple comparison of vocabularies, appeared in 1826. This was a booklet written by H. J. Klaproth, the eminent German Orientalist (author of *Asia Polyglotta*), who endeavoured to analyse the vocabulary appearing in Denham's

---

[28] John Clarke, *Specimens of dialects . . .* , Berwick on Tweed/London, 1848/9 (original vocabularies only – Bugimbinour 37, Houssa p. 59 and numerals 49, 299, Malaba 53, Birni numerals 352; Borno 58, Bernu 265, Bulaqua numerals 127). On Clarke, see Hair, *op. cit.*

[29] F. de Castelnau, *Renseignements sur l'Afrique Centrale et sur une nation d'hommes à queue qui s'y trouverait d'après le rapport des nègres du Soudan esclaves à Bahia*, Paris, pp. 48–60. Of greater interest among the contents of this volume than the Hausa vocabulary (or the report of tailed men) are two vocabularies of small North Nigerian languages, 'Java' = Jaba and 'Courami' = Kurama/Chawai, perhaps the earliest vocabularies of these languages.

[30] S. W. Koelle, *Polyglotta Africana*, London, 1854. Included in this list only for completeness, the material in the Polyglotta was of course immeasurably superior to that in the earlier works on the list, for reasons which the text will shortly show.

[31] J. C. Adelung, completed J. S. Vater, *Mithridates oder allgemeine Sprachenkunde . . .* , vol. 3, Berlin, 1812, pp. 152–3, 231–2.

[32] J. C. Prichard, *Researches into the physical history of mankind*, 2nd edition 1826, vol. 1, pp. 276–7, 3rd edition, vol. 2, 1837, pp. 109–13.

[33] [E. Norris], *Outline of a vocabulary . . .* , London, 1841. In the later 1840s, the ethnographer and linguist R. G. Latham several times discussed the available vocabularies. But as we shall see, though we have listed early vocabularies up to 1850, more serious work on Hausa was available in print after 1843 (and on Kanuri was under way after 1849) and therefore further discussion of the early vocabularies was of little value for the study of the language.

account of the 1822–5 expedition. Klaproth produced only fourteen pages of analysis, to form the first scholarly though very slight study of Kanuri.[34]

The Niger Expedition of 1841–2 marked the end of the period of groping discovery of Hausa and Kanuri, for aboard one of the ships of the expedition was the first serious student of Hausa, J. F. Schön. Schön published his first book on Hausa in 1843 and his last in 1888: the French linguist, Delafosse, said of him – 'on pourrait l'appeler le grand découvreur de la langue haoussa, car c'est lui qui l'a révélée à l'Europe'.[35] Schön, as we shall see, began work on Hausa when he was a missionary of the Church Mission-ary Society in Sierra Leone (and in the essay on the early study of Yoruba, we have already caught glimpses of him at work). On the linguistic side of his missionary activity in Sierra Leone, his successor was S. W. Koelle, who devoted three years to the study of Kanuri and in 1854 published two brilliant works on this language. Meanwhile, on behalf of the British government, yet another expedition had crossed the desert to the Central Sudan. Its most distinguished surviving member, Heinrich Barth, learned to speak both Hausa and Kanuri and, some years after his return to Europe, published linguistic material containing partial studies of both languages. By the 1870s, thanks to the labours of these three men, Hausa and Kanuri were languages unusually well des-cribed by the standards of the day in African linguistics.

*   *   *

James Frederick Schön (christened Jacob Friedrich Schön, but the Anglicised form appeared whenever his full name was given on the title pages of his books) was born at Ober Weiler, in Baden in South Germany, in 1803.[36] His earlier career is not known, but at the age of twenty-seven he offered himself for missionary service. He was trained at the Basel Missionary Seminary, and then at the Church Missionary Society training college at Islington.[37] Ordained in 1832, he was sent to Sierra Leone, where he served six and a half years in various parishes in the peninsula before returning to Europe on leave in 1839. During his first stay in West Africa, he married and buried his first wife, who was the daughter of the pioneer missionary-linguist, G. R. Nyländer.[38] While on leave, Schön married his second wife, who died soon after he brought her back to Sierra Leone. After a year, he married again, this time the widow of a fellow-missionary; his third marriage lasted for forty-seven years – but most of it was spent away from The White Man's Grave. In 1841, Schön travelled on the Niger Expedition, and then to

[34] This work is listed in the bibliography: hereafter, works appearing in the bibliography will not be given a footnote if the reference to them in the text is a general one.
[35] 'We might call him the Discoverer of Hausa, for Europe learned about it through him' (M. Dela-fosse, *Manuel de la langue haoussa*, Paris, 1901, p. ix).
[36] *C.M.S. Register of missionaries* [1905], [privately printed]: *Modern English Biography: Allgemeine Deutsche Biographie.* Part of the biography of Schön, and most of the biography of his linguistic successor, S. W. Koelle, has already been related by the present writer in the Historical Introduction to the 1963 reprint of Koelle's *Polyglotta Africana* (henceforward referred to as Hair/Koelle, *op. cit.*).
[37] The Church Missionary Society, founded in 1799 by Evangelical supporters of the established Church of England, at first had difficulty in recruiting Englishmen as missionaries, and hence employed Germans. The Berlin Missionary Seminary supplied candidates from 1802 (they included G. R. Nyländer, father of Schön's first wife), the Basel Missionary Seminary from 1818.
[38] She had been born on the Bullom shore, opposite Freetown: her father and mother died in Sierra Leone, as did at least three sibs who died in infancy and a sister who also married a missionary. Her daughter by Schön survived, grew up, married a missionary in Ceylon, and produced another generation of this missionary family.

England, but was back in Sierra Leone by late 1843. In 1847, his health broke down, and he left West Africa for good, after fourteen years' service in the mission.

In 1838, Schön began work on the Sherbro (Bullom) language of Sierra Leone, resuming the study started thirty years earlier by his late wife's father; and while on leave in 1839 he had printed two small preparatory works. But in 1840 the mission authorities ordered him to turn his attention to languages relevant to the forthcoming Niger Expedition, which he (together with Samuel Crowther, as we saw in the previous essay) had been chosen to accompany. Schön made inquiries among the liberated slaves in Sierra Leone and read the literature available on the Niger, and selected Ibo and Hausa as the most useful languages. Forty years later, he recollected – 'when the writer commenced the study and reduction of Hausa, he had to begin at the very beginning. A small but notwithstanding valuable vocabulary by Oldfield, a few words in Clapperton's Travels were all he met with as then in existence'.[39] To these, Schön added a manuscript vocabulary of Hausa collected at Freetown by his former colleague, J. Raban (now retired), and made, testified Schön, 'with very great care'.[40] Informants were chosen from among the Hausa ex-slaves in Freetown, and by September 1840 Schön was finding it 'a soft and sweet language'.[41] Schön and Crowther (who was reported to be 'as far advanced in Hausa' as Schön) joined the ships of the Niger Expedition in June 1841 and, once at sea, Schön settled down to translating an Address to the Chiefs and Peoples of Africa, drawn up in England for the use of the expedition. It was ready by the time the ships reached Cape Coast, and was printed there on the government press[42]– thus becoming the first Hausa text in print.

Travelling up the Niger, Schön translated more diplomatic documents, and practised his Hausa on African visitors to the ships and the tribal officials in the riverain towns. As he and Crowther surveyed the linguistic topography of the Niger, he became enthusiastic about the role of Hausa in future exploration and missionary penetration: 'Hausa is now, to these parts of Africa, what the French is to Europe', he wrote.[43] But though the expedition reached areas where Hausa was a commercial lingua franca, it never reached even the fringes of Hausaland proper: mortality among the European members forced it to turn back and leave the river. On the island of Fernando Po, Schön discovered a 'learned mallam', with whom he checked over his translation. But the hard fact remained that he had not had – and was never to have – the opportunity to study Hausa within its homeland.

During his leave in England after the Niger Expedition, Schön saw through the press his journal of the expedition (published together with Crowther's), and a book containing a vocabulary and brief grammar of Hausa – the first printed study of the language. Included with the journal was a report by Schön which stressed the importance of linguistic work, and pleaded with the mission authorities to give it greater priority. Despite official encouragement in the past, Schön complained that little had been done. This, he thought, was mainly because 'it was believed to be compatible with

---

[39] J. F. Schön, 'Sketch of the Hausa Language', *Journal of the Royal Asiatic Society*, n.s. 14, 1882, pp. 176–217, on p. 179.
[40] C.M.S. Archives, CA 1/o 195, letter of 25.9.1840.
[41] *ibid.*, and the letter of 24.3.1841.
[42] *Journals of the Rev. James Frederick Schön and Mr Samuel Crowther, who . . . accompanied the Expedition up the Niger in 1841, on behalf of the Church Missionary Society*, London, 1842, p. 21.
[43] *ibid.*, pp. 74, 116, 120 (quotation), 237, 357: Crowther also tried to speak Hausa and to collect vocabulary, pp. 259, 287, 307.

the other duties devolving upon a Missionary, and has therefore never formed a distinct occupation for some of the Society's labours . . .I must express my conviction that more will not be done in the future, unless the study of the Native Languages be made a separate employment.' The authorities commented in the introduction to the book – 'The Committee have now devolved this branch of labour specifically upon certain Missionaries in Sierra Leone, of aptitude for lingual and philological pursuits, besides engaging the service of one individual exclusively as a linguist'.[44] This was less satisfactory than it sounded. The 'linguist' appointed was a layman who received a meagre salary and little cooperation from his clerical colleagues (so at least he persistently asserted), and who, after a few years with little to show, resigned.[45] Meanwhile Schön found that though he was expected to continue his work on Hausa (in 1843, he regretted that he was unable to accept the suggestion of the home authorities that he should also take up the study of Mandingo and Fula), the local mission authorities tended to grudge him the time spent on linguistic work and away from pastoral duties, and he had several times to resist strongly attempts to make him undertake a more normal missonary routine.[46]

Of the next few years of Hausa study, Schön later wrote: 'on returning to Sierra Leone . . . , I was requested to pursue the study of the Hausa, and to prepare translations of portions of Scripture into it. Three Gospels and the Acts of the Apostles were translated,[47] and materials collected for a Grammar and Dictionary, amidst many interruptions from fever and other circumstances. In the spring of 1847, I was obliged to return to Europe through ill-health: in fact, during the last three years of my residence in Sierra Leone, I do not think I ever enjoyed more than tolerable health to prosecute my labours for a month together.'[48] In 1844, Schön's Hausa work was submitted to Professor Samuel Lee of Cambridge, an Orientalist and the C.M.S.'s principal linguistic adviser.[49] Perhaps on Lee's advice, Schön tried to acquire some Arabic, but he was unable to spare time to advance far in this study.[50] On his return to Europe, Schön

---

[44] *Journals* (*op. cit.*), pp. 359, xiv.

[45] The 'linguist' was W. C. Thom(p)son, a graduate of Glasgow, whose 'original design in coming to Africa [was] the reduction of the native languages spoken in the Colony' (C.M.S. Archives, CA 1/o 214, letter of 21.5.1841): he worked on Temne (see P. E. H. Hair, 'Early vernacular printing in Africa', *Sierra Leone Language Review*, 3, 1964, pp. 47–52, especially p. 52, n. (f)): his report on a visit to Timbo, where he died in 1845, was published: his son served in the Presbyterian mission at Calabar.

[46] C.M.S. Archives, CA 1/o 195, letters 18.12.1843 – 1847.

[47] A manuscript copy of Schön's translation of one of the Gospels, made by John Clarke, the Baptist missionary, in 1846, is in the Library of S.O.A.S. The translation of another Gospel was sent to England in 1845 (C.M.S. Archives, CA 1/o 195, letter of 23.6.1845).

[48] J. F. Schön, *Grammar* . . . , 1862, p. vii: in the C.M.S. Archives, among the reports from Schön 1843–7, in CA 1/o 195, is one of a few pages of 'Observations and answers to questions on the Hausa language', written at Gloucester, Sierra Leone, in 1846. Reports on Schön's progress in Hausa appeared regularly in the annual *C.M.S. Proceedings*: 1842–3, p. 37 ('to confine his labours almost entirely to this department') 1844–5, p. 36 (translation of Matthew revised and copied for fifth time), 1845–6, p. 41 (John completed), 1846–7 (Luke completed).

[49] Samuel Lee 'was a carpenter's apprentice at Shrewsbury, who, while working at his trade, had acquired a knowledge of Latin, Greek, Hebrew, Syriac, Arabic, Persian and Hindustani, before he was twenty-five years of age. He came under the notice of [the Secretary of C.M.S.] . . . and the Committee arranged for him to go to Cambridge at the Society's expense. There he quickly made his mark as a scholar, and for some years he was employed by the C.M.S. Committee, and called 'the Society's Orientalist' . . . He afterwards became Professor of Arabic and Canon of Bristol' (E. Stock, *History of C.M.S.*, 1, 1899, p. 120).

[50] C.M.S. Archives, CA 1/o 195, letter of 23.9.1844.

chose to settle in England, and was naturalised in 1854. Through the good offices of one of the surviving naval officers of the Niger Expedition, in 1848 he was given the post of Chaplain at the Melville Hospital, Chatham, in which town he lived with his family for the remainder of his long life. The salary was small, and Schön had difficulty in supporting his five children, but the post allowed him opportunity to continue linguistic work.[51]

Hausa studies were not immediately continued, however, for reasons described by Schön himself, as follows: 'On presenting the work of my labours to the Committee of the C.M.S., I confess that I was not a little disappointed at its decision, that as the translations were not required for Sierra Leone, and as there was no prospect of commencing a mission in the interior, the Committee would not recommend them for publication. Consequently, all was put aside, or at all events very little attention was paid to it, until the year 1856 . . .'[52] What had happened was that the mission authorities had changed their minds. In the early and mid-1840s, the idea of a chain of mission stations stretching from the coast to the Central Sudan had been canvassed, and work on interior languages encouraged. But the establishment of the first link in the chain, the station at Abeokuta, even though this in itself was a great success, drew attention to the practical weakness of the idea. Since Yorubaland was responding so encouragingly to the advance of the Gospel, was it not wiser to concentrate resources, by consolidating the base in Yorubaland for at least a decade, before making the leap forward across the Niger? Between 1848 and 1850, the proponents of consolidation in Yorubaland (the principal of whom, Henry Townsend, we met in the earlier essay) won the day.[53] Thus, David Hinderer, a recruit from the Basel Seminary, in 1848 was sent to Schön at Chatham to learn Hausa, but in 1849 when he reached West Africa, he was stationed, permanently it was to prove, in Yorubaland, and he dropped his study of Hausa.[54] Crowther, the former student of Hausa, was by now too busy preparing translations in his own language, Yoruba.[55] During the early 1850s, it seemed as if Schön would join the ranks of the many who had studied West African languages but whose work had borne little or no fruit in the form of publications. His grammar and vocabulary of 1843 was self-confessedly a tentative work, incomplete and in parts inaccurate, as he himself later admitted. His only other publication in Hausa was a primer, issued in 1848.[56] The C.M.S. now made use of his linguistic experience in humbler if necessary tasks; assisting Professor Lee in the preparation of a brief set of *Rules for reducing unwritten languages to alphabetical writing in Roman characters, with reference especially to the languages spoken in Africa* (to which we return later); helping Crowther to revise the orthography of his Yoruba translations, and seeing these (and other works from

---

[51] Schön remained nominally 'in connexion' with the C.M.S. until 1853. But from 1847, his letters were no longer filed with the Sierra Leone mission, but with 'Home' correspondance, and hence are more difficult to locate. Letters 1847–53 are in section CH/O: a letter of 20.2.1849 is highly unusual in that in it describes his domestic condition, which was then very difficult, his health being poor and the chaplaincy salary only £100 p.a. to support a family of five children ('not a shilling in hand'). The chaplaincy was not a sinecure, and to speak of 'the leisure of Schön in retirement' (J. F. A. Ajayi, *Christian missions in Nigeria 1841–1891*, 1965, p. 130) is misleading.

[52] Schön, *op. cit.* (1862), p. viii.

[53] Ajayi, *op. cit.*, pp. 95–6.

[54] C.M.S. Archives, CH/O, letters of 6.3.1848, 4.2.1850.

[55] In 1854, Crowther confessed himself 'not yet master of the Hausa' (S. Crowther, *Journal . . . ,* 1855, p. 101).

[56] The date of this undated work is given in Schön, *op. cit.* (1862), p. ix.

missionaries in the West African field) through the press.[57] But the study of Hausa had come to a standstill.

Schön's insistence that a more specialised approach was required if sound linguistic work was to be produced in Sierra Leone, had some result, in that when S. W. Koelle was appointed to the Freetown mission – in effect, as Schön's successor in linguistic duties – he was exempted from normal pastoral responsibilities by being appointed to the teaching staff of Fourah Bay Institute (later College). It was probably also on Schön's advice[58] that Koelle spent a few months at Tübingen, under the great Ewald, learning Arabic. Koelle therefore worked in Freetown with advantages that Schön had never possessed, but which the older man had helped to gain for him. As Nyländer and Raban had laid the ground for Schön, so Schön laid it for Koelle. And Koelle's work at Freetown finally justified the labours of the earlier generations of missionary-linguists.[59]

Sigismund Wilhelm Koelle (his surname was spelt thus on all his publications) was born in 1823 at Cleebronn, in Württemberg in South Germany, and like Schön, he trained at Basel and Islington. He arrived in Freetown in late 1847, and in the next five years and two months carried out brilliant and extraordinary linguistic research. Since it was still thought when Koelle left England that the next venture of the C.M.S. would be in the Central Sudan, with Schön's Hausa studies supporting those who took the first leap beyond Yorubaland, Koelle decided to over-leap Schön and begin by studying the language which led to the shores of Lake Chad, Bornu or Kanuri.[60] Later, Koelle gave this explanation of his choice:

'During my stay on the Western coast of Africa, the cultivation of the Kanuri language occupied me almost three full years . . . The direction of the Committee [of the C.M.S.] required of me, not only to furnish information respecting the whole question of African philology,[61] but also to select some one language for my particular study. In its selection I was to be guided by the probability of "its becoming a sort of key to the study of other languages". At that time, however, the African languages were so little known, that, in deciding this question, I could not be guided by any strictly lingual data. The Committee of Missionaries[62] agreed with me in its being desirable that I should fix upon the Kanuri or Bornu language, as this was spoken by one of the mightiest nations of Central Africa, and in the vicinity of Hausa, of which we already possessed a grammar. Accordingly, I selected one of the most suitable Bornuese of Sierra Leone as my interpreter,[63] and commenced the language.'[64]

[57] C.M.S. Archives, CH/O, letter of 4.2.1850.

[58] 'I know but little of Arabic . . . really it would be well that every missionary had some knowledge of it who proceeds to West Africa' (C.M.S. Archives, CH/O letter of 31.3.1848).

[59] Koelle's work at Freetown, which extended beyond the subject of this present essay, is dealt with in Hair/Koelle, op. cit., p. 9 ff.

[60] It would seem to have been Koelle who first used the term 'Kanuri' with reference to the chief language of the state of Bornu. Earlier, it had been used occasionally in European works to mean the people of Bornu, more usually called 'Bornuese' (e.g. 'the Bornou people or Kanowry', from Denham's account: Bovill, op. cit., 2, p. 514).

[61] This direction led of course to the production of the Polyglotta Africana.

[62] Probably the local committee in Freetown.

[63] Ali Eisama Gazirma, alias William Harding, born c.1788, kidnapped and enslaved c.1813, released in Sierra Leone 1818. A portrait and a short biography can be found in Koelle's Grammar, and an autobiography in the Native Literature.

[64] S. W. Koelle, Grammar . . . , 1854, p. iii: cf. C.M.S. Proceedings, 1848–9, p. lxvii.

Koelle was not the first to study Kanuri in Freetown. Apart from Mrs Kilham's collecting a vocabulary of 'Borno' in 1827, in the year before Koelle arrived, a Sierra Leonean, T. Maxwell, a catechist, was reported to have begun work on 'Bornou' – this most probably at Schön's suggestion.[65] To this extent, Koelle was justified in claiming that Freetown opinion was in favour of a study of Kanuri. But it may be suspected that in selecting this language, Koelle was also following his own inclinations more than he cared to admit, at the time or later. As his subsequent career was to show, he had a yearning to make use of his Arabic, and there was a fair chance that a language in the extreme north east corner of West Africa would turn out to be extensively influenced by Arab culture and might even be genetically related to Semitic – as one scholar had already suggested that Hausa might be. Certainly Koelle can hardly have known as little about Kanuri when he arrived in Freetown as the quotation might be taken to imply. German Orientalists like Ewald had been showing interest in Saharan and Sudanic languages for some decades – Klaproth had written on Kanuri – and it is likely that Koelle had seen some of this literature when at Tübingen. While he was undoubtedly sincere in believing that Kanuri would be of value to the missionary advance, it is unlikely that he really thought that a language with the geographical situation of Kanuri was a possible 'key to the study of other languages', when by 'other languages' the C.M.S. clearly meant languages of immediate use in mission labours, that is, the languages of the Guinea coast and (perhaps) of Southern Africa. Given a vaguely defined task, Koelle selected a language which suited both his own philological inclinations and the most general missionary programme. But when the latter was reshaped and the Central Sudan excluded from the immediate aims, Koelle had some further explaining to do.

> 'In the progress of my studies, it became more and more evident that the Kanuri had no important affinities with other Negro languages, and that, for the present, it cannot be used for direct missionary purposes, from the fanatical Mohammedan character of the Bornuese. . . . But by the time that I had become possessed of this information, I had made such progress in the language, that it was considered advisable that I should proceed still further, and then publish the results for the benefit of philology, and, as it is hoped, for the benefits of future Missionary enterprise.'[66]

Koelle's pessimism about the immediate missionary value of his Kanuri studies was fully justified. Neither *his* work on Kanuri, nor Schön's on Hausa, was of any immediate, direct, evangelistic value to the C.M.S.,[67] since it was another thirty years before direct contact was made with the homelands of these languages; and thus it must have seemed to many of the Society's subscribers and supporters that fifteen years of linguistic research had been financed to no good end.[68]

Koelle's admission of the missionary uselessness of his Kanuri studies was blunt, if not brusque, nevertheless his books on Kanuri were published by the C.M.S.[69] as soon

---

[65] *C.M. Record*, 1847, p. 197.
[66] Koelle, *op. cit.*, p. iv.
[67] Though, as we shall see, Schön's Hausa material was of some use on the Niger where Hausa was a lingua franca.
[68] The study of philology not being considered in itself a good end. Koelle tried to mitigate these reactions by arguing that the study of Kanuri had humanitarian implications (Hair/Koelle, *op. cit.*, p. 10).
[69] Note moreover that the books, although not Scriptural translations or devotional works, were published by C.M.S. itself. It was the usual practice to publish grammars and vocabularies, even if paid for by the C.M.S., without the mission imprint; often they had to be published privately by the author.

as ready – while Schön's Gospel translations in Hausa lay on his Chatham shelf, as they had done since 1848, spurned by the mission and gathering dust. The explanation of this discrimination is undoubtedly that Koelle, a more forceful character than Schön, had the good fortune to be backed at every turn by Henry Venn, the Secretary of C.M.S. and by the 1850s virtual dictator of its policies, who had developed an interest in linguistic problems and who was greatly impressed by Koelle's philological ability, with reason.[70] As a result, Koelle had disposed of Kanuri by 1854; he then turned his back on African languages for ever, and departed to the Middle East. Schön, his lesser genius fortunately compensated for by greater perseverence, slogged on in Hausa for another four decades.

Koelle produced two studies of Kanuri, both published in 1854: a grammar, and a vocabulary drawn from a large number of accompanying texts, some of them of considerable historical or anthropological interest.[71] These works were drafted in Freetown, but Koelle changed the orthography before publishing. Apart from his work on Kanuri, while in Freetown Koelle studied the Vai language[72] and wrote a grammar of it, collected the vocabularies which make up the *Polyglotta Africana*, and taught various subjects at Fourah Bay Institution. In 1850, as his Kanuri material began to take shape, he wrote to the mission authorities in London suggesting that he should be allowed to make his way to Bornu, where he could combine his studies with evangelistic work. He wrote in a tone of burning idealism, but the C.M.S. considered the idea impracticable (as it surely was), and turned down the suggestion, almost curtly.[73] This was perhaps one reason why, when all his African material had been seen through the press in 1854, Koelle decided not to return to Sierra Leone, and instead was transferred to the Society's Middle East mission: the official reason for the transfer was ill-health. Koelle lived another fifty years and published, as well as works of apologetics in English, material on and in the Turkish language, but nothing further on African languages. After his death, some unpublished African language material was printed, but an amount of further unpublished material, including material on Kanuri, cannot now be traced.[74]

For the C.M.S. as a patron of African language studies, 1854 was Annus Mirabilis, with three works by Koelle coming off the press. Considering these and earlier publications – Koelle's Vai grammar in 1853, Crowther's Yoruba grammar in 1852 – and with work on a dozen other languages in progress, Henry Venn could feel that his missionary-linguists were in the forefront of African linguistics. His diary during these years indicates

---

[70] Ability shown as early as 1849, in his first publication on the Vai script.

[71] For instance, the accounts of Bornu history, while the description of an eclipse is one of the sources used by Dr Richard Gray in his current investigation of eclipse-dating.

[72] On the circumstances of Koelle's work on Vai, see P. E. H. Hair, 'Notes on the discovery of the Vai script, with a bibliography', *Sierra Leone Language Review*, 2, 1963, pp. 36–49, on pp. 36–8.

[73] C.M.S. Archives, CA 1/o 135, letter of 31.1.1850.

[74] To the discussion of these points in Hair/Koelle, *op. cit.*, I can now add the following additions and corrections. (a) Koelle died in London on 18.2.1903, aged 78 (from his death certificate; no obituary has yet been traced). (b) His publications from the Middle East were in Turkish, and despite his quarrel with the C.M.S., I now think that almost all the material he prepared in manuscript was eventually published; he also published learned articles on Turkish. (c) Among Koelle's papers in the C.M.S. Archives, are some brief pencilled notes on African languages, apparently made in London in the 1880s or 1890s, hence comment on his later, *total* disinterest in African languages must be slightly modified. Unpublished material on Kanuri was reported in 1912 to be in the possession of Dr Karl Kumm (P. A. Benton, *Notes on some languages . . .*, 1912, p. vi; P. A. Benton, *The sultanate of Bornu*, 1913, p. 228).

something of his excitement, for instance the following entry: 'March 5th, 1853. Went with Mr Koelle to breakfast at Chevalier Bunsen's. Exhibited to him the wonderful results of Mr K.'s investigations of the languages of Africa. . . We stayed with him till 12 and then went to Mr Edwin Norris, at the Royal Asiatic Society, who had compiled the vocabulary of eight African languages for the Niger expedition, and also a Bornou grammar from H. Barth's papers [an error: the papers were J. Richardson's], and was therefore fully prepared to appreciate Mr Koelle's labours in both departments: but, as he said, he was perfectly overwhelmed at the magnitude and importance of them.'[75] On the other side, Koelle appreciated Venn's support and enthusiasm. Writing from Constantinople in 1873, on the occasion of Venn's death, Koelle recollected: 'He caused me one of the sunniest moments in my life when, on my return from Africa, he once took me to the late Chevalier Bunsen, and then I saw his countenance beaming with delight, his eyes full of joy and pleasure, passing from the manuscripts spread on the table to the Chevalier and then back again. If ever I saw a soul-delight, it was in those looks.'[76]

Schön was not entirely neglected, but was called to London to discuss orthographies with Venn, Koelle and others. We can be sure that with his usual humility he welcomed the triumph of his younger colleague; he himself had to wait many years before his work received academic recognition of any kind. In the early 1850s, few among the body of C.M.S. officers and supporters can have shared Henry Venn's liberal approach to African language studies and his enthusiasm for the mission's linguistic achievements. Yet, even when it came to be realised that the work on the languages of the Central Sudan was of little practical advantage to the mission, some consolation was nevertheless derived from the award of a Volney Prize of the Institut de France to Koelle in 1856, and, much later, the award of a Volney medal to Schön in 1877. The official historian of the C.M.S. wrote in 1899 – 'thus the competition instituted in honour of an infidel brought reward to the work of two missionaries of Christ'.[77]

*   *   *

In 1847, Schön returned to England and Koelle arrived in Freetown. Three years later, at the end of 1850, while Schön was despairing of ever resuming his Hausa studies, Koelle was well advanced in Kanuri, and had published his first contribution, a letter to Ewald discussing a few minor matters which the professor put into a German journal.[78] At this point, a rival student of Hausa and Kanuri made his first appearance in print: this was Dr Heinrich Barth, who travelled in the Central Sudan between

[75] Stock, *op. cit.*, vol. 2, p. 102.

[76] Quoted (from the C.M.S. Archives) in J. Spencer, 'S. W. Koelle and the problem of notation for African languages, 1847–1855', *Sierra Leone Language Review*, 5, 1966, pp. 83–105, on p. 101.

[77] Stock, *op. cit.*, vol. 2, pp. 102–3: Koelle received the highest award for work submitted in the years 1855–6, the sum of 1200 francs, for his four books; Schön received a gold medal worth 300 francs, as one of the runners-up to the prizewinner of 1877, for his Hausa books of 1862 and 1876 (*Journal des savants*, 1856, p. 502; 1877, p. 642). Although Schön and Koelle do not appear to have commented on each other's work, it is amusing to note that the former paid tribute to the latter, by copying word for word in the title of a Hausa work published only in 1885, the title of a work on Kanuri published by Koelle in 1854 – 'native literature, or proverbs, tales, fables and historical fragments . . . '.

[78] See the bibliography: the letter was written from Fourah Bay and dated 14.11.1850.

1850 and 1855 and who included a list of Hausa words in a report he forwarded to Europe in 1850.[79]

While the C.M.S. had perforce to make studies of the languages of the Central Sudan at its Freetown base 1500 miles away from the homelands, the British government was repeating its attempts to contact the region directly, by sending expeditions across the Sahara and up the Niger. In 1849, a new trans-Saharan expedition set off, under the direction of James Richardson, an Englishman who had already travelled widely in the northern parts of the desert. In 1851, Richardson died near Lake Chad: his papers were sent back to England, and his linguistic material[80]– collected in the main north of the Sudan – was edited, on behalf of the Foreign Office, by Edwin Norris, Assistant Secretary of the Royal Asiatic Society.[81] In 1853, two works based on Richardson's material were published.[82] The first, in a limited edition, contained dialogues in 'Bornuese' and 'Haussa' (also called 'Soudanese'), together with translations of a few chapters of Scripture – all the non-English matter in Arabic characters. The second was devoted to Kanuri and was in Roman characters: it contained a transliteration of the Bornuese part of the dialogues in the first work, a sketch of the grammar by Norris, and a vocabulary which Norris drew, not only from Richardson's papers, but from some of the earlier vocabularies listed above (from Mrs Kilham onwards). These two works possessed only limited usefulness. Much of Richardson's material was collected hastily in Tripoli or in the desert, and the dialogues which were translated were – as Delafosse later justly complained –'ceux de Mme de Genlis, et on y parle de chambres d'hôtel au premier, de voitures à deux chevaux, de serviettes de toilette, etc'.[83] Koelle, whose own grammar of Kanuri appeared a few months later, referred gracefully in it to the 'attempt at a Kanuri grammar . . . from the pen of the laborious and indefatigable Edwin Norris, Esq. . . . [which] does him great credit', but in fact the appearance of Koelle's work made the Richardson/Norris volume practically valueless.[84] 'Overwhelmed' as Norris was when Venn showed him Koelle's studies, no doubt this was partly due to the polite suppression of very mixed feelings.

---

[79] See the bibliography: written November 1850. Barth first met Hausa in the desert towns. Barth sent a stream of letters and reports to Europe, a large number of which were printed in a variety of journals, both in Germany and England. It is not therefore easy to track down all his comment and material on languages.

[80] References to his collecting linguistic material, together with odd words of Hausa, can be found in J. Richardson, *Narrative of a mission to Central Africa . . .*, 1853, vol. 2, pp. 97, 99, 101, 106, 141.

[81] On the Richardson-Barth expedition, see Boahen, *op. cit.*, chapter 8. On Richardson and Norris, see P. A. Benton, *op. cit.* (1912), passim: some of Richardson's papers are in the Public Record Office, and they include scrappy material in Hausa and Kanuri, according to Benton. On Barth, see A. H. M. Kirk-Greene, *Barth's travels in Nigeria*, 1962, Introduction.

[82] A third work, entitled 'Sentences for the purpose of conversation in the Arabic, Kanuri called Bornuese, and Sudanese languages, London, 1847', although listed in many bibliographies (e.g. de Tressan de Lavergne 1953, International African Institute 1958), is not in the British Museum or the Foreign Office Library and was not known to Bleek in 1858. This is almost certainly a misreference, probably started by Cust in 1883. The two Richardson/Norris works were given a learned review in the course of an article by the German linguist, A. F. Pott, *Zeitschrift der Deutschen morgenländischen Gesellschaft*, 8, 1854, pp. 412–42 (hence another misreference in de Tressan de Lavergne, p. 53, to Apott).

[83] Delafosse, *op. cit.*, p. x ('those by Madame de Genlis [entitled 'Manuel du voyageur', or Traveller's Guide] which talk of rooms on the first floor, of carriages and horses, of towels, etc.'): the dialogues are at times even more ridiculous than Delafosse's examples – e.g. 'Is the post office far from this?', 'Which wine have you? – Red and white; Champagne, Bordeaux and Port', 'I want some visiting cards, where can I get them printed?' – all apparently translated in full into Arabic, Hausa and Kanuri.

[84] Koelle, *op. cit.*, p. ix.

After Richardson's death, the leadership of the expedition passed to the German, Dr Heinrich Barth, whose detailed and accurate account of his journeys and of the parts of the Sudan which he traversed was published in 1857–8 and became a classic of African exploration. Barth's description of the Hausa and Kanuri homelands was full and the topography of the area was firmly established. Barth's geographical achievements are well known and have been rightly praised; his linguistic achievements, though considerable, have attracted much less attention and are more difficult to evaluate. He published the mass of his linguistic material in three volumes, in Germany (but in a German and English text), in 1862–6: the work was incomplete when Barth died in 1865, but a fourth volume would probably have concluded the set.[85]

Barth collected information on many languages of the Sahara and Sudan, and only about one quarter of this material deals with Hausa and Kanuri. Nevertheless, a large part of the Introductory Remarks to his work, as well as many comments in the relevant sections of the text, refer to the publications of Schön and Koelle. When Barth left Europe in 1849, he had a command of Arabic but no knowledge of Central Sudan languages, and he accordingly took with him Schön's Hausa vocabulary of 1843. He engaged Hausa- and Kanuri-speaking servants in Tripoli and began work on both languages. During his travels in the Central Sudan, he spoke both Hausa and Kanuri, the former for a period of years, the latter for a period of months, and claimed to speak both with fluency. Of Hausa he said – 'if I had been able to spend half a year longer among the Hausa people, I should have become fully master of the language'.[86] Among the reports he sent to Europe were some vocabularies, but very little was published before he returned.[87] The only detailed contribution to Hausa and Kanuri studies to find its way into print at this stage was a Hausa vocabulary of 1000 words, compiled at the beginning of his study, in 1850. Meanwhile, he had this to say, in 1851, of Schön and his 1843 vocabulary: it was 'on the whole excellent, although not in the present Katshena [dialect]. He is perfect master of the language.'[88]

In 1856, Barth returned to Europe. He brought back with him two Hausa-speaking youths, Dorugu and Abbega,[89] but while the party was in England, the youths left Barth and attached themselves to Schön. The circumstances in which this happened are in dispute. In 1862 Schön published the following account. After the refusal of the

---

[85] Exceptions to the general disregard of Barth's linguistic work are the useful paragraphs in Kirk-Greene, *op. cit.*, pp. 61–3 and Boahen, *op. cit.*, pp. 199–201. Some of Barth's unpublished material eventually appeared in Benton, *op. cit.*, (1912), pp. 70–114, but none of it relates to Hausa or Kanuri. The existence of other unpublished material, including vocabulary in both languages and a collection of sentences in Hausa, is noted in R. Prietze, 'Die sprachlichen Sammlungen Barth's Nachtigal's und Rohlf's', *Zeitschrift für afrikanische und oceanische Sprachen*, 2, 1896, pp. 195–6.

[86] Barth described how he pursued his linguistic work in the Introductory Remarks to *Sammlung* . . . , part 1, 1862: quotation p. vi.

[87] 'There is evidently a very important difference between the Bornu and Buduma languages . . . Bur when I learned from that indefatiquable examiner into languages, Mr Norris of the Foreign Office, who made his comparison of both these languages by means of specimens received from Dr Barth, that . . . ': S. W. Koelle, *Polyglotta Africana*, 1854, p. 9. 'He [Koelle] mentions expressly my collection of shorter vocabularies [including Buduma] . . . having been forwarded by me to the Chevalier Bunsen before my leaving Bornu for Timbuktu in November 1853, and the Chevalier having shown them to the English linguists, such as Mr Latham, and the missionaries, before he sent them to Mr Lepsius at Berlin.' : Barth, *op. cit.*, part 1, 1862, p. xiv. Note that Koelle does not say that he actually saw the vocabularies.

[88] This remark was quoted by Schön himself (with a reference) in Schön, *op. cit.*, p. vi. Barth's remark that Schön's Hausa was not 'the present Katshena' was queried by Schön a little sharply, but apart from this the references to Barth are dispassionate.

[89] A drawing of the two youths in H. Barth, *Travels* . . . , 4, p. 10.

C.M.S. in the late 1840s to print his Hausa material, 'all was put aside . . . until the year 1856, when I was informed . . . that Dr Barth, who had just returned from Africa, had spoken favourably of my labours, and that my translations and other collections should now be published.[90] Satisfying as this news was to me on the one hand, it was no less embarrassing on the other. Ten years my papers had been lying in the dust: I had nearly forgotten the language. I began to long and pray for help in the person of a Hausa man, and the thought of how to get one engaged me day and night; when to my astonishment and delight, I learned that Dr Barth had brought to London with him two Hausa lads whom I saw, and Dr Barth very obligingly allowed one of them, Dorugu, to spend a few weeks with me and, soon after, both of them were placed under my care. It was the Lord's doing, and it is marvellous in our eyes!'[91] Schön was to regret the last heart-felt phrase. Barth also published in 1862, and his work came out shortly after Schön's – and neither author had apparently seen the other's text before publishing his own. Barth's work contained the following brief but devastating remarks – 'the two youths . . . would have rendered me great service in my linguistical studies . . . if other people had not crossed my intention . . . The Rev. Schön and his friends preferred obtaining by artifice and violence, what they might have obtained easier by fair means.'[92]

Schön was completely taken aback by Barth's charges, uttered in such a venomous tone. Unfortunately the letter which Schön wrote to the Secretary of the C.M.S. refuting the charges seems to have been lost, so the details of the Dorugu Affair may now never be known, though the outline of events is clear enough. What is most extraordinary is that among the C.M.S. Archives there are preserved friendly letters from Barth to Schön (the latter may have presented them as evidence) dating from 1857 and 1858: Dorugu joined Schön in 1856 and the letters, written in an amicable and polite tone, ask Schön to pass on to Dorugu his former master's greetings.[93]

Schön was sufficiently disturbed by Barth's assault to offer a public reply in his next Hausa publication, which as it happened did not go through the press till 1876, when Barth had been dead for eleven years.[94] According to Schön, the youths 'had made up their minds long before I saw or knew them, to remain no longer with Dr Barth'. At first, they wanted to return to Africa,[95] but later, when on the point of embarking, changed their minds and asked to stay with Schön, who chanced to be on the quayside seeing them off. Barth was a somewhat humourless, self-satisfied, tough individual, a bachelor, while Schön was gentle and kindly, and a family man, so that the youths' preference for the latter is not altogether surprising. Although Barth's jealous reaction

---

[90] 'Dr Barth having explained to the Committee the importance of the Hausa language', the C.M.S. requested Schön to resume his translational work (*C.M.S. Proceedings*, 1855–6, p. 58).

[91] Schön, *op. cit.*, p. vii.

[92] Barth, *op. cit.* (1862), p. xvii.

[93] C.M.S. Archives, A 2/U3: letter of 3.3.1856 'I beg you to send Dyrgu immediately off, as soon as you receive this note, as he and Abega have to start tomorrow for Southampton. I heard it not but late on Saturday night.'; letter of 29.5.57 (Barth visiting Schön, bringing him copy of first volume of Travels) 'with many agaisua to the two Africans' [gaisūwā = mutual salutations]; letter of 31.5.1858 (thanks for Hausa translation, delighted to hear Abbega in Abeokuta) 'I did not see his and Dyrgu's palmito. With my best wishes for the latter, Yours truly'

[94] J. F. Schön, *Dictionary*, 1876, pp. iv–v.

[95] Venn noted in his diary for 2.2.1856, 'Went to see Dr Barth, the African explorer. Had some talk with his two African lads and arranged with the Doctor to send them to Mr Schön to be his interpreters for the Yoruba [sic!] language. They were both of them evidently as home-sick as any Swiss, and to all my attempts to lure them to stay in England, their answer was 'Africa! Africa!' (W. Knight, *Missionary secretariat of Henry Venn*, p. 133).

seems unworthy, Schön's own account of the episode suggests some ingenuousness in his actions which Barth was able to construe as sharp practice. The episode, or at least as far as Schön was concerned, the publication of Barth's version, led to a feud between the two Hausa scholars which is reflected in many references in their later texts.

The youths joined Schön in 1856 and he immediately resumed his Hausa studies, making use principally of Dorugu whose mother-tongue was Hausa. Barth concluded his charge against Schön with the sarcastic observation – 'thus the public has a right to expect the perfection of these Hausa-studies from the Rev. Schön'. Schön successfully met this challenge. He described his new informant in enthusiastic terms. 'Dorugu is a real Hausa, speaks the language fluently and beautifully. Never was there an African coming to this country that was of greater use; full of information for his age, probably not more than 16 or 17 years old, energetic and lively in his habits, always ready to speak. He began relating stories to me, or rather dictating them, giving me a description of his own life and travels in Africa in his own language, very often dictating to me for hours together, and even till late in the night; so that I soon had a Hausa literature of several hundred pages before me.'[96] If Dorugu served Schön well, Schön did the same for Dorugu's texts, which he gradually had printed, in publication after publication, when funds permitted and opportunity offered, over the next thirty years.

Both Dorugu and Abbega learnt English, became literate and acknowledged Christianity. By 1862, Schön was able to report of them – 'Abbega has returned to Africa with the Gospels in his hand, has given evidence of his zeal for the conversion of others, and has hitherto maintained his Christian character. Dorugu is still with me, reading and studying, and by God's blessing, preparing himself for still greater usefulness.'[97] Shortly after this was written, Dorugu also returned to Africa. Both men lived until the second decade of the present century; both seem to have slowly lost contact with the mission and with Christianity, but their literacy brought them posts of some local responsibility in European-supervised concerns, latterly in the British administration of Northern Nigeria.[98] But their names are more likely to be remembered because of their appearance on the pages of Barth's and Schön's books. The texts dictated by Dorugu formed the basis for all Schön's later work, and extracts appeared in nearly all his later publications. The most interesting of these texts is Dorugu's autobiography – recounting his childhood, enslavement, liberation by Barth and travels with him in the Sudan, across the Sahara, and in Germany and England. Schön provided an English translation of the autobiography, and sections of the text or the translation have been republished in this century.[99]

---

[96] Schön, *op. cit.* (1862), p. viii.

[97] *ibid.*, p. x.

[98] Abbega on his return worked with Crowther and with Dr Baikie; there are letters from him in the C.M.S. Archives, and see [S. Crowther], *The Gospel on the banks of the Niger, no. II*, 1863, p. 16. He was appointed Chief of Lokoja in 1896, and was then a Moslem; see C. H. Robinson, *Hausaland*, 1896, p. 38; A. H. M. Kirk-Greene, 'Link with Lugard', *West Africa*, 1957, pp. 1179, 1203; H. J. Pedraza, *Borrioboola-Gha*, 1960, pp. 61, 98–9 (as an example of the growth of oral tradition – 'Dr Barth presented him to Queen Victoria. His son relates that the Queen was unable apparently to pronounce his proper name Abubakar, and called him instead 'Abiga', a name which since stayed with him.'). Dorugu returned to Africa in 1864 (*C.M.S. Intelligencer*, November 1864, p. 261) and died at Nasarawa in 1912 (P. A. Benton, *op. cit.* (1913), p. 232). I have not been able to see A. H. M. Kirk-Greene, 'Abbega and Durogu [sic]', *West African Review*, September 1956.

[99] Dorugu's autobiography appeared in parts in the *Grammar* 1862, the *Dictionary* 1876 and the *Reading Book* 1877, and in full in *Magana Hausa* 1885 (text) and *African Proverbs* 1886 (translation). It was reprinted in Hausa in E. C. Marre, *Die Sprache von Hausa*, Vienna [1902], and in *Magana Hausa*, edited C. H. Robinson, 1906, and in English in *The Story of Dorugu*, London [1933]. Probably it has also been reprinted in Northern Nigeria.

Between 1856 and 1862, when both Schön and Barth were busy preparing linguistic material for publication, another person was undertaking a study of Hausa. This was Dr William Baikie, a Scotsman who travelled up the Niger in the expeditions of 1854 and 1857, and who was British consular agent at Lokoja (a settlement he founded), at the Niger-Benue confluence, from 1859 to 1864.[100] This flurry of activity on the Niger had had its distant effect on Schön, for the C.M.S. had seen in it, taken together with Barth's triumphant return across the desert, evidence that the plan for advance into the Central Sudan, shelved in 1848–9, could now be taken up again. It was not only Barth who had recommended to the mission that Schön should resume his Hausa work, but also Crowther, who had accompanied Baikie on the Niger expeditions and who now thought that the Gospel should be carried to the Niger – where Hausa was a lingua franca. Crowther began to make use of Schön's publications, and to request that he prepare more. In his consulate at Lokoja, Baikie was impressed by this missionary zeal, and resolved to help. He began to learn Hausa, and after a year at Lokoja, he wrote a few pages of 'Observations on the Hausa and Fulfulde languages', which he had privately printed (in England) in 1861. In the preface to this booklet, he announced – 'Should I live to return home, I hope to be able to enter at large into the subject'.[101] But on the way home, in 1864, he died at Freetown. He had translated a large part of the Bible into Hausa, and these manuscripts were eventually passed on to Schön who, making full acknowledgement of the value of Baikie's work, incorporated much of the material into his own later Hausa studies and reproduced the manuscript translation of Jonah as an appendix to his 1876 dictionary.[102] A little later, when the C.M.S. was resuming interest in Hausa, it asked the Bible Society to publish Baikie's translation of Leviticus and Psalms, as slightly revised by Schön. Eventually, in 1881, Psalms alone appeared – the only portion of the 1400 manuscript pages of Hausa translation by Baikie to appear as a separate publication.

Schön re-commenced his Hausa studies, with Dorugu at his side, in 1856. The next year he published a small primer, entirely in Hausa and partly in Arabic characters, which was addressed to the Hausa people from the 'mallam Yakubu'.[103] Schön followed this with a series of Scripture translations: Matthew, John and Acts in 1857; Genesis and Luke in 1858; Exodus in 1859.[104] The Gospels and Acts were presumably revisions of the translations he had first prepared fifteen years earlier. Schön's last and most important work of this second period of his Hausa studies was a grammar, published in 1862. Based largely on an analysis of Dorugu's texts, it remained the standard introduction to Hausa, and the fullest study of the structure of the language, until the end of the century. It was also, of all Schön's African language publications, the one which

---

[100] Pedraza, *op. cit.* [a history of Lokoja], chapter 4: Baikie was never formally appointed Consul though his successors were, but his duties were consular, hence the terminology of the text.

[101] Baikie's interest in the languages of the Niger is shown in W. B. Baikie, *Narrative of an exploring voyage* . . . , 1856, passim, especially in the section on languages from p. 419.

[102] Schön wrote – 'I was glad to bring the labours of another person in the Hausa language to public notice' (C.M.S. Archives, Yoruba Mission, 1881/126) and – 'I regret that Dr Baikie's death ensued before he could arrange and publish his collection, as he undoubtedly intended to do. The public would have greatly benefited by his knowledge of the language.' (J. F. Schön, *Appendix to dictionary*, 1888, p. iv). At Schön's suggestion, R. N. Cust searched for more of Baikie's linguistic papers at the Foreign Office (R. N. Cust, *Modern languages of Africa*, 1883, 1, p. 217).

[103] This work was published at Berlin, the only work by Schön to be published in Germany. Possibly publication was organised by Barth?

[104] It may be noted here that the list of his works which appeared in Schön's last book (*Appendix* . . . , 1888) is incomplete and inexact.

represented the most profound study. Now approaching the age of sixty, Schön richly deserved the testimonial he won from the mission in 1860: 'the Committee thankfully acknowledge the very important and extensive literary labours which Mr Schön is carrying forward in the Hausa, Ibo and now in the Nupe languages; they recognise in his residence in this country a gracious provision for the completion of translations sent home from Africa. He is thus able to do far more than he could have accomplished in Africa: so that his great philological talents, instead of being lost to the African missions are more than ever useful to that cause to which he early devoted himself.'[105]

In the same year that Schön published his magnum opus, Barth published the first volume of his *Collection of Vocabularies*. This work, distinguished in the first instance because it served as an introduction to many little-known Saharan and Sudanic languages, in its first and third volumes included lists of Hausa and Kanuri words, with extensive annotation, and brief remarks on the grammar of these languages. But as far as related to Hausa and Kanuri, the work was doubly unfortunate; unfortunate in its date of publication, inasmuch as it could claim no priority in the field and could only confirm – or comment adversely on – the solid works already laid before the public by Schön and Koelle, while it appeared just too early to offer a critique of Schön's best work; unfortunate again in its method of presentation, since the vocabulary was given first, and the collection of sentences, which was required to show that Barth's understanding of the languages was complete (and even to substantiate the technical arguments in his introductory remarks), never appeared because of his premature death. To a layman, it seems that Barth's work on the one hand, and Schön and Koelle's work on the other, did largely confirm each other, and that this in itself is a tribute to the work of all three.

But this was not the view taken by Barth, and later by Schön (Koelle in Constantinople remained silent). It must be said that the volumes of the *Collection* do not give a favourable impression of Barth's character, since, side by side with impressive scholarship, they include an amount of petty and pathetic belittling of the work of Schön and Koelle, supported by an assumption of linguistic infallibility on Barth's part. Either the lionising the great explorer had received for his geographical achievements had gone to his head, or else the shadows of his approaching death were obscuring his judgement and mental balance. The general theme of his criticism of Schön and Koelle contained a germ of truth, that whereas *they* had studied far away from the homelands of the languages, using only single informants, *he*, Barth, had spoken the tongues fluently for months and years within the homelands; but the tone which Barth adopted to make this point was distasteful. His over-frequent references to the dangers of his life as an explorer and traveller, explicitly contrasted with the quiet home life of the missionaries, probably served to remind many readers that The White Man's Grave was not in Hausaland, and that Schön and Koelle, each after more years in West Africa than Barth, had each left because of recurrent ill-health. To substantiate his general point, detailed criticism of the writings of Schön and Koelle was given in the introduction to and footnotes of the Hausa and Kanuri vocabularies: most of the corrections appear to be on very minor points and to be introduced mainly in order to contradict the rival scholar. Schön, who was assaulted more fiercely than Koelle, no doubt because of the Dorugu episode, was sufficiently nettled to reply more or less in kind. His 1876

---

[105] *C.M.S. Proceedings*, 1860, p. 55. The work in Nupe referred to was that of editing Crowther's 1860 Nupe publications.

dictionary (in fairness, it should be borne in mind that it was prepared many years earlier, and the comments on Barth probably written while he was still alive) similarly carried the battle into the footnotes, where Barth is given credit for little and corrected on every other page. At worst, we have the assault direct – (Barth speaking) 'Schön, besides this separates the words without taking the slightest regard neither to their root, nor to the grammatical form' – (Schön speaking) 'The accusation of violating the laws of grammar does not come well from one that has not added one iota to our knowledge of grammar, and from whose work no one can learn how to put a sentence together in the Hausa language.' The controversy, in rather shaky English, added light relief to the somewhat arid pages of Hausa vocabulary, but it indicates that fair appraisal of each other's work is not to be found in these volumes.[106]

With the deaths of Baikie and Barth in the mid 1860s, Schön was left alone again in the field of Hausa studies. But no more publications followed the 1862 grammar until 1876. Reasons for this pause are to be found in the history of the C.M.S. missions. The Hausa translations which Schön produced between 1857 and 1859 were intended for use by Crowther and his assistants in the newly-founded Niger Mission, mainly in the mission-stations above the confluence, on part of the river where Hausa commercial influence was strong. But in the mid 1860's Crowther was forced to withdraw from his more northern stations (partly owing to Moslem hostility), and to concentrate on the peoples further south, those near the confluence, the Igbira and Igala, and those down-river to the Delta, the Ibo and the Ijaw. Schön was requested to resume work on Ibo, the language he had studied for a few months in 1840–1, and in 1861 he produced a fairly extensive grammar. He also helped Crowther's assistant, J. C. Taylor, to produce a series of translations into Ibo, which Schön saw through the press. No sooner had this Ibo work subsided than the mission called on Schön to abandon the Niger altogether and to initiate work on a Sierra Leone language, Mende; and duly, with aid from a Sierra Leonean, Henry Johnson, in the early 1870s Schön produced Scriptural translations in Mende. Thus, once again, Hausa studies lapsed for nearly ten years.

Schön had drawn his grammar from Dorugu's texts, and from the same he added to and corrected his 1843 vocabulary. Though both the texts and the enlarged vocabulary were ready for publication soon after the grammar was printed, Schön could obtain no financial support from the mission, which had always been reluctant to spend funds on works of purely linguistic value.[107] Fortunately for Hausa studies, in the mid 1870s

---

[106] Quotation in Schön, op. cit. (1876), p. 71. Barth claimed that the Hausa discussed by Schön was a minor dialect, and that in any case his knowledge was defective. Schön complained that Barth referred only to his 1843 work, and ignored the improved knowledge he showed in later works. As regards Koelle, Barth began by praising his 'diligent and accurate study' and regretting that it had not been published before he left Europe (p. v), but later he implied that the Kanuri was unidiomatic and out-of-date, that many terms had been coined under European influence, and even that Koelle had made use of, without acknowledgement, a vocabulary Barth had sent to Europe in 1853 (see footnote 87, above). The Polyglotta Africana, said Barth, was 'very far from reliable' (p. v). The essence of Barth's charges against the Freetown missionaries was contained in the following sentence – 'I am sure the missionary himself would have hesitated in adopting such a complicated system of writing an illiterate language, if he had worked upon the living idiom of a whole nation, instead of abstracting all his rules from the pronunciation of a single individual, whom he was holding during five years under the control of European theories and of European schematising' (p. xli).

[107] Except, as we have seen, when Venn backed Koelle. Although Venn at times wrote encouragingly to Schön, e.g. 'My faith is not in contracts or governments, but in your translations of God's Word. He will make a way for its dispersion on the banks of the Niger.' (C.M.S. Archives, A2/U3, letter of 21.4.1860), he was clearly not as impressed by Schön's work as by Koelle's, and was not prepared to

—Continued on following page

changes occurred on the Niger which produced renewed interest in Schön's work. Crowther succeeded in establishing a mission station well above the confluence, in Nupe country, at Egga, and he again found Hausa useful in this region. But a demand for Hausa material came now, for the first time, also from non-missionaries; from European traders who were beginning to operate in fair numbers well up the Niger, and from European officers in charge of the Hausa soldiers recruited for service at Lagos (in the late 1860s) and on Gold Coast (in the 1870s).

In 1874, Crowther asked Schön to publish his Hausa dictionary, and offered £100 towards the cost. The Fowell Buxton family gave a further contribution and, after Schön had revised his orthography slightly, the work was published in 1876.[108] It incorporated vocabulary from Baikie and Barth, and was the standard work for about twenty years. It was probably used more widely than any other of Schön's writings. In 1877, Crowther sent one of his assistants, the Rev. T. C. John, a Sierra Leonean who was Hausa-speaking, to England to study Hausa with Schön.[109] John assisted in the preparation of a rather elaborate primer or reading-book, also entitled a 'traveller's vade mecum', and obviously intended for Europeans who wanted to learn the language. Schön recommenced Bible translation, and published Mark in 1878, the complete New Testament in 1880, and Isaiah in 1881, and in the latter year also saw through the press Baikie's translation of Psalms. All of these were in Roman script, but in 1877 Schön's translation of part of John was published in Arabic script, the transliteration being the work of Henry Johnson, the Sierra Leonean who, since working on Mende with Schön, had learned Arabic.[110]

In 1881, Schön, now approaching eighty years of age, wrote a long and moving letter to the mission authorities. He was under the impression that his work had been criticised, and the letter bears the character of an Apologia pro vita sua. 'I hope the Committee will bear with me, when I pour out my full heart to them. It may be that my labours do not come up to their expectations. I can only say that I have faithfully and conscientiously applied myself to the work. I am no linguist by profession [but] one quality I have. I can work and go on patiently, surmounting difficulties in time . . . I am aware it might be said and has been said – "You took your time to do it." It is true. I have been long at it to my regret, and I must say I have not after all produced a perfect work. I may plead an excuse, the state of the language not being full reduced . . . I trust I have been preserved from gross errors and have exhibited the sense of the Word though it may not be in classical Hausa throughout . . . To the question "Why publish if you cannot say that they are perfect, and will require no alteration in the future?",

---

—Continued from previous page

publish everything Schön wrote. In any case, as Venn grew old, he seems to have taken less interest in linguistic matters, and he was succeeded in the late 1860s as the dominant personality among the officers of the C.M.S. by Edward Hutchinson, whose disinterest in the linguistic labours of the mission was to vex Schön.

[108] C.M.S. Archives, A2/U3, letter of Crowther to Schön of 5.5.1875, and Yoruba Mission, 1881/126, letter of 27.12.1881; Schön, op. cit. (1876), pp. 1–3.

[109] Schön liked John and wanted to keep him longer in England, which led to a clash with Hutchinson of the C.M.S. who ordered him back to the Niger. (C.M.S. Archives, A2/U3, letters of 29.4.1876, 22.3.1878). At Lokoja, John worked on a Hausa translation of the Prayer Book (C.M. Proceedings, 1879–80, p. 21) and he contributed Hausa texts to two of Schön's later works. But he was eventually dismissed during the crisis period of the Niger Mission, and became an instructor in Hausa at Lagos. His son was in the 1930s an Assistant Bishop on the Niger.

[110] C.M.S. Archives, Yoruba Mission, 1881/126, letter of 27.12.1881. Johnson's wife had been a protégée of Mrs Schön.

I would reply, if you wait for that time it will never come, objections will never cease . . . .'[111]

A sympathetic and appreciative letter was sent in reply to Schön, and he henceforward enjoyed the very active support of one member of the C.M.S. Committee, Robert Cust, Honorary Secretary of the Royal Asiatic Society, who in 1883 published a two-volume bibliographical work on the languages of Africa.[112] As a result, in his ninth decade of life, Schön published as much as in any previous decade, and cleared his shelves of almost all his remaining manuscripts (in Mende and Ibo, as well as Hausa). In 1888, he brought out an Appendix to his Hausa dictionary (into which he managed to insert a few more texts) – his final publication; and in 1885 and 1886 appeared his most lasting work, the *Magana Hausa* or Hausa literature, that is, the collection of Hausa texts, here published in Hausa and in English translation. To Dorugu's texts, collected thirty years before, had been added a few collected by John at Lokoja, and by a correspondent, the German scholar G. A. Krause, at Tripoli. During 1888, Schön reported to the mission that he was at work on a translation of the Prayer Book (perhaps a revision and completion of translations by Baikie and John), and the mission asked the publishers to print the manuscript page by page as it came forward 'in view of the advanced age of Dr Schön';[113] but the work was unpublished and was abandoned when Schön died, aged eighty-six, in April, 1889.[114]

Schön published about 3,000 pages in, or on, Hausa, during a period of nearly fifty years. In 1877, as we saw earlier, he was awarded a Volney medal for his grammar and dictionary, and in 1882 he was invited to read a paper on Hausa to the Royal Asiatic Society.[115] Cust arranged this latter honour, and further – as he later wrote – 'I felt so ashamed at the neglect shown to this great scholar by his native and adopted countries, that I prevailed on the three great religious societies (C.M.S., B.F.B.S., and S.P.C.K.) to memorialise the Vice-Chancellor of Oxford for an honorary degree of Doctor of Divinity'.[116] Schön received this degree in 1884. A graceful tribute to Schön was written by Cust and printed in the C.M.S. journal a few weeks before the aged scholar

---

[111] *ibid.* Schön was in effect appealing to the Committee against the continuance of the policies of the unsympathetic Hutchinson, whom Schön reported to have said 'that such books as the Hausa dictionary, translations, etc, were but waste paper, that it was unnecessary because the English language would supersede African languages, and that as far as he was concerned he would not give a penny for their publication.' But wider issues than Hausa publications were at stake. Hutchinson, who was highly critical of the Niger Mission and its African staff and who had initiated a policy which led eventually to the virtual disbandment of this mission, had, under pressure, himself abruptly resigned in early 1881. But Hutchinson's narrow Evangelical views still had support in the counsels of the C.M.S., and in complaining about them, Schön was endeavouring to aid his friend and colleague, Crowther. On the Niger imbroglio, see Ajayi, *op. cit.*, chapter 8.

[112] Cust's book was highly eulogistic of the language work of Crowther and his African assistants, and in the C.M.S. Committee he opposed the critics of the Niger Mission. (For his connection with Crowther's son, Dandeson Crowther, see P. E. H. Hair, 'Archdeacon Crowther and the Delta Pastorate, 1892–9', *Sierra Leone Bulletin of Religion*, 5, 1963, pp. 18–27, on pp. 19–24.) Cust's practical contribution to Schön's cause was that he was able, as a member of the committee of S.P.C.K., to arrange for this publishing body to bring out Schön's unpublished material. On Schön, see Cust, *op. cit.*, pp. 251–2.

[113] C.M.S. Archives, Letterbooks, Niger Mission, 26.6.1888.

[114] *Times*, 4.4.1889, p. 10.

[115] See bibliography: D. Westermann (in Bargery, *op. cit.*, p. xv) gave the date of this article wrongly as 1842, putting it at the beginning instead of at the end of Schön's studies: the wrong date has been copied in most later bibliographies.

[116] *Church Missionary Gleaner*, March 1889, p. 36.

died.[117] The German national biographical dictionary says of Schön – 'Er war, wie sein Name, körperlich und geistig schön'.[118]

*   *   *

F. W. Newman, the British pioneer of Berber studies and one of the first scholars to declare Berber a member of a Hamito-Semitic family of languages, in 1844 wrote a note on Schön's Hausa vocabulary in which he made the earliest attempt to define a relationship between Hausa and Hamito-Semitic.[119] The very suggestion that a 'negro language' was in any way related to Semitic caused surprise at the time.[120] Schön's later studies were extensively drawn on by Fr. Müller, Lepsius and Meinhof during the next half-century to illustrate their varying standpoints in this vexed matter. Schön himself was at a disadvantage in comparative studies since he had little knowledge of Arabic, a state of affairs he often regretted. However, as a result of his theological training, he had a working knowledge of Hebrew, and he employed this in his 1862 grammar to demonstrate, though less convincingly than he supposed, that Hausa was a Semitic language. This showed a more advanced interest in comparative studies than did the 1843 vocabulary, which contained merely a casual attempt to compare terms in Hausa and in 'Celtic' (!). Koelle, who was better equipped because of his Arabic, contributed to comparative linguistics largely through the *Polyglotta*; as regards Kanuri, he was convinced soon in his study that not only had it 'no important affinities with other Negro languages' but that 'it was connected with Indo-European and Semitic languages by a considerable number of roots', conclusions which would not now, in these broad terms, be accepted.[121] Barth, in the course of his *Collection*, had much to say about the inter-relationship of various Saharan and Sudanic languages, but little about their relationship to other language groups, possibly a wise silence at the time. He indicated a limited relationship between Hausa and Kanuri, which would now be explained in terms of a lengthy contact of cultures.

Koelle wrote of his efforts to describe Kanuri as follows:

'When I commenced my Kanuri studies, nothing whatever had been written on the grammar [a slight exaggeration], neither was anything known as to its general character; so that I was left to pursue my way through an entirely unknown region, where

---

[117] *ibid.*

[118] 'He lived up to his name ['schön' in German means 'beautiful, fine'] and was fine in body and soul.' (*Allgemeine Deutsche Biographie*). Cust had made the same play on words earlier – 'his long life has been as his name "beautiful" ' (Cust, *op. cit.* (*1883*), 1, p. 252). Cust stated that Livingstone (who had occasionally visited Freetown and took an interest in West African missions) had said of Schön – 'This man's name will live generations after mine has been forgotten' – intended no doubt as a tribute to the importance of linguistic work.

[119] See the bibliography. On Newman, see *D.N.B.* and Cust, *op. cit.* (1883), pp. 101–3. On Hausa and Hamito-Semitic, see M. Cohen, *Essai comparatif sur le vocabulaire . . . du chamito-semitique*, 1947.

[120] J. C. Prichard, edited E. Norris, *Natural history of man*, 4th edition, 1855, p. 324.

[121] However, in the sense in which Koelle was probably thinking of 'other Negro languages', *i.e.* meaning the languages of the Guinea coast and Southern Africa, there was some truth in his first conclusion; Kanuri's close relations are with languages to the north east and east and there is no affinity with languages to the south and south west. Koelle's attempt to relate Kanuri to Indo-European and Semitic (in the *Grammar*, p. 2) was justly criticised by another distinguished African linguist of this generation, see W. H. I. Bleek, 'On the languages of Western and Southern Africa', *Transactions of the Philological Society*, 1855, pp. 40–50, on p. 49.

every step brought new and strange objects under my notice, contrary to everything I could have anticipated. Under such circumstances, two opposite errors are to be avoided: on the one hand, there is the danger of being carried away by a desire for the new and the strange, so as to make common things look uncommon; and, on the other hand, that incredulity is to be guarded against which postulates that the languages, hitherto unknown, cannot present features entirely new. I endeavoured to avoid these extremes . . . but I must confess, that in spite of my honest wish not to *make* a grammar for the Kanuri, but modestly and diligently to *learn* the grammar which the Kanuri has long ago made for itself, it from time to time required fresh exertion to keep my mind free from prejudice and preconceived notions.'[122]

This discriminating appraisal of the task of descriptive linguistics, and of the psychological difficulties of the student of a previously unstudied language, was uncommon in contemporary linguistic writings. In view of the criticism sometimes made, that the early students of African languages distorted their descriptions by shaping them to Indo-European models,[123] it is worth noting that Koelle, Schön and Barth each had some knowledge of Semitic as well as of Indo-European languages, which gave them a wider approach to African languages.[124] Barth was originally a student of Graeco-Roman culture, but he acquired a fair practical and academic knowledge of Arabic. Koelle taught Arabic and Hebrew as well as Greek at Fourah Bay Institution (though no doubt at an elementary level): in his grammar, he included a few pages of roots in these languages (and also in Sanskrit, but this probably only indicates that he had read some of the German philologists). Schön had theological-college Greek and Hebrew. Lacking comparative African studies, the early students of African languages naturally drew heavily on the methods of description already worked out for Indo-European and Semitic languages, and these were for a time sufficiently adequate to enable striking advances in knowledge and practice to be made. Barth, from his examination of a dozen Saharan and Sudanic languages, was the best placed of the three men to observe where the standard descriptive methods failed, and his claim that his own work in Kanuri was in some respects more penetrating than that of Koelle because the latter was unacquainted with Hausa, though hardly convincing in the detail cited, showed some theoretical perception.

Evaluation of early work in Hausa and Kanuri has been made more difficult by the comparatively recent introduction of another dimension of analysis, that of tone. Some of the early exponents of tone-analysis in West African languages found the new technique so revolutionary that they were inclined to ignore all the language study that had gone before. Thus, in the 1930s, Abraham on Hausa, and Lukas on Kanuri, produced grammars and vocabularies which contained virtually no references to previous work, not even in their prefaces (there were no bibliographies), while each insisted that

---

[122] Koelle, *Grammar*, p. iii.
[123] 'The great majority of writers on Bantu grammar have unhesitatingly accepted their own mother tongue or Latin as the basis for everything classical' (C. M. Doke, *Bantu linguistic terminology*, 1935, p. 2: cf. P. D. Curtin, *The image of Africa*, 1964, p. 396). Perhaps the earliest critic on this point was Burton, who said of Crowther's Yoruba grammar that it was 'copied too servilely from Murray, itself an Anglo-Latin modification' (R. F. Burton, *Abeokuta and the Camaroons Mountains*, 1863, 1, p. 305, footnote).
[124] Cf. J. H. Greenberg, 'The history and present status of African linguistic studies', *Proceedings of 1st international congress of Africanists*, 1964, pp. 85–96, on p. 87.

'to neglect the tone is to neglect the essentials of the language'.[125] Lukas writing on the Lake Chad languages, remarked that Barth's work was 'incomplete, especially phonetically, and therefore of little value'.[126] Possibly there was an element of exaggeration, bred of enthusiasm, in these statements, yet it cannot be doubted that tonal analysis produced a considerable advance in the understanding of the structure of the languages. The exact extent to which the failure to appreciate the tone-system vitiates the early analyses – this is something which the layman cannot determine. However this can be said: it is clear that, in the case of Hausa and Kanuri, tonal analysis is necessary to present a fully systematic description, but it is also clear that tones enter into the description less vitally than they do in the case of certain other African languages, for instance, Ewe, Yoruba and Ibo.[127]

The pioneers took little notice of intonation. Koelle ignored it completely in Kanuri.[128] Barth perhaps had some awareness of its existence in Hausa, since he criticised Schön for ignoring 'accentuation' which he described as of lexical significance.[129] In his 1862 grammar, Schön referred to both accentuation and intonation, but only in the following terms. 'The intonation must be distinguished from accentuation, neither of which is sufficiently ascertained to enable us to lay down rules. The few lines we can give with regard to the former are designed to direct the attention of the learner to the subject, rather than to develop the system. Besides that, we may safely assert that it is altogether impossible to represent intonation by any marks or signs. It consists in the raising or sinking of the voice (not so prominent in the Hausa language as in the Ibo and others) and dwelling upon and prolonging one syllable according to the will of the speaker.'[130] The assertion that it was impossible to mark intonation, and the rather vague apprehension of the role of tone, are both surprising, in view of contemporary interest in the tonality of West African languages.

Granted that the tonality of Hausa and Kanuri is not as obvious as that, for instance, of the Kwa languages, nevertheless there were reasons why both Koelle and Schön should have been on the look-out for tone at an early stage of their research. In 1853, both men took part in discussions in London on a universal orthography, and one of the points discussed was the marking of tones in Romanised Chinese: Venn's diary actually records – 'Koelle in the evening. Three hours' hard discussion upon Chinese orthography'.[131] Moreover, Schön's colleague and friend, his former collaborator in Hausa,

[125] R. C. Abraham, *Principles of Hausa*, 1934, p. 4: cf. 'The tone-system of Kanuri has hitherto been overlooked . . . It is imperative to observe the tone-system of the language, as otherwise the accidence cannot be grasped' (J. Lukas, *A study of Kanuri*, 1937, p. vii). On pp. 49, 133 of the latter work, the name Koelle occurs twice, without a bibliographical reference or explanation.

[126] J. Lukas, 'The linguistic situation in the Lake Chad area', *Africa*, 9, 1936, pp. 332–49, on p. 332.

[127] 'Tone [in Hausa] is of restricted significance etymologically, but has morphological value in as far as it builds up tone-patterns which are morphologically characteristic' (D. Westermann and M. A. Bryan, *Languages of West Africa*, 1952, p. 170). Abraham has amusingly noted that he himself for a time was unaware of the existence of tone in Hausa – 'that I did not hear the distinction of tone from tone was more than remarkable, as I had come to Nigeria from Burma with its tonic language' (Abraham, *Dictionary*, 2nd edition, 1962, p. iv–v).

[128] Koelle stated that his informant was weak on 'accents' (allegedly because he had been away from his homeland for many years) – which might indicate that Koelle detected some tone patterns but did not grasp their logic or significance (Koelle, *Grammar*, pp. viii–ix).

[129] Barth, *Collection*, p. ciii.

[130] Schön, *Grammar*, p. 7.

[131] Stock, *op. cit.*, 2, p. 647. No doubt partly because the Chinese had written about them themselves, the tones in Chinese were recognised by the first European students of the language in the sixteenth

—Continued on following page

Crowther, was one of the first to stress tonality in certain West African languages.[132] Crowther pointed out that tone was an essential element of his own language, Yoruba, and must be marked; he did this first, hesitatingly, in his vocabulary of 1843, and then, more insistently and explicitly, in his 1852 grammar. Although Crowther never published in Hausa, he remained in close contact with Schön while the latter was preparing material in the later 1850s, and made use of the material as soon as published, and in 1864 he expressed in print his regret that tone-marks had been omitted from the Hausa translations of the Scriptures – 'a very great mistake, from whatever cause it was done'.[133] The wording leaves us in doubt whether Schön completely ignored tone in these translations, or whether he made some attempt to show it in the manuscript but was persuaded to abandon tone-marking in print (possibly for reasons of economy in printing). However, it can be assumed that Crowther's strong views on tonality and tone-marking were known to Schön, and hence, most likely, to Koelle, by the early 1850s.[134] Later, Schön himself was clear about the importance of tone in another language, Ibo, and marked two tones in the grammar which he was preparing concurrently with his 1862 Hausa grammar. His failure to deal adequately with tone in Hausa may therefore have been due to a belief that tone was of very limited importance in this language.

Except as regards tone, modern students of these languages have failed to specify the deficiencies and errors of the early works, and have confined themselves to general statements of appraisal. Of Barth's work, Lukas wrote in 1939 (modifying his harsher, earlier judgement) – 'Even today this material can render valuable service. From a phonetic point of view, it is, of course, not always what we should like, but it enables the linguist to draw up a grammatical analysis, at least up to a point'.[135] We have already

---

—Continued from previous page

century. Tones were henceforth marked in at least some of the works intended for non-Chinese students, e.g. the writings of the British missionary, Morrison, c.1815. But tone-marking had to be rediscussed when, in the 1840s, missionaries began to prepare Bible translations for Chinese readers, using Roman script. The C.M.S. had a few missionaries working on Chinese translations, hence Venn's concern about orthography. On all this, see J. de Francis, *Nationalism and language reform in China*, Princeton, 1950, early chapters; also, P. E. H. Hair, 'A nineteenth century link between Chinese and African language studies', *Bulletin of S.O.A.S.*, 29, 1966, pp. 143–5.

[132] Statements about tonality in West African languages by other early workers were perhaps not known to Schön and Koelle, e.g., J. G. Christaller, [a mission report from Akropong], *Magazin für die neueste Geschichte der evangelischen Missions- und Bibel-Gesellschaft*, pp. 51–6; A. W. Hanson, 'On the grammatical principles of the Gha (Accra) language, *Journal of the Ethnological Society of London*, 4, 1856, pp. 84–97, on p. 87 [Hanson had tone-marked a translation as early as 1843]. For a comment on early tone marking, see Greenberg, *op. cit.*, p. 90.

[133] S. Crowther, *A grammar and vocabulary of the Nupe language*, 1864, p. iii. Crowther went on to say – 'The Yoruba language has often been remarked by the Missionaries as musical; this is perfectly correct; so also are the Hausa, Nupe and in some degree, the Ibo' [perhaps a slip? – 'in some degree' should refer to Hausa?].

[134] Unfortunately, contemporary correspondence between Crowther and Schön is not generally to be found in the C.M.S. Archives (the latter being no longer, strictly, a C.M.S. agent); but we know that the two were in contact since in 1861 Schön referred to a comment by Crowther on a point in the recent Hausa translations (J. F. Schön, *Oku Ibo*, p. 26).

[135] J. Lukas, 'Linguistic research between the Nile and Lake Chad', *Africa*, 12, 1939, 335–48, on p. 336. The phonetic analysis of the pioneers seems to have been at least moderately acute: for instance, in Hausa Schön noted implosive b, though ignoring the glottal stop and implosive d (cf. Westermann in Bargery, *op. cit.*, p. xvi): in Kanuri, comparing Koelle and Lukas, Koelle noted but did not mark the second of the f forms, but failed to distinguish the two l forms. Of course, the early workers described vowels much less exactly than modern scholars – indeed, it must be said, that some of their examples of vowels appearing in English words are so misleading that it is clear that their command of spoken English was very far from perfect.

57

quoted Delafosse's tribute to Schön as the pioneer of Hausa studies, and Westermann remarked in 1934 that his name 'will for ever be connected with the language'.[136] The works on Hausa produced up to about 1920 were, in the main, either self-confessedly based on Schön's studies, or were merely supplementary to his researches.[137] Koelle's Kanuri grammar, according to Lukas, 'shows a mastery which is unequalled, and it remains one of the greatest achievements in African linguistics'.[138] In general, it may be said that the writings of the pioneers remained useful for academic purposes, even when they had been improved in detail by other students, for roughly three-quarters of a century after they were produced (although academic interest in West African languages was so limited in this period that only one of the works went into a second edition[139]). But all of them have now, even for academic purposes, been superseded, and their interest is purely historical.[140]

The feud between Barth and the Freetown missionaries, though unseemly, was not without value for academic linguistics. Barth made his challenge unequivocably – 'I am fully convinced that succeeding inquirers who may penetrate into these regions [of the Central Sudan] will have full opportunity of acknowledging the greater exactness of my labours in this respect with reference to those of the Rev. Schön';[141] and at many points in his writings, Barth argued that his own work was necessarily better than the Free-town work, because he alone had worked in the homelands and made use of a large number of informants. But this argument cannot be accepted, since it is clear that the work of Schön and Koelle was at least as accurate as that of Barth.[142] In fact the feud demonstrated this – that though the optimum conditions for linguistic research are undoubtedly residence in the homeland of the language, research of very high quality can be done, even with a single informant, anywhere in the world, provided that the informant is a good one and that the inquiry is intensive. Contrariwise, lengthy travel or residence in the homeland and a multitude of informants are of little avail if the inquiries are casual and the inquirer unskilled – while it has to be realised that inquiry within the homeland may raise as many problems of practical procedure as does inquiry from a single informant outside. Almost all the great linguistic research carried out before the days of Schön and Koelle – that, for instance, into the languages of Arabia,

---

[136] Westermann in Bargery, *op. cit.*, p. xvi.

[137] R. Basset, 'Rapport sur les études Berberes et Haoussa', *Actes du 11e Congrès International des Orientalistes*, sect. 5–7, 1899, p. 51; M. Delafosse, *op. cit.*, p. xiv; A. Mischlich, *Lehrbuch der hausa-nischen Sprache*, Archiv für das Studium deutscher Kolonialsprachen, 1, Berlin, 1902, p. ix; F. W. Taylor, 'Hausa and the late Canon Robinson', *Journal of the African Society*, 26, 1926–7, pp. 145–59. An exception to the statement in the text that the work of this period was not original should be made for the writings of R. Prietze from the 1890s.

[138] Lukas, *op. cit.* (1939), p. 344.

[139] Schön's *Magana Hausa*.

[140] A rash assertion to make, of course; I noted that a paper on Hausa given at the 1963 West African Languages Congress included Schön's 1862 grammar in its bibliography. . . . Perhaps new insights will turn out to be early suggestions, since forgotten.

[141] Barth, *Collection*, p. ciii.

[142] Though usually he did not comment on his sources, Müller, the Austrian linguist, noted in his encyclopedic study of world languages, that – 'in my estimation, Koelle, although he was obliged to pursue his studies in Sierra Leone, went much deeper into the subject than H. Barth, who was in Bornu. I find the latter's complaints about Koelle's excellent work unfounded, and on the other hand can point out many much worse faults in Barth's linguistic work' (Fr. Müller, *Grundriss der Sprachwissenschaft*, Band 1, Abth. 2, Wien, 1876, p. 192). Commenting on Barth's Saharan vocabularies, Newman stated that 'his ear cannot have been good' (F. W. Newman, 'Notes on the Libyan languages', *Journal of the Asiatic Society*, n.s. 12, 1880, p. 424).

India, China, Brazil and Peru – had been undertaken by residence in the homeland, and this residence had been considered a sine qua non of research. But the importance rather of intensive inquiry into the speech of a single individual, demonstrated by the success of Schön and Koelle, has been recognised since, during a century in which most of the linguistic research has been on these lines.[143]

Koelle had a talent approaching genius for linguistic research, and Barth too was highly talented: Schön, as he noted himself, compensated for lesser gifts of intellect by the undaunted perseverance which led him through long years of research, despite the frustration of periods when he received neither financial nor moral support. Although they all contributed to academic linguistics, for none of them was linguistic research either a profession[144] or a main aim of life. For Barth, African linguistics was a by-product of his geographical research, for Schön and Koelle it was a means of assisting the missionary endeavour to which they were primarily dedicated.

To evaluate the work of Schön and Koelle simply in terms of the contribution to academic linguistics would give an incomplete picture of their achievement. What, we now ask, was the practical value of their labours? As we have seen, the writings of the two men were of no immediate direct value to the C.M.S., since the attempt to penetrate to the homelands in order to establish mission stations had to be abandoned. As far as Kanuriland is concerned, even after a century has passed the sum of Christian endeavour there is trifling – the greater part of the Bible is still untranslated, for instance – and secular interest in the Kanuri language has been negligible, for the number of literate Kanuris is very small and only a handful of non-Kanuri (mainly Europeans) has ever attempted to learn the language. It seems therefore that Koelle's work has had virtually no practical value. The same, however, cannot be said of Schön's writings on Hausa: though their circulation was limited, they had for a time real practical value, mainly by enabling Europeans to acquire a knowledge of the language.

The Bible translations never circulated in Hausaland, but they were used to a limited extent by Crowther and his assistants on the Niger. It is likely that very few copies were distributed, and Crowther complained (as we have seen) that the Hausa lacked tone-marks.[145] Nevertheless, the books must have been of some use, since Crowther encouraged Schön to resume his Hausa studies later. The primers of 1848 and 1857 were probably used, if at all, only by the Sierra Leoneans in the Niger Mission when they were trying to acquire some knowledge of the lingua franca. The appearance of portions of Christian Scripture in these primers must have discouraged from using them any Moslem who thought of learning to read and write Hausa in Roman script. The 1877 reading book was addressed more to European students, and together with the 1862 grammar and the 1876 dictionary, was undoubtedly of use in the late 1870s and in the

---

[143] One of the earliest successful attempts to obtain linguistic information outside the homeland occurred a little before the Freetown/Chatham studies; this was the work of Karl Tutschek, on four languages of the Eastern Sudan and Ethiopia (Fur, Tumale, Galla, Berta), between 1838 and 1843, using as informants four youths purchased in the slave market at Alexandria and brought to Germany by Duke Maximilian of Bavaria (K. Tutschek, *Dictionary of the Galla language*, Munich and London, 1844, Introduction).

[144] On the evidence given earlier in this essay, it will be clear that Koelle and Schön were not 'professional linguists' or even 'full-time' ones, as stated in Curtin, *op. cit.*, pp. 321, 393.

[145] S. Crowther and J. C. Taylor, *The Gospel on the banks of the Niger*, 1859, pp. 59, 61, 129; S. Crowther, *Nupe grammar*, 1864, p. iii. Three thousand copies of the early Hausa translations were printed between 1856 and 1861, but no more printings were called for during the next twenty years (*Annual report of B.F.B.S.*, 1858, 1861, 1879).

1880s to a number of European missionaries, traders and soldiers – possibly a total of several score. Apparently a small mission school at Lokoja in this period also made use of Schön's books, presumably for teaching Hausa-speaking youths.[146] In numbers of readers, all this added up to very little, yet there is no doubt that it was Schön's books which enabled a start to be made in literate instruction in Hausa and the literate employment of the language by non-Hausa.

In the late 1880s, there arrived on the Niger a band of young English missionaries whose perfervid enthusiasm made them excessively critical of all that had been done before.[147] They proposed a mission to Hausaland, but the leaders died before the mission got under way. In memory of the attempt, a Hausa Association was formed in England, with a studentship at Cambridge University,[148] and the first student of the Association, C. H. Robinson, brother of one of the dead men, began to study and produce works in Hausa. In this milieu, there was much severe criticism of Schön's work: of his translations, Robinson wrote – 'they will require a large amount of correction before they can be of use'.[149] A new translation of the Bible was begun, and Schön's translations have not been used in the present century. The major criticism made of them was that they were too European in idiom and, considering the circumstances in which they were produced, it need not be doubted that there was at least a measure of justice in the criticism.

Schön's critics made much of the fact that he was unaware that Hausa had been written in the homeland in the Arabic script for some time before the language was put into Roman script,[150] and they argued that Arabic rather than Roman script was the more suitable for translations. Schön had in fact sometimes wondered about the suitability of Roman script and had provided transcriptions in Arabic in two of his works, but his very limited knowledge of the Arabic language forced him to work in Roman script. This was perhaps fortunate, since the enthusiasm for Arabic script, displayed for instance by Robinson, seems now a misreading of the situation. Only a very little

---

[146] C.M.S. Archives, Yoruba Mission, 1881/126, letter of 27.12.1881.

[147] Ajayi, *op. cit.*, pp. 250 ff. It must be pointed out that the current avid search for a racialist explanation of all activities by Europeans from 1880 onwards is leading to a disregard of other important factors in the Niger crisis. The young men referred to in the text were the product of a new wave of narrow Evangelicalism in Britain, and their attitudes on the Niger to the bishop and his archdeacons were partly theological in origin. They were also the product of the public schools, and their social status on recruitment was very different from that of earlier British volunteers or the Germans who were recruited until the 1860s, hence their haughty airs. Statements like – 'It will certainly be several generations before the West African native, however carefully trained he may be, will have gained that force of character which an Englishman now inherits as a sort of birthright, and which will fit him to be placed in an independent position of authority' (C. H. Robinson, *Hausaland*, 1896, p. 194) – are less patriotic, and racialist, than they seem, when it is considered that the 'Englishman' whom the author had in mind was almost certainly not the British man-in-the-street (or in-the-fields-or-factory), but the public-school trained 'gentleman'. Compare the attitude of Kipling's public-school boys (in 'Stalky and Co.') to the natives of Devon.

[148] A. H. M. Kirk-Greene, 'Cambridge and the Hausa language', *West Africa*, 2056, 8.9.1956, p. 675.

[149] C. H. Robinson, *Specimens of Hausa literature*, 1896, p. xviii; C.M.S. Archives, Niger Mission, letterbook 1889/124, letter from G. W. Brooke ('too European in idiom and far from correct'); B.F.B.S. catalogue in the Society's Library, manuscript addition ('Dr Miller has never found a Hausa who could understand Schön's version').

[150] Schön had in fact heard of, but had never seen, Hausa literature in the Arabic script (Schön, *op. cit.* (1882), pp. 179–80). For the criticism, see Robinson, *Specimens*, p. xviii, *Dictionary*, 1899, p. viii. In 1882 Schön wrote – 'I am convinced that sooner or later it will be necessary to write our Hausa books in the Arabic characters, in order to make them more generally useful' (C.M.S. Archives, Yoruba Mission, 1881/126, letter of 17.1.1882).

Hausa literature had ever been produced in Arabic script,[151] and it can be contended that the language can be represented more easily and perhaps more effectively in Roman than in Arabic. A very large proportion of printed Hausa literature today is in Roman, and it would appear that the Hausa prefer not to use Arabic. The more credit is therefore due to Schön as the pioneer of Hausa in Roman. Whether his writings, if they had been in Arabic script, would have circulated in Hausaland in his lifetime, is doubtful, since their theology would have distressed the only literates, the Moslem mallams.

In 1896 and 1897, Robinson produced a dictionary and a grammar of Hausa: each went into several editions during the next thirty years, and they superseded, as they were intended to, Schön's grammar and dictionary. Robinson spent only short periods studying Hausa at first hand (in Hausaland and at Tripoli), and it is therefore no discredit to his work that it was largely based on Schön's, though this was perhaps not made as clear as it might have been by Robinson himself. His dictionary, in its earlier editions, was a slightly enlarged version of Schön's, with revisions which in some cases were no improvement. Both grammar and dictionary showed a tendency to popularise Hausa studies by presenting a simplified form of the language: while this made them useful to learners who wished to acquire only a smattering of the language, it may be doubted whether in soundness of linguistic theory they represented any advance on Schön's works.[152] While Robinson catered for English-speaking learners,[153] works in

---

[151] During the Fulani jihad, some literature was written in Fula and Hausa. Whether Hausa was written in earlier centuries is uncertain. It is clear that the official literature of the Western and Central Sudan before colonial days was entirely in the Arabic language, and there seems to be no conclusive evidence that vernaculars were put into writing much before the nineteenth century. On the other hand, the recent discovery of a seventeenth century copy of a Koran with glosses in Kanembu, while providing at the moment merely an exception to the general conclusion, might indicate that more vernacular literature of an early date may yet be found, or that some which did exist has been destroyed (for instance, during the Fulani conquest of Hausaland when the state archives disappeared). See A. D. H. Bivar, 'A dated Koran from Bornu', *Nigeria magazine*, 65, June 1960, pp. 199–205. A general study of vernacular literature in Arabic script is badly needed. Curiously, the earliest Christian text we know of in Hausa was written in Arabic script, and twenty years before Schön began his research: the following account relates to a slave in Brazil (for references to some of the literature on Hausa or 'Malê' in Brazil, see G. Freyre, *The masters and the slaves*, New York, 1946, p. 298). 'Le nègre Francisco est plein d'intelligence et de probité. Il a été prêtre mahométan et maître d'école dans sa patrie, il connaît fort bien l'arabe, il sait compter et écrire, comme vous vous en convaincrez par une traduction du Pater Noster en langue haussah, écrite par lui en caractères arabes, que je vous envoie . . . ' (*Journal des voyages*, 32, 1826, p. 305).

[152] In fairness to Robinson, it must be said that he always acknowledged some debt to Schön, but he tended to stress differences rather than similarities, *e.g.* Robinson, *Dictionary*, pp. viii–ix. Thanks to contributions received from other workers in Hausaland, the later editions of the dictionary were quantitatively a distinct improvement on Schön. A less favourable comment on Robinson's work appeared in J. Lippert, [a review], *Mittheilungen des Seminars für Orientalischen Sprachen*, 4, 1901, pp. 280–7; and another in A. Seidel, *Die Haussasprache*, 1906, pp. iii–v. (It is worth noting that these comments display nationalistic animus, the German Schön being contrasted favourably with the Englishman Robinson. Fifty years earlier, before the Unification of Germany, tribalism infected West African language studies – Barth boasted that 'the ear of a native of South Germany [*i.e.* Schön and Koelle] is much less capable of catching the difference of these sounds than that of a native of North Germany [*i.e.* Barth]' – while Koelle remarked in the *Polyglotta* that an Ijebu-man would no more call himself a Yoruba, than a Wurtemberger [like himself] would call himself a Prussian.) For an English attack on Robinson, by the pioneer of the next stage of Hausa studies, see an intemperate article, F. W. Taylor, 'Hausa and the late Canon Robinson', *Journal of the African Society*, 26, 1926–7, pp. 145–59.

[153] The bibliography contains two works by J. Numa Rat, published in 1889. Though of no linguistic value, they deserve a note. Numa Rat was a Jamaican doctor in the Colonial Medical Service, and

— Continued on following page

French and German presented Hausa to speakers of these languages; the latter works were similarly based on Schön but admitted it rather more freely.

During his half-century of Hausa studies, Schön had had the field almost to himself, as the bibliography that follows shows. But between the late 1880s and 1914 about a score of authors published books on Hausa. This came about because Hausaland, and those neighbouring districts in which Hausa was spoken as a lingua franca, passed under colonial control during this period. British, French and German administrators were introduced into the area and called on to learn Hausa. (The very first volume in a series entitled 'The Library of Research into the languages of the German Colonies' was on Hausa.) Gradually, the writing of the vernacular in Roman spread among educated Hausa; and today the Hausa language has certainly the largest printed literature of any African language of the Sudanic zone, and probably the fifth or sixth largest of any African language in any part of Africa.[154]

*　　*　　*

Schön and Koelle, with whom so much of this essay has been concerned, worked together on one project of far-reaching practical importance. In 1848, shortly after returning to Europe and settling at Chatham, Schön assisted Professor Lee in the production of *Rules for reducing unwritten languages to alphabetical writing*.[155] This was not the first time Lee had been consulted on the problem of a standard orthography,[156] while Schön's contribution was undoubtedly his practical experience with three West African languages, Bullom, Ibo and Hausa. The *Rules* were moderately successful: through Schön's work on Ibo, they shaped the development of Ibo orthography up to the 1920s, while they were even more influential in Yoruba orthography, through Schön's influence on Crowther, so that Yoruba orthography today is a modified version of the one suggested in 1848. However, the 1848 orthography was insufficiently detailed to suit Koelle, and when in London in 1853 he encouraged Henry Venn to review the matter. Venn had already had discussions on the subject of a possible 'scientific, universal orthography' with Richard Lepsius, the German philologist; and during 1853, Lepsius (quoting his own words) 'was again induced to direct his attention to this subject, by a visit from the Rev. S. W. Koelle, in consequence of which he determined to bring forward his own long-prepared project, after discussing it minutely with this

---

Continued from previous page—

his other writings include a work on yaws, and a translation of a Gospel into 'the French patois of the West Indies' (1894). His Hausa writing was done on Gold Coast and was produced for the officers of Hausa troops. In 1881, Schön noted that he had had a complaint from Gold Coast to the effect that his dictionary omitted the term 'revolver' (C.M.S. Archives, Yoruba Mission, 1881/126, letter of 21.12.1881): this could well have been from Dr Numa Rat, whose pamphlet giving the commands for physical training exercises on the parade ground, in Hausa, is surely the oddest work in the early literature. The text in his grammar, the autobiography of one of the Hausa soldiers, has some interest.

[154] Larger are probably Swahili, Ganda, Xosa, Sotho, perhaps Yoruba.

[155] This section of the essay leans heavily on a recent paper, J. Spencer, 'S. W. Koelle and the problem of notation for African languages, 1847–1855', *Sierra Leone Language Review*, 5, 1966, pp. 83–105.

[156] Lee provided the C.M.S. with 'Rules for the guidance of persons who have to fix a language' in 1814 (C.M.S. Archives, Minutes, 1813–17, p. 232, minute of 28.12.1814). Again, thirty years later, he provided 'some valuable general rules for fixing these [Hausa and Yoruba] and other languages' (*C.M.S. Proceedings*, 1844–5, p. 36).

gentleman'.[157] Lepsius listened to the sounds in various languages outside his previous experience, and among other speakers, he heard Schön in Hausa (and Ibo), and Koelle in Kanuri (and Vai). After a conference in London in 1854, Lepsius produced a 'Standard Alphabet', which was almost immediately accepted by the C.M.S. The first book to be printed in the Standard or Lepsius Alphabet was Koelle's Kanuri grammar. In 1860, when it was felt that slight revisions were required and Lepsius was preparing a second edition of the booklet describing the alphabet, Schön was sent to Berlin, with one of the officers of C.M.S., to discuss the revision.[158] The Lepsius Alphabet, though possessing defects, has been a most effective instrument in the spread of literacy into many new tongues, in translation work, and, for a time at least, in linguistic research. It was the basic orthography for most African languages for about seventy years, and in variant forms is still employed in some languages. It is pleasant to record that Schön and Koelle – much of whose work was very little used by others, most of whose work is superseded – were connected with a device still of some practical importance, a device still employed in the work to which they were dedicated, 'the evangelisation of Africa', and hence (as Koelle wrote) the demonstration of 'the common humanity which the Negro shares with the Caucasian'.[159]

All the three pioneers of study of the Central Sudan languages, Barth, Koelle, Schön, would have approved of the recent intensification of interest in the languages of West Africa, whether from the practical or the academic side. In his Kanuri grammar, Koelle wrote in 1854 – 'Africa is still an unknown country in many respects. Its numerous languages are a wide field, the cultivation of which would be sure to reward the professional philologist with many interesting discoveries. Hitherto the Christian Missionaries have done by far the greater part of the work: may we not expect that the linguists will join them in this enterprise?'[160]

---

[157] R. Lepsius, *Standard alphabet*, 1855, pp. 18–23.
[158] *ibid.*, 2nd edition, 1863, pp. xiii, 2.
[159] S. W. Koelle, *Grammar of Vei*, 1853, p. 4.
[160] S.W. Koelle, *Grammar of Kanuri*, p. x.

1790–1854 [Early vocabularies have been listed in the text, on pp. 34–36]

1841* [James Frederick/Jacob Friedrich Schön, a handbill, 'Address to the chiefs and people of Africa' in Hausa, printed at Cape Coast]

1843 J. F. Schön, Vocabulary / of the / Haussa language / Part I – English and Haussa / Part II – Haussa and English / and / phrases and specimens of translations. / To which are prefixed, / the grammatical elements / of the / Haussa language. / By the Rev. J.F.S., / missionary of the Church Missionary Society, / author of a journal of the Niger Expedition, and of a vocabulary / and specimens of translations of the Sherbro language / , C.M.S., London

pp. i–v Introduction; 1–30 Grammatical elements of the Haussa language; (1)–(157) A vocabulary of the Haussa language, Part I English and Haussa, Part II Haussa and English; (158)–(165) Translation of medical terms; (166)–(169) Phrases; (170)–(190) Specimens of translations [Lord's Prayer, Scripture portions, Address to the kings and their people (with English), Intended treaty between the Queen of England and the chiefs of the interior of Africa (with English)].

1844 Francis William Newman, 'Remarks on the Haussa language, based upon "the vocabulary" of the same "with grammatical elements, by the Rev. J. F. Schön, 1843" ', in James Cowles Prichard, Researches into the physical history of mankind, 3rd edition, vol. 4, London, Appendix 3, pp. 627–631.

[1848] J. F. Schön, Primer / of the / Haussa language, / by the / Rev. J.F.S., / missionary of the C.M.S., / member of the German Oriental Society. / London: printed by William Watts

pp.[2] note on orthography; 3–36 [words, phrases, lessons, Scripture portions, all in Hausa].

1851 Heinrich Barth, 'Progress of the African mission . . . ', *Journal of the Royal Geographical Society*, 21, pp. 130–221

On pp. 169–88, in a letter written November 1850, 'Vocabulary of the language of Agádèz' [vocabulary in 'Haussa, Emghedesie, English', 1000 words and phrases]; pp. 188–90, Parable of the Prodigal Son, Lord's Prayer, both in Hausa and English.

1853 [James Richardson, edited Edwin Norris], Dialogues / and / a small portion of the New Testament, / in the / English, Arabic, Haussa, and Bornu languages / , London: Printed by Harrison and Sons

Large size (22 × 33 cm.); no indication in text of author or editor; pp. 1–102, conversations or useful dialogues, Bornouese, Soudanese [i.e. Hausa], Arabic, and English, in columns, the first three in Arabic script; pp. 103–16, verses from Matthew, chapters 2–4, in Soudanese and Bornouese, with literal English, the translation in Arabic script.

1857 [J. F. Schön], Fārawā / letāfin māgána Haúsa / ko / mākóyi māgánan gáskía / da / haínya ga raí hal ábbabá / wónda / góni māllámi Yakúbu ya rūbúta ya aiké ga / Haúsawa dúka tāre da gaísuānsa / , Berlin

i.e. primer of the Hausa language . . . by Mallam Yakubu: pp. 1–2 Alphabet; 3–53 words and phrases in Hausa, in Roman and Arabic scripts; new pagination, 1–46 Hausa Primer [Hausa only, Roman script; mainly Scripture portions].

1857 J. F. Schön, The Gospel / according to / St. Matthew. / Translated into Hausa by the / Rev. J.F.S. / missionary of the C.M.S. / , B.F.B.S., London

1857   J. F. Schön, The Gospel / according to St. John. / Translated [etc, as previous item], B.F.B.S., London

1857   J. F. Schön, The / Acts of the Apostles. / Translated [etc, as previous items], B.F.B.S., London

1858   J. F. Schön, Lĕtâfin Musa nãfâri / The / First Book of Moses. / Translated from the original into Hausa / by the / Rev. J.F.S., / Chaplain of Melville Hospital, Chatham, / member of the German Oriental Society, and / late Church Missionary at Sierra Leone / , B.F.B.S., London

1858   J. F. Schön, Labâri nãgarí kámmãda anrūbúrasi / dagá Lukas / The / Gospel according to St. Luke. / Translated [etc, as previous item]///// late Church Missionary in Western Africa / , B.F.B.S., London

1859   J. F. Schön, Letafin Musa nabiu / The / Second Book of Moses, / called Exodus. / Translated [etc, as previous items]///// late Church Missionary in Sierra Leone / , B.F.B.S., London

1861   [William Balfour Baikie], Observations / on the / Hausa and Fulfulde / languages / with examples / For private circulation. / London
pp. iii–iv Preface, signed W. B. Baikie; 5–12 [discusses Hausa dialects]; 13–15 Decalogue, Lord's Prayer, Apostles' Creed, in Hausa; 15–19 [on Fula]; 20–1 Decalogue, Lord's Prayer, in Fula; 22–9 Geographical and proper names.

1862   J. F. Schön, Grammar / of the / Hausa language, / by / Rev. J.F.S., / Chaplain of the Melville Hospital, Chatham, / member of the German Oriental Society; and / late missionary of the C.M.S./, C.M.S., London
pp. i–xiv Prefatory remarks; i–[viii] Contents, Corrigenda; 1–163 grammar; 165–234 Appendix containing specimens of a Hausa literature, taken from natives in their own tongue and accompanied with an English translation [165–214 stories, 215–34 'The life and travels of Dorugu, as dictated by himself. One chapter only.']

1862   H. Barth, Sammlung und Bearbeitung / Central-Afrikanischer Vokabularien / von / H.B. / Erste Abtheilung / Umfassendere Vokabularien der Kanúri-, Tédā-, Hausa-, Fulfúlde-, Soṅγai-, Lógonē-, Wándalā-, Bágrimma- und Mãba-Sprachen / Einleitung Kap. 1–6. Fürwörter. Partikeln, Zahlwörter, Zeitwörter.//Collection / of / vocabularies of Central African languages / compiled and analysed / by / Henry Barth, C.B.D.C.L. [sic] / 1st Part [etc, in English translation]//// Gotha
pp. ii–cx Einleitung / Introductory Remarks [ci–cx on Hausa and Schön, concluding with a revision of part of Schön's translation of Matthew, 1857]; (1)–(141) vocabularies of all the languages named in the title, in columns; German and English versions of text on opposite pages throughout.

1863   H. Barth, Sammlung [etc, as previous item]/// Zweite abtheilung. / Einleitung, Kap. 7–12. Analyse der Fulfúlde-, Soṅγai-, Lógonē-, Wándalā-, / Bágrimma-, und Mãba-Sprachen. / [etc, English translation]/// Gotha
pp. cx–cccxxxiv.

1867   H. Barth, Sammlung [etc, as previous items]/// Dritte abtheilung / Nennwörter / [etc, English translation]/// Gotha
pp. 144–295 vocabularies, arranged as in the 1st Part.

1876   J. F. Schön, Dictionary / of / the Hausa language. / Part I / Hausa-English. Part II / English-Hausa. / With / appendices of Hausa literature, / by J.F.S., / Chaplain of the Melville Hospital, Chatham: late missionary of the C.M.S. in West Africa/, C.M.S., London

> pp. i–vi Preface; vii [contents of Appendix]; viii–x Corrigenda; 1–281 Hausa vocabulary Part I Hausa-English. Part II English-Hausa; i–xxxiv Appendix Hausa Literature [i–xii Second chapter of the life and travels of Dorugu, in Hausa only; xii–xxviii stories, in Hausa only; xxix–xxxiv one story, in Hausa and English]; unnumbered pp. 9, Translation of the Book of the Prophet Jonah by the late Dr Baikie [a reproduction of a manuscript].

1877   J. F. Schön, Haúsa reading book: / with the / rudiments of grammar and vocabularies, / and / traveller's vade mecum. / By / James Frederick Schön- / Chaplain [etc, as previous item], C.M.S., London

> pp. iii–iv Preface; v–viii Contents; 1–96 lessons; 97–103 Addenda kindly contributed by the Rev. Th. C. John, native missionary at Lokojah [lessons]; i–xxxix Appendix Hausa Literature [this section is identical with the one under the same title in the previous item].

1877   Friedrich Müller, Grundriss der Sprachwissenschaft, Wien, 1/2, pp. 215–237
> 'Die Hausa-Sprache', an analysis based on earlier sources.

1877   [J. F. Schön], Labari nagari (ko linzila na Yahaya) / [title in Arabic script] / (The Gospel of St. John) /, C.M.S., London
> chapters 1–9 only, in Hausa in both Roman and Arabic script.

1878   J. F. Schön, Labāri nāgarí kámada Marku / ya rubútaši / The Gospel according to St. Mark. / Translated into Hausa from the original by / J.F.S., / Fellow of the Royal Geographical Society /, C.M.S., London

1880   [J. F. Schön], Letāfi na alwāši sābo / na / ubangīžimu Isa Kristu / The New Testament / of / Our Lord and Saviour Jesus Christ. / Translated into Hausa /, B.F.B.S., London

1881   [J. F. Schön], Letāfi na Yesāya annabi / da magána / Haúsa / The Book of Isaiah / Translated into Hausa /, B.F.B.S., London

1881   W. B. Baikie, Letāfi ta zabúra / The Book of Psalms, / translated into Hausa / by / William B. Baikie, Esq., M.D. / late Her Majesty's Consul at Lokajah, River Niger /, B.F.B.S., London

1882   J. F. Schön, 'A sketch of the Hausa language', *Journal of the Royal Asiatic Society*, new series 14, pp. 176–217
> Erroneously dated 1842 in several previous bibliographies.

[From 1885, material on Hausa by French and German scholars begins to appear; for the period 1885–90, this bibliography lists only the publications in English.]

1885   J. F. Schön, Magána Hausa. / Native literature, / or / Proverbs, tales, fables and historical fragments in the Hausa language. / To which is added / a translation in English / by J.F.S., D.D., F.R.G.S., Church Missionary /, S.P.C.K., London

> pp. iii–x Introductory Remarks; xi–xii Alphabet; xiii–xx Contents; 1–4 Introductory sentences [with English]; 5–10 Proverbs; 10–18 Letters of Dorŭgu [1857–8]; 113–230 Narratives, tales and descriptions, chiefly by Dorŭgu; 231–68 Contribution forwarded by the Rev. T. C. John, Lokoja [stories and local gossip]; 269–88 Contributions by Mr Gottlieb Adolphus Krause sent from Tripoli [stories]; Hausa only (despite the title) from p. 5.

1886 J. F. Schön, African proverbs, tales / and / historical fragments / English translation / Hausa text / by J.F.S. [etc, as previous item], S.P.C.K., London

pp. v–vi Preface; 1–182 Translations, of all the Hausa material from p. 5 in the previous item; English only (despite the title).

1888 J. F. Schön, Appendix / to the / Dictionary of the Hausa language / (published 1876) / Hausa-English part / with / additions of Hausa literature. / By J.F.S., .DD., F.R.G.S., / late Chaplain [etc, as 1876 item], C.M.S., London

pp. iii–iv Preface; 1–182 Appendix to Hausa dictionary; 183–198 Sentences and short stories contributed by the Rev. T. L. [sic] John [Hausa and English]; 198–204 Letter from Mr Uriah H. Bennet 1886 [Hausa and English]; 204–6 Continuation of proverbs.

1889 J. Numa Rat, The elements / of / the Hausa language, / or a / short introductory grammar of the language, / prepared by / J.N.R., / Assistant Colonial Surgeon of the Gold Coast, / for the use of the Gold Coast Constabulary, / respectfully dedicated to / His Excellency, Sir W. Brandford Griffith, K.C.M.G., / Governor of the Gold Coast Colony. / London: / Waterlow and Sons

pp. [iii] Preface; [v]–vi Introduction; [1]–47 grammar; 48–60 Account of his life dictated by Sergeant Augustus, to the author, at Hythe, England, August 1888 [Hausa and English]; interleaved with blank pages throughout; errata slip stuck on last page.

1889 J. Numa Rat, Physical training. / English-Hausa, / translated from the / Infantry Field Exercise, 1889. / By / J.N.R., / Assistant Colonial Surgeon of the Gold Coast, / for the use of the / Gold Coast Constabulary /, London, Waterlow and Sons

pp. 23: Hausa and English, in columns. Copy in the possession of the compiler.

1790–1854 [Early vocabularies have been listed in the text, on pp. 34–36.]

1826 Heinrich Julius Klaproth, Essai / sur / la langue du Bornou, / suivi des vocabulaires / du Begharmi, du Mandara et de Timbouctou; / par M. J. Claproth [sic]. / Paris.

pp. 5–18 Essai; 19–28 Vocabulaire du Bornou; 29–33 Vocabulaire du Begharmi; 34–6 Vocabulaire du Mandara; 37–40 Vocabulaire de Timbouctou; 41 Table. A copy of this work is in S.O.A.S. Library. The Essai also appeared as an appendix to the French translation of D. Denham, H. Clapperton, W. Oudney, *Travels* . . . , vol. 3, Paris, 1826.

1850 Sigismund Wilhelm Koelle, 'Aus einem Briefe des Missionar S. W. Kölle an Herrn Prof. Dr v. Ewald', *Zeitschrift der deutschen morgenländischen Gesellschaft*, 4, pp. 509–12

Letter dated 14.11.1849, from Fourah Bay, Sierra Leone: brief comment on few points in Kanuri.

1853 [James Richardson, edited Edwin Norris], Dialogues . . . [see bibliography of Hausa]

1853 [J. Richardson and E. Norris], Grammar / of the / Bornu or Kanuri language; / with / dialogues, translations, / and / vocabulary / London

pp. 1–31 Dialogues in Bornu and English, from Richardson's manuscripts; 31–6 Additional phrases [Kanuri and English]; 36–9 translation of Matthew, chapters 2–4; 40–6 Agreement intended to be entered into with the petty kings and chiefs of the interior of Africa [Kanuri and English]; 47–101 Grammatical sketch of the Bornu or Kinuri [sic] language by Edwin Norris [49–53 Introductory Observations, 54–74 Grammar, 75–101 Vocabulary].

1854 Heinrich Barth, 'Schreiben Barth's an Prof. Lepsius', *Zeitschrift für allgemeine Erdkunde*, 2, pp. 372–4, 384–7

Letter dated 18.1.1853, discusses a few Kanuri terms, and refers to a vocabulary sent to Europe.

1854 S. W. Koelle, Grammar / of the / Bórnu or Kā́nurī language. / By / Rev. S.W.K. / missionary of the C.M.S. / , C.M.S., London

Engraving of the informant, Ali Eisama Gazirma; pp. i–ix Preface; [x] Contents, Corrigenda; 1–326 Grammar.

1854 S. W. Koelle, African / native literature, / or / proverbs, tales, fables and historical fragments / in the Kanuri or Bornu language. / To which are added / a translation of the above / and / a Kanuri–English vocabulary: / by / Rev. S.W.K., / Church Missionary / , C.M.S., London

Cover entitled 'Koelle's Kanuri proverbs, etc'. pp. v–xii Preface; [xiii]–[xv] Contents, Corrigenda; 1–6 Proverbs and sayings [Kanuri and English]; 7–64 Stories; 65–121 Historical fragments [including pieces on Serpents, Locusts, Eclipse of the Sun, the Bode people, Bornu kings, biography of the informant]; 122–256 translation of the Kanuri texts; 257–434 Vocabulary, Kanuri–English.

1854 A. F. Pott, 'Sprachen aus Afrika's Innerem und Westen', *Zeitschrift der Deutschen Morgenländischen Gesellschaft*, 8, pp. 412–42

Reviews Richardson/Norris and Koelle on Kanuri, together with works on other languages.

1862, 1867 Barth, Sammlung [see the bibliography of Hausa]

On pp. xli–xlv of the 1st Part, a discussion of Kanuri and Koelle; vocabularies in both parts.

1877 F. Müller, Grundriss der Sprachwissenschaft, Wien, 1/2, pp. 192–214

'Die Kanuri-Sprache', an analysis based on earlier sources.

[Earlier bibliographies of Hausa and Kanuri are included on p. 106.]

THE EARLY STUDY OF THE LANGUAGES OF THE LOWER NIGER AND BENUE, 1840–1890

This essay is concerned with languages whose homelands lie along the banks of the lower Niger, from the Delta five hundred miles upstream to the Bussa Rapids, and along the banks of the lower Benue, the Niger's main tributary, from the confluence upstream for three hundred miles. Only the two most northern of these languages were mentioned in Arabic sources on the Sudanic region before 1800;[1] only the two most southern were mentioned in European sources on the Guinea coast before 1800.[2] Knowledge on the part of the outside world of the mere existence of the remainder – and the linguistic study of all of them – had to await the discovery of the course of the Niger, completed in the 1830s, and the opening-up of the river to European influence, inaugurated by a series of expeditions up-river between 1832 and 1857. Immediately after, major work was begun on the lower Niger-Benue languages. The early students of these languages and the founders of written literatures in them, were, in the main, missionaries; and the majority were African members of the C.M.S. Niger Mission.

A dozen different African languages are spoken today on the banks of the lower Niger and the lower Benue, not including the commercial and administrative lingua franca, Hausa. Eight of these languages, all of which received some attention before 1890, will be considered in this essay: they are as follows.[3]

(a) *Ijaw*,[4] spoken in the Delta.

(b) *Ibo*, spoken for about one hundred miles upstream, above the Delta, on each bank of the lower Niger (and also, in the nineteenth century, at the Delta port of Bonny).[5]

(c) *Igala*, spoken on the east bank of the Niger, for about one hundred miles, above Ibo and below the Benue confluence.

(d) *Igbira*, spoken between the Niger and the Benue immediately north of the confluence, but for only a short distance on the banks, with another section west of the confluence in the near interior.

(e) *Idoma*, *Tiv* and *Jukun*, spoken, in that order, ascending the Benue from the confluence, probably in the nineteenth century on both banks, with the last extending to about three hundred miles up from the confluence.

(f) *Nupe*, spoken on both banks of the Niger above the confluence for about two hundred miles.

---

[1] Strictly, the names mentioned indicated peoples, not languages: (a) *Nupe* – Ibn Battuta in the fourteenth century referred to 'Yufi', downstream from Timbuktu and Gao, thought to be Nufi or Nupe (for sources discussing, see T. Hodgkin, *Nigerian perspectives*, 1960, p. 73, n. 3); (b) *Jukun* – apart from references in recently-composed works allegedly based on oral traditions, e.g. the Kano Chronicle, a seventeenth century poem refers to the 'Kwararafa', almost certainly the Jukun (Hodgkin, *op. cit.*, p. 132). In general, very little can be learnt about these peoples from pre-1800 Arabic sources.
[2] The Ijaw and the Ibo, as described later in the text.
[3] Three languages, Yoruba, Edo and Sobo, which are spoken along stretches of the west bank of the Niger, are not considered here; partly because the homeland centres are well away from the Niger; partly because Edo and Sobo were not studied before 1890, while the study of Yoruba has of course been dealt with in the earlier essay.
[4] Ijɔ: perhaps the best excuse for using the older spelling is that visually it is more distinct from Ibo than Ijɔ.
[5] These are indications of where the language was encountered by Europeans during our period. Its total extent was of course not known.

These languages are spoken today by about fifteen million persons – between one quarter and one third of the population of Nigeria – and were spoken in the nineteenth century by probably around ten million.[6] But one language, Ibo, today accounts for half the total, and except for Nupe which has about two million speakers and Tiv which has about one million, the other languages are well under the million mark: it is likely that in the nineteenth century, proportions of the total population for individual languages were much the same. Early students recognised after a time that the languages represented populations of very varying sizes, and more attention was eventually devoted to the most widely-spoken languages, Ibo and Nupe.

Before the nineteenth century, European knowledge of even the coastal peoples of this area was extremely limited. A Portuguese account of the coast written around 1500 noted that the 'Jos', i.e. Ijaw, lived in the rivers of the Delta region: it briefly described their economic activities, and included one word in the vernacular which might be an earlier form of a modern Ijaw term.[7] This account remained in manuscript until the nineteenth century. Nothing in fact appeared in print about the languages of this part of the coast during the period of Portuguese ascendancy in the trade there, though it is conceivable that vocabularies were collected and may yet be discovered in the largely unexamined archives of Portugal and the Catholic missionary orders.[8] The earliest material in print in any of these languages was apparently collected by a Dutch sailor, no doubt while the Dutch were opening out trade at New Calabar and Bonny in the mid-seventeenth century. The material was somewhat slight, being only the first five numerals in Ijaw: it was published as part of an account of Dutch trade at these ports, in 1668.[9] During the next hundred years, various writers described the Ijaw traders and chiefs at New Calabar and Bonny (without, however, using the term 'Ijaw'), and an

---

[6] Present-day figures are very approximate because of the confusion arising from recent Nigerian censuses. As regards earlier population, our guess is that it remained steady during the first two-thirds of the nineteenth century, the Fulani razzias compensating for the ending of the Atlantic slave trade.

[7] 'A jente d'este Rio [Rio Real, or Bonny River] sam chamados Jos . . . todos comem carne . . . e ha ho carneiro chamam "bozy" . . .' (Duarte Pacheco Pereira, *Esmeraldo de situ orbis*, liv. 2, cap. 9, Bissau edition, 1956, pp. 144, 146). A sheep is not called 'bozy', or any word like that, in any language of this part of the West African coast. But – remembering that to the visiting European, West African sheep and goats look very much alike – a common Bantu term for 'goat' is '-bozi' (H. H. Johnson, *A comparative study of the Bantu and semi-Bantu languages*, 1919, 1922), with present-day forms in Ibibio and the Cross River languages of 'ebut', 'ebu', 'ebweli', etc., and in Ijaw (personal communication from Miss Kay Williamson) of 'obori'. The suggestion by G. I. Jones (*Africa*, 28, 1958, p. 44) that in later contexts 'bozy' means 'bracelets' seems to me irrelevant to the present issue. Pacheco Pereira's account, but not the vernacular term, is discussed in G. I. Jones, *The trading states of the Oil Rivers*, 1963, pp. 33–6.

[8] No early linguistic material is however noted in A. F. C. Ryder, *Materials for West African history in Portuguese archives*, 1965, or in R. Gray and D. Chambers, *Materials for West African history in Italian archives*, 1965, though these authors make it clear that parts of the extensive archives investigated have only been sampled.

[9] O. Dapper, *Naukeurige Beschrijvinge der Afrikaensche Gewesten . . .*, Amsterdam, 1668, second pagination, p. 135. The numerals can also be found in the second Dutch edition 1676, in the German translation of 1670, and in the shamelessly unacknowledged translation into English of 1670 which goes under the name of J. Ogilby; but they are missing from the French translation of 1686. (It cannot be repeated too often that the French version is a paraphrase, with many cuts, and the translation sometimes inaccurate; African historians who persist in using it, or the loosely translated Ogilby version, do so at their peril. An excellent account of the early Delta trade, for instance, is marred by ignorance of these numerals and the evidence they afford of the Ijaw presence, arising from the use of the French version – Jones, *op. cit.* (1963), pp. 36–8.) The numerals were reprinted, without a reference, in J. C. Adelung and J. S. Vater, *Mithridates*, 3, Berlin, 1812, p. 206, under the name 'Calbra'.

English work of 1732 referred to the inland 'Hackbous' (probably a misprint for 'Hick-bous'), i.e. Igbo/Ibo,[10] but no more linguistic material appeared in print. Thus, the first two hundred and seventy years of European contact with the Niger Delta region proved almost entirely profitless as far as the study of African languages was concerned.

Meanwhile, however, representatives of these various peoples and languages were being transported across the Atlantic as slaves. In the Americas, slaves from the Delta region were usually known as Caravali/Carabali/Kalbary/Calabars, after the two Calabars, New and Old, the ports from which so many of the slave-ships sailed;[11] and this name concealed their ethnolinguistic identity. But in 1627 a Spanish priest who had worked among slaves at Cartagena, listed in print the names given by 'Caravalies' when questioned further about their provenance. Of nineteen names, ten are the same as those of modern Ijaw settlements in the Delta, while among the other names is the name 'Ibo'.[12] We can be certain from this evidence that Ijaw slaves were to be found in America, though the name 'Ijaw' seems never to have been used in records of the slave trade. We cannot be so sure that 'Ibo' had the modern ethnolinguistic meaning, but since it is likely that there were Ibo-speaking slaves in the Americas from at least the early seventeenth century, this could well be the earliest reference to the Ibo people in print. Much later, in the second half of the eighteenth century, the name 'Ibo' began to appear regularly in slave trade records and the term 'Calabar' was much less used: this may indicate that Iboland was providing a larger proportion of the slaves shipped from the Calabars and neighbouring ports. Several accounts describe Ibo slaves in the Americas,[13] and one of these also provided the earliest substantial linguistic information on the lower Niger-Benue languages.

In 1766–7, G. C. A. Oldendorp, a German pastor of the Moravian Brethren, visited the West Indies to collect material for a history of the Caribbean mission of the Brethren.

---

[10] J. Barbot, *A description of the coasts of North and South Guinea* . . . , 1732, p. 461. The name was supplied by Barbot's brother who visited the Bonny River in 1700. It may be noted here that the vocabulary of the 'Old Calabar language' in Barbot (p. 383), is pidgin Portuguese with some Ibibio, perhaps more of the vernacular than stated by M. D. W. Jeffreys, *Old Calabar and notes on the Ibibio language*, Calabar, 1935, p. 34.

[11] See, for instance, G. Aguirre Beltran, 'Tribal origins of slaves in Mexico', *Journal of Negro History*, pp. 269–352, on pp. 325–6 (taken from the same author's *La poblacion negra de Mexico 1519–1810*, Mexico City, 1946, on pp. 134–5). The name 'Calabar' was first used by Europeans to mean the section of the Delta around Bonny and Degema (see the map of 'Calbaery' dated 1638 in K. Ratelband, *Vijf dagregisters van . . . Mina 1645–7*, 1953, p. lxxxiv, ignoring the confused comment in the text). It supposedly derives from an Ijaw name Culeba/Okolaba (but now Okoloma) for the port of Bonny, the latter European name supposedly deriving from the Ibo name for the port, Obani. Around the middle of the seventeenth century, the name 'Calabar' was also applied to a second trading area, that on the Cross River; hence, in 1668 Dapper had to distinguish between 'Old' Calabar on the Cross, and 'New' Calabar in the Delta (up-river from Bonny and near modern Degema). The earlier inhabitants of New Calabar and Bonny were Ijaw and those of (Old) Calabar Efik: but during the period of the Atlantic slave trade, all three acquired an Ibo element in the population which in Bonny became dominant. See P. A. Talbot, *The peoples of Southern Nigeria*, 1926, pp. 182–3, 238–9; K. O. Dike, *Trade and politics in the Niger Delta 1830–1885*, 1956, pp. 19–46; Jones, *op. cit.* (1963), pp.9–42.

[12] Alonso de Sandoval, *Naturaleza . . . de todos Etiopes*, Seville, 1627, lib. 1, cap. 16, f. 59r. Details are given in my forthcoming paper on 'Ethnolinguistic continuity on the Guinea coast' in the *Journal of African History*. Father Sandoval recommended the preparation of an 'abecedario de costas, lenguas et interpretes' (p. 236) for use in American missions dealing with slaves, but it would seem that he did not himself study any African language.

[13] *E.g.*, B. Edwards, *History of the British colonies in the West Indies*, 1793, 2, p. 50; Moreau de Saint Méry, *Description de la partie française de l'Ile de Saint-Domingue* (1797–8), edition of 1958, 1, pp. 50–1.

He became interested in the slave population he encountered, and wrote at length about their African origins and languages: the account was edited and published in Germany in 1777. Among Oldendorp's twenty-eight brief vocabularies of African languages were two of Ibo, under the names 'Ibo' and 'Karabari'. Despite the individual orthography, the words (numerals and thirteen nouns) can be seen to be close to modern Ibo, the 'Karabari' being probably a more southern and the 'Ibo' a more northern dialect.[14] These Ibo vocabularies, together with an accompanying vocabulary of 'Mokko', which in this case is Efik, represented the earliest deliberate information in print, not only on the languages of the Nigerian coast, but on the languages of any part of modern Nigeria.[15]

The interior peoples of the lower Niger-Benue were almost completely unknown to European scholars before 1800. It is true that the kingdoms of 'Noofy' (i.e. Nupe), and of 'Korofa' (i.e. Kwararafa, on the Benue, usually meaning the Jukun state), were marked on maps of Africa from about 1720.[16] But the exact position of these interior districts was uncertain, because of contradictory reports about the course of the Niger. A few slaves from the interior reached the Delta ports (or, from Nupeland, the ports further west), and hence found their way to the Americas, but it was not till the Fulani razzias after 1800 that large numbers of interior slaves were exported. In the nineteenth century, Nupe slaves were sufficiently common in Brazil and Cuba to be known by the Yoruba term for a Nupeman, 'Tapa'.[17] Slaves from the Benue area were still often

---

[14] G. C. A. Oldendorp, *Geschichte der Mission der evangelischen Brüder auf den caraibischen Inseln S. Thomas, S. Croix und S. Jan*, Barby, 1777, table opposite p. 346. Oldendorp also provided a sentence translated into each of the African languages: the two Ibo sentences are on pp. 345–6, and a first attempt to find an equivalent sentence in modern Ibo can be found in, P. E. H. Hair, 'Languages of Western Africa ca.1770: a note and a query', *Bulletin of the African Church History Society*, 1, 1963, pp. 17–20. Oldendorp interviewed five 'Karabari', but in detailing their provenance, they could tell him only that their neighbours were the 'Ibo', who spoke the same language, and the 'Bibi', i.e. Ibibio. An Ibo, interviewed in Pennsylvania (which Oldendorp later visited), said that he came from the interior, some distance from 'Alo', presumably Aro; Oldendorp gained the impression that Iboland was vast and that 'Alo' was Egypt (pp. 285–6). Thus Oldendorp threw little light on the geography of the Delta region. It is worth adding that there is a certain amount of anthropological information on the Ibo and Ibibio in Oldendorp, which perhaps deserves more attention than it has so far been given.

[15] These vocabularies were collected a little earlier than Niebuhr's Hausa and Kanuri vocabularies (1773: see the essay on the early study of these languages), and were printed very much earlier.

[16] De Lisle's map of Africa of 1722 shows, to the south of a River Niger erroneously flowing into a lake in 'Bornou', three kingdoms, the 'Royaume de Nouffy' (south of 'Cano' on the north side of the river), the 'Royaume de Yaourry' (immediately south of 'Nouffy'), and to the east and very much larger the 'Royaume de Courourfa' (its northern boundaries not quite reaching the river and the lake). Relative to each other, the three kingdoms are almost correctly placed, as they are in relation to 'Cano' and to the lake, if this be taken to be Lake Chad. But the river, which seems to be a conflation of several, is of course hopelessly misplaced. Since these kingdoms are not on De Lisle's earlier maps (1707, 1714), the information presumably came into his hands in the late 1710s. It is possible that it came from French exploration of the Senegal River and inquiries in that area; but it is more likely that it came from the other side of the desert, from Tripoli, where it has recently been shown that, between 1700 and 1710, missionaries and diplomatic agents were making inquiries about the Central Sudan, and particularly about 'Canorfa' or 'Corurfa' (R. Hallett, *The penetration of Africa*, 1, 1965, pp. 102–3, but Hallett misunderstands 'Canorfa', and in his section on maps, pp. 93–4, has overlooked the De Lisle map; R. Gray, 'Christian traces and a Franciscan mission in the Central Sudan' – for further details, see footnote 6 to the essay on the early study of Hausa and Kanuri). The meaning of the term 'Kwararafa', which was later sometimes applied to the Benue River, is obscure: see C. K. Meek, *A Sudanese kingdom*, 1931, pp. 16–18. On some eighteenth century maps, the name 'Dauma' appears roughly in the Benue area, but it is unlikely that this has anything to do with Idoma: it is probably rather a misplacement of a version of 'Dahomey'.

[17] A. Ramos, *The Negro in Brazil*, 1951, pp. 25, 44, etc.; Aguirre Beltran, *op. cit.*, p. 132 (quoting a source on Cuba, where the the 'Tapa' are listed among the 'Locumi', i.e. Yoruba).

known as 'Calabars', but the term 'Appa', apparently derived from a Jukun word, also came to be used.[18] Nevertheless, no information about the languages of the interior peoples was collected, either in Africa or in the Americas, before the 1820s.

Systematic exploration of the lower Niger-Benue area began when Friedrich Horne-mann crossed the Sahara in 1800: he made his way to Nupe country, but died there and all his papers were lost.[19] Five years later, Mungo Park died, probably in the waters of the Niger, just as his expedition was about to enter Nupe country. In 1826, Clapperton and Lander passed through the western part of Nupeland, on their way from Badagry to Sokoto, and in 1830 the Lander brothers became the first Europeans to pass down the lower Niger, from Nupeland to the Delta. None of these early expeditions provided material on the languages under discussion. But, in 1832–4, the first expedition up-river, under the direction of Macgregor Laird, explored the Niger up to Rabba in Nupeland and the Benue up to about 150 miles from the confluence, and returned with a small quantity of linguistic material. Again, in 1841, an official Niger Expedition penetrated to the confluence and a little farther, and though it failed to do most of what had been purposed, it achieved a measure of success in one respect: with the expedition travelled two missionary-linguists from Freetown, who successfully studied the distri-bution of languages along the river. Though the lower Benue languages had yet to be investigated, for the first time a connected view of the lower Niger languages became available.

*   *   *

After Oldendorp's vocabularies of 1777, a half century elapsed before further vocabu-laries of lower Niger-Benue languages were published. The first to appear were, like Oldendorp's, collected far away from the homelands. In Freetown, in the 1820's, vocabularies were collected from liberated slaves by C.M.S. missionaries and by Mrs Hannah Kilham, the Quaker educationalist (as described, at length, in the first essay). Mrs Kilham published a collection of vocabularies in 1828, and this included vocabu-laries of Ibo, of 'Tapua', i.e. Nupe, and of 'Appa', a language not Jukun but probably neighbouring and to date still unidentified – numerals, and about 50 nouns in each.[20] Though slight and only moderately accurate, these vocabularies were the first linguistic material in print on two of the languages, Nupe and 'Appa'. The next vocabularies were collected in the homelands, during the Laird expedition of 1832–4; the account of the expedition, published in 1837, included a vocabulary of 70 words of Ibo, a vocabulary of 30 words of 'Nufie or Nupaysee', i.e. Nupe, and a vocabulary of half a dozen words of 'Kacundah or Shabbe', i.e. Kakanda, a language probably only a dialect of Nupe and spoken nearer to the confluence than Nupe proper.[21] These two

---

[18] Hugh Crow, *Memoirs of the late Captain H. C. of Liverpool*, 1830, p. 200. According to Meek, *op. cit.*, pp. 14–15, 'appa' means 'men, persons': the same author states that the term was sometimes even applied to the people of Calabar. The Jukun, Koelle noted, were called 'Kurorofa' by the Bornuese, Hausa and Nupe, and 'Apa' by the Igala and Ibo (S. W. Koelle, *Polyglotta Africana*, 1854, p. 21).

[19] Hallett, *op. cit.*, pp. 250–263.

[20] [H. Kilham], *Specimens of African languages* . . . , London, 1828, and see footnote 23 to the essay on Hausa and Kanuri. Mrs Kilham printed vocabularies of the neighbouring languages, Sobo ('Uhobo') and Ibibio ('Karaba'), but not one of Ijaw. On 'Appa', see footnote 43 of this essay.

[21] M. Laird and R. A. K. Oldfield, *Narrative of an expedition* . . . , 1837, vol. 2, pp. 421–3, 427, 441–6. The numerals were also given in each language.

sets of vocabularies were made use of by Edwin Norris, the Assistant Secretary of the Royal Asiatic Society, when in 1840 he prepared a handbook of vocabularies for the use of the forthcoming Niger Expedition. The list of Nupe words in this book was based on the two earlier vocabularies noted above, with the addition of about 100 words taken from 'MS lists collected by various persons', most probably members of the Laird expedition. The Ibo list added to the earlier vocabularies noted,[22] some words from an unknown manuscript source and others collected (perhaps by Norris himself?) from an Ibo in London. Numerals in 'Bonny', i.e. Ijaw, were also supplied; their source was not stated and must have been a manuscript one; these were the first words in print in Ijaw since the five numerals of 1668.[23]

Public interest in the Atlantic slave trade during the early decades of the nineteenth century led to the appearance of a number of accounts of the Delta ports. Two descriptions of Bonny contained vocabularies. One, published in 1830, contained a list of 60 words and phrases of 'Eboe' which a Liverpool sea-captain had collected around the beginning of the century.[24] This vocabulary seems to have been overlooked by Norris when compiling his handbook. The second vocabulary was collected at Bonny in 1841 by a German doctor aboard a British vessel, and appeared in the account he published in a German periodical in 1843.[25] The language was Ijaw, and the vocabulary a lengthy one of 600 words, including many medical terms; it has probably never been adequately examined. Dr Köler pointed out that this 'Bonny' language was not the same as Ibo, or as the language of Calabar (i.e. Efik); but he was not so sure what its relation was to the languages of neighbouring ports, New Calabar and Brass (where in fact other dialects of Ijaw were spoken). Köler's account also contained an interesting section on the pidgin English of the Delta.

While Norris was preparing his guide to the languages of the Niger, the Church Missionary Society was arranging to send two missionary-linguists on the expedition. Two men on the mission staff in Freetown were selected, the German missionary J. F. Schön and the African school-teacher Samuel Crowther – the leading figures of the earlier essays. Schön, who had previously been studying a Sierra Leone language, began to study Ibo and Hausa. By September 1840, he was able to report to the mission authorities that he had collected a vocabulary of 1600 words in Ibo, and had translated a few prayers.[26] When the Expedition sailed from Freetown in July 1841, Schön and Crowther took with them twelve interpreters, selected from among the ex-slaves in Sierra Leone and representing the languages believed to be spoken 'on the banks of the Niger and in the adjacent countries . . . Haussa, Ibo, Kakanda, Yoruba, Bornou, Nufi,

---

[22] Except, apparently, Oldendorp's, although the 'Ibo' and 'Mokko' numerals in Oldendorp were reprinted, with a reference to the source, in J. C. Prichard, *Physical history of mankind*, 3rd edition, vol. 2, 1837, p. 127.

[23] [E. Norris], *Outline of a vocabulary of a few of the principal languages of Western and Central Africa, compiled for the use of the Niger Expedition*, London, 1840.

[24] Crow, *op. cit.*, pp. 229–30.

[25] Hermann Köler, 'Nachrichten über die Eingeborenen von Bonny, am Bonny-Fluss an der Sklavenküste Guineas mit besonders Beziehung auf die Sprache dieser Völkerschaft', *Monatsberichte über die Verhandlungen der Gesellschaft für Erdkunde zu Berlin*, 4, 1842–3, pp. 69–90, 146–58; reprinted as H. Köler, *Einige Notizen über Bonny . . . seine Sprache und seine Bewohner*, Göttingen, 1848. The 1843 articles were overlooked in England: hence, R. G. Latham, 'Remarks upon a vocabulary of the Bonny language', *Proceedings of the Philological Society*, 4, 1848–50, p. 73.

[26] C.M.S. Archives, CA 1/o 195, letter of 25.9.1840.

Benin, Filatah and Eggara'.[27] By late August, the Expedition was sailing up the Niger through Ibo country, and Schön attempted to communicate in Ibo. To his great disappointment, he found 'that the dialect of the Ibo language on which I had bestowed so much labour in Sierra Leone, differs widely from that spoken and understood in this part of the country. It never escaped my observation, that a great diversity of dialects existed: but I must blame myself much for not making stricter inquiries about that which would be most useful for the present occasion.'[28] However Schön persisted in his efforts to put his Ibo to use, and prepared and read an address in the language to the chief of Abo: the chief, no doubt baffled by the pronunciation and intonation, soon grew bored and interrupted the reading.[29] Higher up the Niger, Schön turned to Hausa as a medium of instruction; and nearly twenty years elapsed before he resumed his study of Ibo. His unhappy experience with Ibo dialects in 1841 was unfortunately significant: it can now be seen as an ill omen of the problems that lay ahead in the development of Ibo literature, problems which have persisted to the present day.

When the Expedition reached the confluence of the Niger and the Benue, a site was prepared for a settlement from which European influence could extend up both rivers. Schön noted the many languages of the district – Igala on the east bank down-river, Nupe on the Niger to the north west, varieties of 'Kakanda'[30] on the west bank above

---

[27] J. F. Schön and S. Crowther, *Journals of the Rev. J.F.S. and Mr S.C. who . . . accompanied the Expedition up the Niger in 1841*, London, 1842, pp. 2–3, the list of languages given by Schön expanded to the fuller list given in W. Allen and T. R. H. Thomson, *Narrative of an Expedition . . .*, London, 1848, 1, p. 78.

[28] Schön and Crowther, *op. cit.*, p. 47.

[29] *ibid.*, p. 55: according to an observer, when Schön addressed another chief up-river (in Hausa), the chief laughed at Schön's spectacles (Allen and Thomson, *op. cit.*, p. 289).

[30] In the mid-nineteenth century, the term 'Kakanda' (Kakanja, Akanja) was used by the Igala and Ibo, and also in Sierra Leone, to describe the peoples of the west bank of the Niger, opposite the confluence with the Benue, and up-stream for about one hundred miles, and the peoples of the hinterland of this stretch of the river. Hence the following groups found themselves at times labelled as 'Kakanda' – (a) speakers of the four north-eastern dialects of Yoruba (Bunu, Ijumu, Owe and Aworo); (b) speakers of the Nupe dialect, Basa (a group later transferred to the east bank of the Niger); (c) speakers of the Nupe-like language, Shabbe (Ihabe). It was believed, perhaps correctly, that these 'Kakanda' languages were intermediate between Yoruba proper and Nupe proper.

That Kakanda then possessed this loose, general meaning was made clear by Koelle, *Polyglotta*, 1854, pp. 6, 9, and perhaps independently by W. B. Baikie, *Narrative of an exploring voyage . . .*, London, 1856, p. 271. Modern writers however limit the term to the Shabbe – D. Forde, *The Yoruba-speaking peoples*, 1951, pp. 71–4; D. Forde *et al.*, *Peoples of the Niger-Benue confluence*, 1955, p. 20; D. Westermann and M. A. Bryan, *Languages of West Africa*, 1952, pp. 85–6.

Partly because of the contemporary general meaning, early writers regularly failed to distinguish between the constituent groups, and references were confused. 'Kacunda . . . below the Confluence', 'Yarriba George, a native of Kacundah', 'Kacundah or Shabbe', Laird and Oldfield, *op. cit.*, 1, pp. 133, 375, and 2, pp. 25, 132, 294, 325: 'Kakanda spoken from Egga to below the Confluence . . . Shabi . . . a dialect of Yoruba', 'Bunu . . . dialect between Nufi and Kakanda', Schön and Crowther, *op. cit.*, pp. 119, 134, 206, 294, 307; Allen and Thomson, *op. cit.*, 1, pp. 334, 344, 379, and 2, p. 115: 'a dialect of Yoruba . . . inhabit chiefly below the confluence', S. Crowther, *Journal of an expedition . . .*, 1855, p. 201: 'Bunu more resembles Ishabe than Bassa, but yet they contrive to understand each other', 'Igara, Igbira and Kakanda are all related to Yoruba', Baikie, *op. cit.*, pp. 271, 420: 'Of the Owe tribe of Kakanda', 'Kakanda, called Bunu or Shabe', S. Crowther, *The Gospel on the Banks of the Niger*, 1859, pp. 53, 74. (It will be noted that Crowther's contribution to the discussion was disappointing: though a Yoruba speaker, he confused Yoruba dialects with Shabbe, which is closer to Nupe.)

Koelle and modern writers distinguish between the Basa of the confluence (Basa-Nge) and the Basa of the Benue (Basa-Komo). The 1854 expedition failed to do this, but Crowther, possibly as a result of studying the Polyglotta more carefully, got it right in 1857 – Crowther, *op. cit.* (1855), p. 50; Crowther, *op. cit.* (1859), p. 69; Baikie, *op. cit.*, p. 271.

—Continued on following page

and below the confluence – and feared this might hinder missionary work. 'To study all of them and reduce them to writing is almost impracticable' he wrote, and he suggested that the mission should concentrate instead on Hausa, the lingua franca.[31] One ship of the expedition made its way up the Niger as far as Egga in Nupeland, and here Schön and Crowther were able to make contacts with Hausa and Yoruba traders in their own languages.[32] So far, the experiences of the Expedition were discouraging for the study of the Niger vernaculars; and had permanent contacts been established with the lands above the confluence, the mission would probably have followed Schön's advice and endeavoured to evangelise the riverain peoples through Hausa.[33] But the Expedition ended in near-disaster; high mortality among the European members forced it to retire from the river; a Freetown Yoruba was left at the confluence settlement, partly in order to study further the distribution of languages, but he was brought away when the settlement was abandoned a few months later.[34]

In England after the Expedition, Schön prepared a report on missionary prospects on the Niger. In this report, he gave the first connected account of the languages of the lower Niger, naming six encountered – 'Brass' (i.e. Ijaw), Ibo, Igala, Nupe, Hausa and Fulani[35]– and briefly describing their extent and range of use. The account was wrong in one respect (Schön thought that the Brass language was the same as the language at Benin), and the brevity of the information supplied showed how limited was even the best knowledge at this date.[36]

Schön never returned to the Niger. He worked at Freetown, studying Hausa, until 1847, when ill-health drove him to England. But his companion on the 1841 expedition, Crowther, returned almost immediately to Yorubaland, and a few years later to the Niger itself. Since much of what follows will concern Crowther, it will be appropriate at this point to remind the reader of his earlier history. Born in a small town in Yorubaland, he found himself, at the age of twelve or so, aboard a slave-ship bound for America, but was rescued by a British gun-boat and brought to Freetown in 1822. He was educated there by the C.M.S. missionaries, eventually at the institute which offered the highest level of education then available, Fourah Bay, and on leaving became a school-teacher. He was selected to accompany Schön on the Niger Expedition, presumably because of interest already shown in his mother-tongue, Yoruba, and on the expedition he helped to collect information on the Niger languages. Ordained in England in 1843, the next year he became a member of the first C.M.S. mission to

---

Continued from previous page—

The confusion in the earlier references, the migration of some of these groups during the nineteenth century, and the lack of an authoritative modern treatment of the languages of the area (N.B. the maps in Forde, *op. cit.* (1951) and in Forde *et al.*, *op. cit.* (1955) are not in entire agreement over the present location of the peoples around the confluence) makes it impossible to be sure exactly how the groups were located topographically, and related linguistically, a century ago.

[31] Schön and Crowther, *op. cit.*, pp. 120.

[32] *ibid.*, p. 134.

[33] Exactly how much Hausa was spoken along the river is difficult to say; probably non-Hausa traders at the riverain towns had only a smattering of the language. Certainly Hausa would not have served to evangelise the interior.

[34] Schön and Crowther, *op. cit.*, p. 215.

[35] Fulani was spoken only by some officials and soldiers of the northern emirates, now extending their power towards the confluence.

[36] Schön and Crowther, *op. cit.*, pp. 356–7. The mistake over the Brass language may have been due to the presence of small groups of Edo (Benin) speakers in the Delta, not far from the town of Brass (R. E. Bradbury, *The Benin kingdom*, 1957, p. 13, n. 1).

Yorubaland, and in his homeland he worked for a decade as a missionary, in particular translating portions of the Bible and schoolbooks into Yoruba. Experienced both as a missionary and as a student of African languages, in 1854 he ascended the Niger again.

The headquarters of the C.M.S. Yoruba mission was at Abeokuta, where in the early 1840s a colony had been formed of ex-slaves of Yoruba extraction who had returned to their homeland from Freetown. The idea that the ex-slaves living in Sierra Leone could further the cause of civilisation by returning, educated and Christianised, to their homelands, was popular in humanitarian and missionary circles at this period. The Niger Expedition attempted unsuccessfully to establish a settlement of Sierra Leoneans at the confluence in 1841. Twelve years later, a small party of Sierra Leoneans of Ibo extraction set out from Freetown, under the direction of the Principal of Fourah Bay Institute (himself an Afro-American), with the intention of visiting Iboland to prepare the ground for a general return of the Ibos in Freetown. But the party got no farther than Bonny, where the members were told that it was impossible to penetrate up the Niger because of the hostility of the Delta peoples.[37] That this was an exaggerated view was shown by the successful expedition of the very next year, but meanwhile the Ibo party had returned to Freetown. It was left to Crowther to establish centres of Freetown culture on the Niger.

While the ex-slaves were returning, or attempting to return, to Nigeria, their languages were still being studied, away from the homelands, in the places of liberation. Slaves from ships stopped by the British navy were released either at Freetown or, in much smaller numbers and for a shorter period, on Fernando Po Island, east of the Niger Delta. At both these places, the study of the lower Niger-Benue languages was furthered in the 1840s. In 1848, John Clarke, a Baptist missionary who had served in a mission to Fernando Po (as well as in the West Indies), published a collection of vocabularies of African languages.[38] The original vocabularies in this collection had been collected by Clarke and by an Afro-American colleague, Merrick: though very brief and unsystematically arranged, they included a large number in lower Niger-

---

[37] *C.M. Intelligencer*, 4, 1853, pp. 253–8; C. P. Groves, *The planting of Christianity in Africa*, 2, 1954, p. 73; Dike, *op. cit.*, p. 117; J. F. A. Ajayi, *Christian missions in Nigeria 1841–1891*, 1965, pp. 41–2.

[38] John Clarke, *Specimens of dialects . . . in Africa*, Berwick-upon-Tweed/London, 1848/1849: vocabularies reprinted in this work from earlier sources (e.g. Mrs Kilham, sometimes without acknowledgement) are not listed below; the list gives the names under which Clarke presented his vocabularies, and the number each has in his book; in the list below, numbers in brackets refer to Clarke's vocabularies of numerals: (a) *IJAW* – New Calabar 112, 146, (155); Bonny 145, (148); Numbe 219, (159); Akrika (147); Okkulabur 152: (b) *IBO* – Amitsh 107, (158); Ibo/Iboe 111, 121–4, 137, 152, (138–141), (145), (323), (365), pp. 51–3; Oss 113, (151); 'Nkissi 114; Iswama 115, 250, (310), (325); Loopa 125, (153); Aru/Aro 126, 260, (154), (372); Bonny 127, 130, (150); Bretshi 129, (348); Orata 148, (162); Enishi 172, 242; Otam 176, (355); Okori 235, (157), (313); Niko 247, Elugu/Olugu 251, (304), (311), (384); Bwidi 259; 'Ndoki 287; Owa (142); Alugiekwa (291); Oboya (302); Obagwa (324); 'Nkresi (330); Omowo (334); Abadja (354): (c) *NUPE* – Nufi 61, (130), p. 35; Biyanni 63; Jappa [?Tappa] 64; Tshamba 224, (?256); Tappa Anuba 137; Anuba (206): (d) *IGALA* – Bidji 50, (108); Eggara/Iggara 56, 214, (163), (164); Iddah/Ida/Idda 212, 263, (117), (366), p. 56; ? Benin 55: (e) *IGBIRA* – Igberra/Igbera 232, 264, (109), (367), p. 57: (f) *TIV* – Appa 67, 68, 101, (120), (123), (?335): (g) unidentified 228, 244 – see footnote 43 below.

Clarke was a Scotsman. He worked in Jamaica from 1829 to 1839, and in Fernando Po and the Cameroons from 1841 to 1847. Although some of his vocabularies were collected in the West Indies, it is likely that the vast majority of these Niger-Benue vocabularies were collected in Fernando Po. Merrick was a missionary in Fernando Po and the Cameroons from 1843 to 1849. On Clarke, see P. E. H. Hair, 'An introduction to John Clarke's "Specimens of dialects . . . "', 1848/9', *Sierra Leone Language Review*, 5, 1966, pp. 72–82.

Benue languages, as follows – Ijaw (numerals and 10 words, in 4 versions); Ibo (numerals and about 250 words, 10 of them in 27 versions); Nupe (numerals and about 50 words, 10 of them in 6 versions); Igala (numerals and about 50 words, 10 of them in 7 versions); Igbira (numerals and about 50 words, 10 of them in 2 versions); Tiv (called by Clarke 'Appa': numerals and 10 words, in 3 versions). This was the first appearance in print for three of the languages, Igala, Igbira and Tiv. The versions provided by Clarke were in many cases different dialects of the language, and in the case of Ibo, Clarke published vocabularies of more dialects than have since been recorded in print. But the value of this collection of Niger-Benue vocabularies was very greatly reduced by the brevity of most of the vocabularies, by the poor arrangement of the material, and by the failure to provide any but the vaguest topographical references, which made identification and comparison of the vocabularies difficult at the time. An error in the book has until recently concealed the identity of a further Niger-Benue language. It was pointed out in 1955 that a vocabulary of six nouns entitled by Clarke 'Gold Coast' is in fact a vocabulary of Idoma, and the first words in print in this language – adding a fourth to the three other languages noted above.[39]

Clarke's Specimens, collected mainly from ex-slaves in Fernando Po, was superseded for all practical purposes within a few years of its publication by a volume of vocabularies collected mainly from ex-slaves in Freetown, the famous *Polyglotta Africana*, compiled by the German missionary, S. W. Koelle. Koelle began to collect vocabularies soon after he arrived in Freetown in late 1847, although he probably did not begin systematic work on the *Polyglotta* until 1850.[40] It is not known whether he became acquainted with Clarke's book during his stay in Freetown, but he must have been inspired to some extent by Mrs Kilham's collection of vocabularies, collected in Freetown and in collaboration with C.M.S. missionary-linguists, a quarter of a century earlier.[41] Koelle's vocabularies were immeasurably superior to both the earlier collections: in the number of languages represented, in the orthography, in the number of words in each language, and in the detail of topographical location of each. Published in 1854, the *Polyglotta* was a work of genius: a century later, it has not been totally superseded as a standard reference work for comparative West African language studies. A modern scholar has commented that 'Koelle's dependability, in the light of the conditions under which he worked, the speed with which he accomplished his task, and the limited knowledge of the field in his day, is nothing short of fantastic'.[42] The *Polyglotta*'s contribution to knowledge of the lower Niger-Benue languages was as follows: vocabularies of about 300 words in each of two dialects of Ijaw, five dialects of Ibo, five (perhaps six) dialects of Nupe, in Igala, in three dialects of Igbira, in Tiv, Jukun and 'Eregba' (a mystery language[43]).[44] Jukun now appeared in print, the last of the languages we are considering

---

[39] R. G. Armstrong, in Forde *et al.*, *op. cit.* (1955), p. 93. The vocabulary is no. 149 in Clarke.

[40] Koelle, *op. cit.*, p. v; on p. 12 of the Historical Introduction to the 1963 reprint, I give the erroneous impression that Koelle had not thought of a collection of vocabularies before 1850.

[41] A manuscript collection of vocabularies of nine African languages, including 'Heboe', i.e. Ibo, was circulating in Freetown in the 1840s and possibly much earlier (see footnote 20 to the essay on Yoruba): the manuscript is now in the South African Public Library.

[42] W. M. Welmers, *Language*, 32, 1956, p. 556, in a review of J. H. Greenberg's 'Studies in African linguistic classification'.

[43] This note deals with some unidentified vocabularies which appear to come from the Benue area. The vocabularies are Mrs Kilham's 'Appa', some of Clarke's 'Appa', and Koelle's 'Eregba'. We have seen that 'Appa' referred loosely to the Benue-Cross River District. (a) Several of Clarke's 'Appa'

—Continued on following page

to achieve this. The vocabularies were accurate, and for most of the languages, longer than any previously in print. Koelle established very precise locations for almost all the languages, and his arrangement of the vocabularies gave in many cases a reasonable indication of the linguistic relationships involved. His work presented a linguistic ground-plan of the lower Niger-Benue area which was not surpassed during the remainder of the nineteenth century.

In the year that the *Polyglotta* appeared, Samuel Crowther returned to the Niger. Another expedition up-river had been organised by Macgregor Laird, who arranged for Dr William Baikie to lead it, and for Crowther to be released from his mission duties in Yorubaland to accompany it. Crowther took with him a copy of the *Polyglotta* (possibly a manuscript copy), and collected linguistic information while the expedition successfully made its way up the Niger to the confluence and then some 300 miles up the Benue. The expedition was successful in three respects: the distance of penetration up the Benue; the timeliness of the journey, inasmuch as it coincided with a Fulani razzia near the confluence, whose destructive results the expedition witnessed and was able to report on; and the relatively unaffected health of the European members, all of whom survived the expedition, in contrast to the 1841 experience. Crowther and Baikie each published an account of the expedition, and each account had an appendix of linguistic information. Crowther's text appears to have been forwarded from Yorubaland, while Baikie's preface was written in hospital in England. Baikie was highly impressed by Crowther's bearing during the expedition, as he acknowledged in his book, and the two men enjoyed friendly relations during the succeeding ten years in which they were in intermittent contact, mostly on the Niger.

Baikie included in his linguistic appendix a short vocabulary of Ibo and the numerals in Ijaw, together with a comparative list of half a dozen terms in various dialects of the latter language. His description of the disposition of 'the languages of the countries bordering on the Kwora [i.e. Niger] and Binue' did not notably improve on the picture already given by Koelle. Perhaps the only point of special interest was his support of the view, then being put forward in several quarters, that the lower Niger-Benue languages lay along a dividing line between the 'Kafir' (i.e. Bantu) languages and the

---

Continued from previous page—

vocabularies are Tiv, without any doubt. (b) But Mrs Kilham's 'Appa' is not Tiv, nor is it Plaoui (M. Delafosse, *Vocabulaires comparatifs . . .* , 1904, p. 269), nor is it Yergum (M. Delafosse, in A. Meillet and M. Cohen, *Les langues du monde*, 2nd edition, 1952, p. 803); while it is the same as Koelle's 'Eregba', which does not seem to have been noted previously. (c) 'Eregba' has not been further reported since Koelle, and it has been suggested that it may be extinct (Westermann and Bryan, *op. cit.*, p. 113). Koelle unfortunately forgot to add his usual notes on the location of the language, but he placed it in his tables next to Jukun, which might indicate that he believed it to have a Benue location. In vocabulary, 'Eregba' has little resemblance to Jukun, but a general resemblance to many other Benue-Cross River languages. Its numerals seem fairly close to those of Efik, and rather less close to those of two languages, Boritsu and Mbarike, placed by Koelle just north of the Benue: its other vocabulary shows some affinity with Ekoi and other Cross River languages reported by Northcote Thomas. Since the languages of this district are still little known, 'Eregba' may yet be rediscovered. (I understand that Dr David Crabb, who has recently published on the Ekoid Bantu languages, is now searching in the field for 'Eregba'.) (d) Two of Clarke's 'Appa' vocabularies (228, 244) are not Tiv, Jukun, not any language in Koelle or Northcote Thomas, and not 'Eregba'; yet they also show an affinity in vocabularly to the Benue-Cross River languages. (e) Clarke's additional 'Appa' vocabulary on p. 37, though not so stated, is taken from Mrs Kilham.

[44] Koelle, *op. cit*: (a) *IJAW* – Ukolōma, Udṣọ; (b) *IBO* – Isoāma, Iṣiēle, Abadṣa, Aro·, Mbọfia; (c) *NUPE* – Nūpe, Kupa, Eṣitāko, Basa, Ebē, perhaps Musu·; (d) *IGALA* – Igala; (e) *IGBIRA* – Opanda, Egbīra-Hīma; (f) *TIV* – Tiwi; (g) *JUKUN* – Dṣuku·; (h) Erēgba.

languages of Western and Northern Africa; Tiv and Jukun, Baikie thought, were, with little doubt, 'Kafir' languages.[45] Crowther also gave a short account of the lower Niger-Benue languages, and he discussed the problem of dialects in Ibo, concluding that the most suitable for translation work was the 'Isoama'. He misread the *Polyglotta* in a curious way, for he included a vocabulary of 'Mitshi', which he stated was a language not known to Koelle, whereas in fact it had appeared in the *Polyglotta* under the name of Tiwi, i.e. Tiv. He also gave a short vocabulary of Igala.[46] But in general, both Baikie and Crowther, despite their visit to the homelands of the languages, added very little to what had already been published by Koelle, working fifteen hundred miles away at Freetown; and some of the information they gave was not as sound as that drawn from informants by Koelle. An exception to this summing up is that Crowther collected and published a vocabulary of Idoma, a language not recorded by Koelle.[47] The vocabulary of about 300 words and phrases was based on the standard list in the *Polyglotta* and is therefore easily comparable with the material there.

One of the objects of the 1854 expedition was to collect information about, perhaps even meet, Dr Heinrich Barth, who, after crossing the Sahara, was travelling in the Sudan on behalf of the British government. In 1851, Barth had journeyed from Bornu into Adamawa, and thus crossed the upper Benue, being the first European recorded to have done this. He found himself on the borders of Jukun country and visited some Jukun settlements: he wrote back to England – 'You will be delighted to see that a large step has been made to a better knowledge of this mighty, industrialised [sic], half-civilised and very interesting nation: for the Koana, whose vocabulary I am sending, do belong to the Korrorofo'.[48] In his *Travels*, Barth again referred to this vocabulary, but did not print it. Possibly he intended it to appear in the last volume of his *Collection of Vocabularies*, but this never appeared because of his sudden death. The Jukun vocabulary, of about 200 words, did not reach print till 1912. Barth, like Crowther, misread the *Polyglotta*, and thought that Koelle had missed a language which only exploration on the spot revealed; Koelle had not, and his vocabulary was longer than Barth's.[49]

The 1854 expedition did not meet Barth (who spent early 1854 in Timbuktu), and it had left the river by the time Barth's colleague, Vogel, in turn crossed the upper

[45] Baikie, *op. cit.*, pp. 419–22.

[46] S. Crowther, *Journal of an expedition up the Niger and Tshadda rivers , . . ,* London, 1855, pp. 65, 71, 200, 208–27.

[47] Although the *Polyglotta* has no Idoma vocabulary, it does have a vocabulary of Yala (Iyala), which is spoken in an isolated district south-east of Idoma, and which appears to be closely related to both Idoma and Igala (see R. G. Armstrong, in Forde *et al.*, *op. cit.*, p. 92; but Yala is referred to as 'the Idoma dialect spoken in Ogoja' in R. G. Armstrong, *The Study of West African languages/An inaugural lecture*, Ibadan, 1964, p. 12). For another early reference to Yala, see Baikie, *op. cit.*, p. 346. According to Cust, who was probably told this by Crowther himself, some translations into Idoma and Tiv were given by Crowther to Baikie; they were not found later in Baikie's papers (R. N. Cust, *Modern languages of Africa*, 1883, 1, p. 231). With reference to Igala, a footnote in Crowther, *op. cit.*, p. 208, reads – 'See my remarks on this language in my Journal of the Expedition 1854, p. 355'. This note was apparently added by Schön who saw the work through the press, but the date must have been added by another hand, and is wrong: the journal referred to is that of the 1841 expedition, published 1842.

[48] P. A. Benton, *Notes on some languages of the Western Sudan, including 24 unpublished vocabularies of Barth*, 1912, p. 74.

[49] H. Barth, *Travels* . . . , 1857, 1, p. 581. Barth noted that his 'Koana' was unlike Koelle's 'Tiwi', implying that he had not seen Koelle's 'Dṣuku'.

Benue. Vogel, who was murdered in 1855, in one of his last letters to reach Europe remarked that 'on the 1st of April we crossed the river Benue exactly on the spot from where the steamer had returned, numerous empty pickle and brandy bottles giving sure evidence that the Englishmen had been there'. This observation has been often quoted, but it does not seem to have been noticed that Baikie, in his account of the expedition, stated – 'there were no spirits on board'.[50]

The 1854 expedition might have made a notable contribution to the study, not only of the Niger-Benue, but of all African languages, if one aspect of the original plan had succeeded. Attached to the expedition when it left England was a young German philologist, Dr W. H. I. Bleek, who intended to make a study of the lower Niger-Benue languages. But Bleek took ill on the journey to West Africa, and from Fernando Po was invalided home. He later went to South Africa, where he coined the term 'Bantu' and became the pioneer of comparative Bantu studies. Linguistic material which he had collected for the 1854 expedition, some from missionaries at Freetown, became part of the Grey Library at Cape Town, of which Bleek issued a splendidly detailed catalogue. Bantu studies gained what West African language studies lost. (Or would Bantu studies have taken a vastly different form if Bleek's scholarship had been concentrated, not on the lately-dispersed regular Bantu languages of Southern Africa, but on the variegated, allegedly-ancestral, Bantoid languages of the Benue?[51])

On his way back to Europe from the Niger, Baikie discussed the prospects of mission-ary activity on the river with Crowther, who travelled as far as Lagos, and with Bishop Vidal of Sierra Leone who joined the ship at Lagos after an episcopal visit to Yoruba-land. Simon Jonas, a Sierra Leonean who had acted as Ibo interpreter on both the 1841 and the 1854 expeditions, was directed to return to Freetown to help in the training of a group of catechists who hoped to be allowed to proceed to Iboland. Aboard ship, Vidal showed Baikie the Yoruba translations he was editing, and told him he was about to begin the study of Ibo. A few days later, Vidal took ill, and died before the ship reached Freetown. No subsequent Bishop of Sierra Leone was as interested in linguistic work. When Baikie arrived at Freetown, he was approached by deputations of liberated slaves who asked for news of their Niger homelands, and expressed eagerness to return.[52]

From Yorubaland, Crowther wrote to the C.M.S. authorities recommending that a mission be commenced on the Niger, with a station at Onitsha in Iboland. The recom-mendation was accepted, for two reasons: a station at Onitsha satisfied the wishes of the Freetown Ibos, while the Niger was seen as a new route to a long-considered objective, Hausaland. Crowther was instructed to prepare for a mission to Iboland.[53] He sent for Simon Jonas, and the two of them settled down in Lagos to study Ibo. Crowther asked Schön in England to resume the study of Hausa, and it is likely that he seized the

---

[50] Benton, op. cit., p. 282; Baikie, op. cit., p. 178 – however Baikie stated that the expedition's doctor carried wine, presumably in bottles.

[51] It was Bleek who noted that Crowther's 'Mitshi' was the same as Koelle's 'Tiwi' (see the last page of Crowther, op. cit.), and it may have been Bleek who told Baikie that Tiv was definitely a 'Kafir' language. Bleek had published a thesis on the Bantu languages before joining the expedition. On his return to Europe, he gave a lecture in 1855 – 'On the languages of Western and Southern Africa' (see P. E. H. Hair, 'Temne and African language classification before 1864', Journal of African Languages, 4, 1965, pp. 46–56, on pp. 48 ff.)

[52] Baikie, op. cit., pp. 357, 362, 374.

[53] C.M.S. Proceedings, 1855–6, p. 58.

opportunity to borrow from him the vocabulary of Ibo compiled in 1840–1.[54] The comparative success of the 1854 expedition led the British government to arrange with Macgregor Laird for further exploration of the Niger and Benue, and a steamer was ordered in England. In readiness for the expedition and the setting up of the Onitsha mission, in 1857 Crowther had printed the first book in a lower Niger-Benue language, a short primer in Ibo. Little more than a spelling book, the primer in its 17 pages gave words and sentences in Ibo and concluded with a few prayers and verses of Scripture in translation.

Humble though this work was, its publication marked the beginning of a new period in the study of the lower Niger-Benue languages. The works to be considered from 1857 onwards were of a more advanced character than those described earlier – not merely pages of vocabulary but whole books of vocabulary and grammar; not merely material of interest to the foreign academic but, in the case of most of the languages, the beginnings of a printed literature intended for the use of the peoples who spoke them. These advances were largely due to the activities of Crowther's Niger Mission.

* * *

In mid 1857, the first steamer of Laird's new venture entered the Niger: Dr Baikie was again in charge, and a C.M.S. party had been given a passage aboard. The party comprised Crowther, a number of Ibo-speaking catechists from Freetown, including Simon Jonas, and the Rev. J. C. Taylor. Taylor was a native of Freetown, but his parents had been born in Iboland and he himself had some command of Ibo.[55] Like Crowther, he had been a student of Fourah Bay Institution in his younger days, and he had now been ordained in order to serve at the Onitsha mission. Crowther had discussed the possibility of the establishment of a mission station at Onitsha with the leading men there during the 1854 expedition, and the arrival of Taylor and his assistants was welcomed. While Taylor organised the station, Crowther and Baikie continued up the Niger. The expedition stopped at Igbebe near the confluence, and here Crowther began mission work on this stretch of the river. His first evangelistic meeting gave a glimpse of the difficulties to be faced in a district where no one language served: Crowther first spoke in English which was translated into Nupe by an interpreter, then he read a portion of the Bible in Hausa (from Schön's translation) and another interpreter read the same portion from an Arabic Bible for the benefit of the local mallams – but nothing could be done for the Igala-speakers who must have formed a fair part of the congregation. Before leaving Igbebe, Crowther tried to teach some young men to read in Roman characters, employing the only primer he had with him, the Ibo one. When the steamer moved on after a few days, two Freetown men were left at Igbebe to start a school.[56]

The expedition now moved up-river into Nupeland, but came to an abrupt end when the steamer was wrecked on the rocks at Jebba. The crew and passengers had to live in

---

[54] In Ajayi, *op. cit.*, p. 127, the impression is given that the Ibo vocabulary prepared by Schön in 1840–1 was published in 1843; this is not so, as the work was never published. I am not aware that the manuscript is extant, though conceivably Professor Ajayi may have discovered it in the C.M.S. Archives. Schön hoarded his linguistic material, and it would be very reasonable for Crowther to ask for a loan of, or a copy of, the vocabulary, when Ibo studies were resumed.

[55] Ajayi, *op. cit.*, pp. 97, 130; S. Crowther and J. C. Taylor, *The Gospel on the banks of the Niger . . .*, London, 1859, passim.

[56] Crowther and Taylor, *op. cit.*, pp. 35, 59–61.

the vicinity for several months, and Crowther made use of the time by commencing a systematic study of the Nupe language, in the following manner. He wrote – 'I engaged Ibrahima, a native of Jebba, a Mohammedan, who is master of both the Nupe and Hausa languages, as my teacher. My servant, Henry, who speaks Nupe and Hausa a little, becomes most useful, as he also speaks English and Yoruba. Ibrahima speaks a little Yoruba also. Thus we have the advantage of three languages, viz. the English, the Hausa, and the Yoruba, to fix the fourth, which is Nupe: and as this is carefully done, much error cannot creep into the work. It was very amusing to hear some of the visitors [to the camp], when a word is given in Hausa, joining to give it in Nupe and Yoruba, and, if their knowledge extended beyond these, in Borgu and Kambari also. They felt very much interested in seeing their language being reduced to writing.'[57]

In early 1858, Crowther moved to Rabba, formerly the capital of Nupeland, and set up a mission post.[58] He then descended the river to Onitsha and inspected the station organised by Taylor. Later in the same year Crowther returned to Rabba, while Taylor made his way to Sierra Leone and eventually England, taking with him journals for the years 1857–8 by Crowther and himself, which the C.M.S. immediately published, as testimony of the early success of the Niger Mission. Taylor's journal contains many references to his translation work in Ibo, but it also makes it clear that the knowledge of Ibo he had acquired in Freetown from his parents was insufficient, without further study, for the work he had undertaken in the homeland of the language.[59] This, as we shall see, was a common defect among Crowther's assistants. Taylor's coming to England was therefore not only to report, but to obtain a better grasp of Ibo from the only European who had studied it in any depth, Schön. Crowther's temporary release of his assistant from duties at Onitsha illustrates the extreme importance that he attached to the linguistic side of mission work.

On arrival in England, Taylor went to Chatham and lived for several months with Schön. (Among the many West Africans who at various dates lived in the Schön household were several other linguists or linguistic informants – Dorugu the Hausa, Henry Johnson studying Mende, T. C. John studying Hausa.) With Taylor beside him, Schön resumed the work on Ibo which he had begun seventeen years earlier, and guided by Schön on theoretical points Taylor began to publish in Ibo. His journal, published in 1859, included a small collection of Ibo proverbs, and in the same year he published a catechism in Ibo. In 1860, he followed these with an Ibo sermon (preached in Freetown[60]) and translations of a Gospel and extracts from the Prayer Book, and he also revised Crowther's primer. Taylor returned to the Niger during 1860 and continued

---

[57] *ibid.*, pp. 121, 134–5.

[58] Crowther left at Rabba, as a catechist, Abbega, one of two youths whom Barth had brought back to Europe from the Central Sudan, and who had subsequently lived in England for some years with Schön – see the essay on Hausa and Kanuri.

[59] According to Ajayi, *op. cit.*, p. 130, one of Taylor's difficulties was that his parents spoke different Ibo dialects; and perhaps neither was the Onitsha dialect. At Onitsha, Taylor relied at first on Simon Jonas for interpretation, but the latter died in November 1858 (Crowther and Taylor, *op. cit.*, pp. 37, 157, 271, 274, 279, 336, 356, 359). Exactly how much Ibo Taylor spoke or understood before he left Freetown is uncertain. As early as 1854, he had shown some translations to Bishop Vidal, who gave him instructions in orthography, asked him to collect idioms and proverbs, and said – 'Press the work of translation forward!' (*C.M.S. Proceedings*, 1854–5, p. 40).

[60] As shown in the bibliography, the publishing date of this and two other works is uncertain, and may have been either 1860 or 1861.

83

his translation work there.[61] Schön meanwhile had applied himself to the grammar of the language, and in 1861 he produced a study of this. Schön's grammar was the only work on the subject until the 1890s and the only important academic study of Ibo in this period.

During 1859, Crowther travelled overland from Rabba to Lagos, and then made a brief visit to the Niger to inspect the stations at Onitsha and Igbebe, before returning to Lagos – journeys totalling about 1500 miles, a figure which gives an indication of the practical problems in the administration of the Niger Mission. In 1860 and 1861, he and Taylor were prevented from returning up-river by the hostility of some of the villages along the Delta channel and the subsequent withdrawal of Laird's vessels, and had to limit their activities to the founding of a Delta station at Akassa. But in 1862, a British gunboat transported a large party of missionaries, all Freetown Africans, to Onitsha and Igbebe. This new evidence of the success of the Niger Mission, together with the belief that Africans should take over the direction of missionary work whenever feasible – a belief most strongly held by Henry Venn, the Secretary of the C.M.S. – led to the appointment, in 1864, of Crowther as bishop, nominally of a vast diocese, in practice in charge of the Niger Mission.[62] He made his home at Lagos and travelled up the Niger whenever a government or trading vessel could give him a passage.

While the Onitsha station flourished, the more northern activities were less successful. Crowther's study of the Nupe language led to his publishing a primer and a translation of one Gospel in 1860, and a grammar and vocabulary of the language in 1864 – the earliest books in and on Nupe.[63] But within Nupeland, the mission met with resistance, partly because of Moslem hostility; and on the advice of the British authorities, who often provided him with transport on the river, Crowther withdrew from the Rabba post.

Baikie remained up-river after the wrecking of the steamer in 1857, and made his headquarters at the new settlement of Laird's Town, soon rechristened Lokoja, at the confluence. Here he acted as semi-official British consul until 1864, when ill-health forced him to leave the river.[64] His interest in languages led him to translate part of the Bible into Hausa, and to collect vocabularies in many of the then-unknown languages in the interior between the river and Hausaland. On his way back to England, Baikie died at Freetown in 1864, and his papers were dispersed and lost; they appear to have included a few vocabularies of languages near the confluence.[65]

To the south, Taylor at Onitsha continued his translation of the New Testament into Ibo throughout the early 1860s and had completed the work in 1866. The remaining

---

[61] On Taylor with Schön, *C.M.S. Proceedings*, 1859–60, p. 55: a letter in Ibo from Taylor to Schön, dated 21.6.1860, is in the C.M.S. Archives, A2/U3. The Gospel translation was done 'under Schön's roof', B.F.B.S. Archives, Editorial 9.12.1859.

[62] On Crowther as bishop, see Ajayi, *op. cit.*, chapter 7. His nominal diocese was both wide and vague, all of West Africa except the British colonies and except the missions already supervised by the Bishop of Sierra Leone, although it was hinted that this latter exception was to be but temporary. Professor Ajayi has therefore argued (p. 206) that it is wrong to refer to Crowther as bishop merely in relation to the Niger Mission. To this it can be replied that on the title-page of his Nupe grammar of 1864, the year of his appointment, a work published by the C.M.S. itself, Crowther was described as 'Bishop of the Niger Territory', a title repeated on a Nupe work of 1877. A later work, the Ibo vocabulary of 1882, merely names him as 'the Right Rev. Bishop Crowther'.

[63] [S. Crowther], *The Gospel on the banks of the Niger, No. II*, 1863, p. 13.

[64] On Baikie at Lokoja, see H. J. Pedraza, *Borrioboola-Gha*, 1960, chapter 4.

[65] J. Kirk, 'Notes of a journey from Bida in Nupe to Kano in Hausa performed in 1862 by Dr W. B. Baikie', *Journal of the Royal Geographical Society*, 36, 1867, pp. 92–108 (on p. 108, vocabularies listed include Basa and 'Bonu'); Cust, *op. cit.*, 1, pp. 217–19, 230 (vocabulary of Gbari). In Pedraza, *op. cit.*, p. 60, it is stated that Baikie translated 'the Church Service' into Nupe; no reference is given.

Gospels, Acts and most of the Epistles were printed between 1864 and 1866. But differences of opinion about points in translation had arisen between Taylor and Schön, and the latter recommended that Taylor revise his translation before the whole New Testament was printed, a view at which Taylor took offence.[66] Taylor and his assistants at Onitsha also prepared some liturgical material – a few hymns were printed in 1871 and most of the Prayer Book in 1871–2. Taylor's connection with Ibo now came to an end; he was transferred from Onitsha to Igbebe, and then to the Sierra Leone mission, allegedly because of ill-health, his formal service with the Niger Mission apparently ending in 1871.[67] Though his knowledge of Ibo at the start, and perhaps his capacity for improvement, disappointed both Crowther and Schön, Taylor was the pioneer of Ibo literature.

Crowther had always hoped to establish mission stations in the Delta, and his retreat from Nupeland in the early 1860s encouraged him to compensate by expansion in the south. After the opening at Akassa, in the same year (1861) the mission was invited to Bonny, and in 1867 was invited to Brass. In preparation for the move into Ijaw country, Crowther persuaded Taylor to prepare a primer of Ijaw. An account by Taylor of an early Sunday school at Akassa, before Crowther or himself knew more than a few words of Ijaw, shows the importance attached to literacy in the vernacular within the Niger Mission. 'Mr Crowther took the first class at the head of the table in the centre of the room, a capital place for him, with his venerable silver-bound spectacles, a [rod] in his hand, pointing to the phonetic alphabet characters, calling out loudly the well-known letters, a, b, d, e . . .'. Taylor stood at the door of the room, inviting bystanders to enter, by calling 'Ebi diri ebima!' ('Good Whiteman's book best!') or 'Ebi! Ebim! Ebima! Aa, beke diri ebima!' ('Good! Better! Best! Yes, Englishman's book is best!'). The class was silent until Crowther discovered the Ijaw term for 'repeat together', then all imitated 'the pronunciation of those wonderful characters which will in due time be beneficial to them and would not fail of preparing them to read the Word of God for themselves hereafter'.[68] Taylor never learnt much Ijaw and his primer, published in 1862 was, he admitted in the introduction, a 'hasty' work. But it was the first book in Ijaw.

A little later, two Sierra Leoneans who were stationed as catechists at Bonny began to study the two languages spoken there. In 1870, F. W. Smart, who was with the Niger Mission from 1868 to 1876, published a revised primer and some hymns in Ibo, while W. E. L. Carew, who served from 1868 to 1889, published a primer and translations of two small religious works in Ibo. Nearly three hundred miles to the north, at the mission station at the confluence, primers in two local languages were also produced, and were published in 1866 and 1867. The author of these first works in Igala and Igbira was a young Sierra Leonean clergyman, A. G. Coomber, who joined Crowther in 1861 and died at his station in 1869. All the works mentioned were edited and seen through the press in England by Schön. Thus, by 1870, five Niger languages (Ibo, Nupe, Ijaw, Igala and Igbira) had achieved their earliest printed literature.

The 1870s found Crowther still travelling up and down the river at irregular intervals. The Lokoja consulate, formally established after Baikie left, was closed in 1869, and

---

[66] Ajayi, *op. cit.*, p. 130, where, as the printed works are not mentioned, a rather different impression is given.
[67] *C.M.S. Proceedings*, 1866–7, pp. 29, 31; *C.M. Intelligencer*, March 1875, in Crowther's report.
[68] Ajayi, *op. cit.*, p. 132, quoting from C.M.S. Archives, CA 3/0 37, entry for 22.12.1861.

for a time no gunboats entered the Niger; Crowther was forced to rely on trading vessels for transport until the C.M.S. provided him with a ship of his own in 1878. Although the various mission stations failed to win thousands of converts – as apparently the home authorities expected – they exerted considerable educational and cultural influence on the districts in which they stood. Crowther's own son, Dandeson, was in charge at Bonny from 1871, and by the end of the decade, the mission was well-established in the Delta. Higher up, the stations at Onitsha and Lokoja (formerly Igbebe) were maintained, and Crowther was able to advance again into Nupeland, establishing a new station at Kipo Hill, near Egga. This advance to the north led him to renew interest in Hausa and Nupe. He subsidised the publication of Schön's Hausa dictionary in 1876, and sent a Hausa-speaking assistant, the Sierra Leonean T. C. John, to Chatham to study with Schön. He himself returned to his Nupe studies, and in 1877 published a translation of a Gospel.

In 1878, the C.M.S. steamer reached the Niger, and to assist the ageing bishop, two archdeacons were appointed, Dandeson Crowther for the Delta and Henry Johnson for the upper stations. Johnson, a Sierra Leonean, had some knowledge of Arabic and had already done much linguistic work, in particular on Mende in collaboration with Schön. Crowther now left Nupe studies to Johnson, and turned to Ibo, where nothing had been published for some years. He came to the conclusion that translation work was held back by the problem of dialects, and that more must be learnt before a firm policy could be evolved. To this end, in the late 1870s he ordered the missionaries at Onitsha to begin work on a comparative dictionary of Ibo dialects. This ambitious enterprise was not carried out, mainly because of lack of able researchers, but such material as did become available Crowther put together to form a dictionary of Ibo, published in 1882 (with an English-Ibo supplement by Schön in 1883).[69] Although Crowther continued to take an interest in the revision of the Bible in his mother-tongue, Yoruba, this Ibo dictionary was the last linguistic work published under his name.

Henry Johnson reached the Niger in 1880 and began to learn Nupe. In 1882 he published a reading book, in 1883 a catechism, and in 1886 and 1887 translations of all four Gospels. He translated more of the New Testament, and was preparing to print this at a mission press set up at Lokoja, when the C.M.S. decided to abandon the station.[70] Another Sierra Leonean, P. J. Williams, who was first catechist then pastor at Lokoja, under Johnson's supervision prepared a reading book in Igbira, published 1883, and a translation of the whole of the Bible and of the Prayer Book, of which only

[69] C.M. Intelligencer, September 1876, p. 536; H. Johnson, A journey up the Niger in the autumn of 1877, London, 1878, p. 18; S. Crowther, Vocabulary of the Ibo language, 1882, pp. v–vii. Crowther explained that a vocabulary of Ibo had not been published earlier, because the vocabulary he had used in 1856–7 when preparing the primer had been passed on to Taylor, who had not returned it when he left the Niger. (We have suggested above that the 1856–7 vocabulary may have been based on Schön's 1840–1 collection.) Crowther himself never spoke Ibo fluently, and the material in the dictionary was mainly collected by the mission staff at Onitsha. The Sierra Leoneans, S. Perry and J. Buck, collected a vocabulary of 'Isuama, Onitsha and Abo' (C.M.S. Archives, Niger Mission, G3/A3, letterbook 1880–1, paper 103 dated 6.10.1881). The dictionary was apparently ready in manuscript by 1880 (ibid., letter of 3.2.1882). This was not the only work done at Onitsha on Ibo in the 1870s: Perry translated the Psalms, but the manuscript was destroyed during the British bombardment of the town in 1879 (D. C. Crowther, The establishment of the Niger Delta Pastorate Church, Liverpool, 1907, p. 30), and some hymns were apparently produced.

[70] Johnson was helped by another Sierra Leonean, C. Paul, catechist and pastor at Lokoja and Kipo Hill from 1869, who had translated a Gospel and other material into Nupe (C.M.S. Archives, G3/A3, letterbook 1880–1, paper 103, dated 6.10.1881; Cust, op. cit., 1, p. 229). Paul also contributed a little Hausa material to Schön's collection of texts.

one Gospel was published, this in 1891. The vigour of the linguistic activity at Lokoja in the 1880s in itself raises doubts about the wisdom of the C.M.S. in closing the station.[71] From Lokoja, Johnson was transferred to Onitsha, and he turned his attention to Ibo. By 1891, he had translated two Gospels, and these were published in 1893,[72] but by then Johnson himself had left both the Niger and the C.M.S., in protest against the changes in the Niger Mission. In his enthusiasm for linguistic work, Henry Johnson was a man after Crowther's heart, and would have made a worthy successor in the direction of the Niger Mission. But disappointed and frustrated, he did no more work on languages after leaving the Niger.

The same decade – the last decade of Crowther's Niger Mission – also saw a flurry of linguistic activity in the Delta, where the work was done under the supervision of Dandeson Crowther. A printing press had arrived, and the works to be mentioned were printed locally, at Bonny or Brass. Thomas Johnson, a Sierra Leonean who was first schoolmaster, then catechist, then pastor at Delta stations between 1861 and 1884, prepared two Ijaw catechisms and a translation of the Book of Common Prayer: after passing through the hands of a translation committee at Brass, the three works were printed in 1885–6. J. D. Garrick, a Sierra Leonean who served as catechist and pastor at Nembe between 1879 and 1894, prepared an Ijaw translation of a Gospel which was published in 1886. Finally, a translation committee at Bonny prepared translations of two catechisms, the Prayer Book, a Gospel and several Epistles, into the local dialect of Ibo, and all of these were printed between 1886 and 1893.[73]

---

[71] Williams and Johnson also translated Watts' Catechism into Igbira and Williams collected a vocabulary of Igara; neither was published and the manuscripts do not appear to be in the C.M.S. Archives (*C.M. Intelligencer*, November 1877, p. 677; December 1882, p. 745; October 1890, p. 700; *C.M.S. Proceedings*, 1880–1, p. 28; Cust, *op. cit.*, 1, p. 226; C.M.S. Archives, G3/A3, paper 109 of 24.6.1882).

[72] At Onitsha, assisted by J. O. Mba, an Ibo catechist, Johnson also prepared a hymnbook (1889), a catechism, parts of the Prayerbook, and a reader; these were printed on the mission press before 1891. One account says that the printing was done at Lokoja, another at Onitsha. None of these works has yet been traced. On the press and the publications, see *C.M. Intelligencer*, May 1884, p. 323; *Niger and Yoruba Notes*, 1896, p. 52; H. H. Dobinson, *Letters*, 1899, pp. 111, 128, 180; *Western Equatorial Africa Diocesan Magazine*, July 1904, p. 13; December 1907, p. 98.

[73] The printing press, a gift from a C.M.S. association, was installed at Bonny in 1881, moved to Brass in 1884, and was back in Bonny in 1888. Parts of the Prayerbook had been translated into Ibo by D. Crowther (who had more command of the language than his father) and his Sierra Leonean assistant, J. Boyle, by 1878 (C.M.S. Archives, G3/A3, paper 103). A tentative version of the Ijaw Prayers and Hymns was apparently printed in 1885 (*C. M. Intelligencer*, May 1885, p. 380). In 1888, D. Crowther compiled a list of translations in Ibo and Ijaw, 'some printed at the Delta Mission Printing Press'. Apart from those which appear in our bibliography, they included in Ibo portions of Matthew, possibly a tentative version of that listed under 1892–3, and '100 Texts', probably a handbill; and in Ijaw, portions of Psalms and Acts, translations not otherwise known to have existed. The list is not altogether accurate (it omits the 1886 John in Ijaw) and it is possible that the additional works, Psalms and Acts, should have been listed as in manuscript, not as in print. The list mentions Ephesians, Colossians and part of Mark in Ibo in manuscript; only Ephesians appears to have been printed later. On the Delta printing press and for this list, see D. C. Crowther, *op. cit.*, pp. 29–31. The Sierra Leoneans in the Delta were assisted in their Ibo translation work by an Ibo catechist, D. O. Pepple (*Niger and Yoruba Notes*, August 1898, p. 14). One final point about the Ibo translation work carried through by the Delta missionaries is that it was claimed to be in a different dialect of Ibo from that employed in the translations made at Onitsha (at least from 1880). B.F.B.S. catalogued the dialects as 'Lower Ibo' and 'Upper Ibo'. Apart from his work as chairman of Delta translation committees, Dandeson Crowther made a slight contribution to academic linguistics. In 1881, he compiled an account of the languages of the lower Niger, based mainly on published material but with a little original information on their distribution, including a list of work accomplished or in process (C.M.S. Archives, G3/A3, paper 131). This was prepared at the request of R. N. Cust, who incorporated the material in his volumes of 1883.

Between 1857 and 1893, over fifty books and booklets were published in the languages of the lower Niger-Benue. Almost all were produced by West Africans, and all were due to the activities of the Niger Mission under Crowther. Nevertheless, from 1875 onwards Crowther and his mission came under increasingly severe attack from European missionaries of the C.M.S., who complained that the mission was not carried forward with sufficient energy and that many of the West African agents, clergymen and laymen, were leading lives unworthy of their vocation. As a result, in 1883 and again in 1889, several agents were dismissed: Archdeacon Crowther was at one point threatened with dismissal by a European mission official, without reference to his father, the bishop, but the threat was later withdrawn, with an apology; Archdeacon Johnson was transferred from his station and his archdeaconry was suppressed. English missionaries were introduced into the mission, though disease rapidly reduced their numbers. Bishop Crowther died in 1891, his passing in extreme old age robbed of its serenity by the tragicomical débâcle of the Niger Mission. His son formed the Delta stations into an independent pastorate which seceded for a time from C.M.S. control, though it remained under Anglican episcopal supervision.

We call a halt to our chronological survey of the study of the lower Niger-Benue languages and the development of their printed literatures, in the early 1890s when Crowther's Niger Mission collapsed. The unique feature of the study of these particular African languages between the early 1850s and the early 1890s was that it was undertaken almost wholly by Africans. After the early 1890s, the study continued and the literatures expanded: Africans (even Sierra Leoneans) participated, but they no longer undertook the major, and the directing, part of the labour. We shall conclude this essay by evaluating the work done up to the early 1890s in terms of, first, its linguistic and literary value, and secondly, its ultimate cultural and historical influence.

*   *   *

In quantity, the output of linguistic material of the Niger Mission was rather smaller than that (during the same period) of the German mission in Gold Coast, or of the American mission in Liberia, or of the British Baptist mission in Cameroons, or of the British Presbyterian mission at Calabar, or even of the neighbouring C.M.S. Yoruba mission. But the output was respectable enough when we consider the educational attainments of the personnel of the Niger Mission. If we count in the unpublished material, we have evidence that almost every literate agent of the mission tried to do linguistic work; if we count in contributions to books, two out of three literate agents of the mission put material into print. It is doubtful if any of the other missions mentioned above achieved such a high rate of attention to linguistic work.[74] The devotion of the Niger Mission to this work is apparent in Crowther's published reports and even more in the pages of the unpublished Niger correspondence in the C.M.S. Archives.[75]

---

[74] It is therefore peculiarly unsatisfactory that a recent work touching on the Niger Mission should have to say of its linguistic endeavour only the following – 'Crowther had to rely on Sierra Leonean helpers, not all of whom were well qualified or reliable. . . . He never learned an east-Nigerian language, and was dependent upon unsatisfactory interpreters.' (S. Neill, *A history of Christian missions*, 1964, p. 377).

[75] The following summaries of a selection of letters (C.M.S. Archives, G3/A3) give some idea of the activity: 18.11.1881 Johnson studying Hausa, will take up Nupe next; 3.2.1882 Crowther's grandson helps in preparing MSS for Hausa and Yoruba translation – MS. Ibo dictionary sent to

—Continued on following page

Yet none of the members of the Niger Mission had a full university training; most of them had attended only a West African secondary school or the largely theological courses at Fourah Bay Institution, and a fair number of them had attended only elementary school.[76] Their educational attainments were therefore on the average inferior to those of the largely-European staff of the other missions. Moreover, the Niger Mission agents had been drawn from a small community of English-speaking West Africans – not more than 30,000 – of whom less than half were literate; and in this Freetown community, at least by the 1870s, those who were the intellectual cream were aspiring after secular and more remunerative occupations in medicine and law. Crowther's staff were almost wholly men of no special intellectual distinction, by normal standards; they were a very ordinary set of men who in other circumstances would not have been expected to produce what they did. Indeed, one must go further and say that they had not even the normal advantage of contemporary ordinary men in Europe who grew up in a literate society. Many of the agents of the Niger Mission had (it may be assumed) illiterate parents, and all grew up in a society the vast majority of whose members were only introduced to literacy when in their middle years they were brought to Freetown. Regarded against this background, the linguistic work of the Niger Mission was extraordinary, and can be interpreted as a notable achievement of human endeavour. It is pleasant to note that it was so regarded by a few percipient contemporaries. The best-informed of these was R. N. Cust, who in 1883 published a two-volume work on African languages and the history of their study.[77] Especial attention was paid in these volumes to the linguistic work of Crowther and his assistants – Cust had sought and obtained detailed particulars from Archdeacon Crowther – and many flattering remarks were made about the two Crowthers, Henry Johnson, and the team of Sierra Leoneans working on the Niger. The only full-page photographic portrait in the book was that of Samuel Crowther.

One point implicit in Cust's text has been ignored or denied by some recent writers on the Niger Mission – the extent to which the mission, not least on its linguistic side, operated within a framework of European approval and collaboration. That for long no European was employed within the mission was, as Professor Ajayi has shown, not strictly Crowther's responsibility or wish.[78] When it came to linguistic publications,

---

—Continued from previous page

England; 19.11.1882 Archdeacon Crowther forwards language map; 1.6.1883 Johnson forwards texts in Igbira, Nupe to follow; 24.6.1883 Johnson forwards Igbira MSS. – will Schön read proofs; 30.6.1883 re 10 copies of Ibo vocabulary; 4.9.1884 prayers in Ibo, Hausa, Nupe from Johnson; 30.11.1885 Schön sends Hausa translations for Crowther; 21.12.1888 request by Schön that Nupe Gospel be reprinted.

[76] In 1879, Crowther had a staff of nine clergy and sixteen laymen: of these, eleven had had only elementary schooling. Carew, who did language work, had only this, and had been a ship's steward before joining the Mission and eventually becoming a clergyman. T. Johnson, who did linguistic work in the Delta, had only elementary schooling and had been a shoemaker. These particulars are taken from Crowther's list of staff (C.M.S. Archives, CA 3/0 43, paper of 14.2.1879). It may be noted here that it is not possible to obtain the particulars of the mission careers of the Niger Mission staff from *List of C.M.S. missionaries and native clergy*, London [1905], because this is limited to clergy and gives only the date on which clerical service began; most of the Niger Mission clergy had earlier served for years as catechists and schoolteachers. As regards the staff of the Mission trained at Fourah Bay, any linguistic training given there was slight and indirect: see P. E. H. Hair, 'The contribution of Freetown and Fourah Bay College to the study of West African languages', *Sierra Leone Language Review*, 1, 1962, pp. 7–18, on pp. 12–13.

[77] Cust, *op. cit.*

[78] Ajayi, *op. cit.*, p. 208.

the mission depended on the London authorities of the C.M.S. who arranged publication, or latterly, sent printing presses to the Niger. There is some evidence that the authorities were more generous to Niger Mission linguistic material than they were to material produced by European missionaries, for instance, to Schön's Hausa works, publication of which sometimes depended on a request from Crowther. In the case of some of the poorer work from the Niger, the contrast between the limited value of the contents and the care taken in London in producing a neat and attractive book is striking. The authorities obviously had a special interest in publishing works whose title-page announced African authorship, for such works justified mission propaganda and served to score points in debate against racialists or other enemies of missionary endeavour. On the academic side, the mission work was underpinned by European scholarship, though this meant largely, in the circumstances of the time, the scholarship of one man, Schön. We have seen Taylor being introduced to phonetic orthography by Vidal, and then later improving his Ibo at Chatham: and we have seen Schön producing an Ibo grammar and 'seeing through the press' nearly all the London-published works of the mission. What is less well documented is the extent to which Schön edited the published works. The B.F.B.S. catalogue, drawing its information from unpublished correspondence, credits Schön with editing, for instance, not only the Nupe material of Crowther and Johnson, but also some of Crowther's early Yoruba material. The work of editing probably ranged from correcting English (as admitted to be necessary in the 1859 print of Taylor's journal) – though in view of Schön's own less than perfect English, he probably received help here from his family – to giving advice on orthography, idiom, and suitable material for translation, and checking incoming translations for consistent orthography, vocabulary and grammar. Schön's practical contribution to the Niger Mission publications, which included such lowly tasks as copying manuscripts and proof-reading, may well have been equalled by his academic contribution. Admiration for the extent of the African contribution to the early study of the lower Niger-Benue languages need not blind us to the fact that this contribution was made possible only by European approval, support, and collaboration.

The quality of the output of the Niger Mission must now be considered. Only three works were formal contributions to academic linguistics. The Ibo dictionary of 1882 was a disappointing work: the idea of a dictionary giving dialect forms was sound, but the work was done carelessly.[79] No doubt this was partly because the editor on the Niger and the adviser in England, Crowther and Schön, were both by the date of compilation nearly eighty years of age. Schön's Ibo grammar of 1861, which was produced *for* the mission if not strictly by an agent, is a difficult work to evaluate, since it drew no reviews at the time and with one exception has drawn no comment from later workers who seem to have been unaware of its existence.[80] Whatever its shortcomings – and as we shall see, it was at least sophisticated enough to discuss tonality – it dealt with the language in fair detail, and provided the only introduction to Ibo grammar available during this period. Crowther's Nupe grammar of 1864 was 'a tentative effort', according to its author, and judgement on it is further complicated by the fact that, unlike Ibo,

---

[79] In the introduction, Crowther wrote – 'The present work is the beginning of a large and comprehensive work' (p. v).
[80] A French missionary-linguist made an unfavourable reference to it, but went on to say that the differences between his own findings and Schön's may have been due to their studying different dialects (P. A. Ganot, *Grammaire Ibo*, 1899, Preface).

Nupe is not even today a well-studied language. But the Nupe grammar was the vehicle for an extremely important contribution to African linguistics, since in the introduction Crowther made his firmest statement about the tonality of certain West African languages.

'As in the Yoruba', he began, 'the knowledge of intonation is an important part in the study of the languages: nothing makes speaking these languages so difficult to foreigners [i.e. Europeans] . . .'. Later Crowther listed the 'musical' or tonal languages known to him, not only Yoruba, but also Nupe, Hausa, and 'in some degree' Ibo. He then argued for the necessity of tone-marking. A Yoruba just taught to read could pronounce the correct tones in reading the book from which he had been taught, because he knew the context and therefore the vocabulary that would appear: 'but if a new book be brought before him, treating on different subjects, without any mark to guide his tone in the pronunciation of words, he will try it in three ways before he arrives at the exact sense'. Hence, 'some marks of intonation are made in the Yoruba translations, which have been of material use to foreigners and natives. . . . The reading of these translations will *ever continue to be uncertain and incorrect* without some marks to distinguish the tone. . . . I do not mean that every word in the translation is necessary to be marked but, in many cases, the distinctive marks are indispensable.'[81]

Crowther chose to make these observations on tone and tone-marking in his Nupe grammar because his previous work on a language other than his mother-tongue had, in his estimation, been spoilt by the failure of the C.M.S. authorities to understand the importance of tone. In his Ibo primer of 1857, he had originally marked two tones: but in the printing of this – and of Schön's contemporary Hausa translations – 'the acute accent only is employed, and the grave, to mark depressed tone, is entirely discarded. This is a very great mistake, from whatever cause it was done.'[82] Crowther had first tried to indicate tone in his Yoruba vocabulary of 1843, and he had explicitly indicated its importance in his 1852 grammar. It is not known whether Schön detected tones in Ibo when studying the language in 1840–1, but it is probable that he did not. Crowther's appreciation of Ibo tonality in the 1857 primer no doubt influenced Schön, who wrote in his 1861 grammar of Ibo: 'We point out a great peculiarity, not only of Ibo, but of many African languages, in speaking of intonation (Betonung) which must not be confused with accentuation. It consists in the raising or sinking of the voice . . . this does not merely affect the form of the word itself, but its import likewise. . . We would strongly recommend to all who may write in Ibo to pay special attention to this subject.'[83] The discovery of tonality in West African languages became known to international linguistic scholarship when Lepsius referred to the matter in the second edition of his *Standard Alphabet* in 1863: he noted the tone-marking of Yoruba by Crowther and Bowen and of Ibo by Crowther and Schön (also of Ewe by Schlegel in 1857), and he concluded, 'we find here in a smaller extent the same principle of intonation as in the Chinese' – a comparison already made by Crowther in 1852.[84]

[81] Crowther, *Nupe grammar*, pp. iii–vi.
[82] *ibid.*, p. iii.
[83] Schön, *Oku Ibo*, p. 5.
[84] C. R. Lepsius, *Standard Alphabet*, 2nd edition, 1863, pp. 275, 277; Crowther, *Yoruba grammar*, 1852, introduction. A modern linguist, discussing the importance of tonal analysis in the study of the Kwa languages (i.e. Yoruba, Ibo, Nupe, Igala, Igbira, Idoma, etc), writes – 'The great stumbling block lies in the systematic transformation which the sounds and tones undergo in various morphological and syntactic contexts. Until these are worked out, there can be no secure grammar or lexicography, and the interpretation of printed texts remains largely guesswork' (R. G. Armstrong, in Forde et al., *op. cit.*, p. 78).

On the whole, Crowther was unsuccessful in persuading the mission authorities that tones should or could be marked, and translations in the lower Niger-Benue languages normally ignored tone. Nevertheless, interest in tonality, or at least awareness of it, filtered down to Crowther's assistants, for the author of a humble reading book in Igbira (published 1883) found it necessary to comment that his book 'being designed solely and wholly for the natives', he had not 'burdened the syllables with tone-marks and accents'.[85]

The vast majority of the publications of the Niger Mission consisted of translations, naturally in the main translations of the Bible or other religious works. It is noteworthy that, apart from the few Ibo proverbs printed by Taylor in 1859 and a few Nupe proverbs in Crowther's 1864 grammar and vocabulary, no free texts were collected in the languages studied, a serious lapse. The point was discussed by Schön in the introduction to his Ibo grammar: why had Taylor worked on translations instead of collecting 'native literature'? Though Schön defended Taylor, on the grounds that translations were needed (and Schön knew perfectly well from experience that pressure was put on missionary-linguists to produce translations as soon as the study of a language had begun), he added – 'while we would never make the Missionary a mere linguistic inquirer, we would still recommend to him to devote some time to the collection of a native literature'.[86] Schön himself had recently collected many texts in Hausa, on which his later study of the language was based, and we may suspect that he urged Taylor in vain to collect Ibo texts. We may further suspect that on this point Schön's views were sounder than Crowther's – for even in Yoruba Crowther appears to have collected very little in the way of free texts – and that therefore Crowther failed to encourage his Niger assistants to collect texts. Very likely it was felt on the Niger that while texts might be necessary for the European studying African languages in Europe, they were unnecessary for the African who spoke the language before he began the study and who worked in the homeland. If so, it was a wrong view.

The translations made by the Niger Mission were, as far as can be judged, in the main of mediocre quality, and quite unlike Crowther's translations into Yoruba. While they were perhaps no worse than the translations produced when African languages in other areas were first studied by European missionaries, there is evidence that they were certainly no better.[87] This is significant, for it points to two delusions which undermined the linguistic activities of the Niger Mission. The first was the delusion, still widely-held and not only in Africa, that, without training or study, any person who speaks a language as a mother-tongue can translate material into it. The second was the delusion that the Sierra Leoneans of the Niger Mission in fact spoke an African language as their mother tongue.

Because of their lowly education, and the fact that they had spoken English only in West Africa and not in England, the English of many of the Sierra Leoneans, though

---

[85] P. J. Williams, *Igbira Otakida* . . . , 1883, p. [3].

[86] Schön, *op. cit.*, p. 2.

[87] Johnson, a fellow Sierra Leonean, reported of one of Taylor's translations that it required 'alterations and emendations in about every line of every page, in order to bring it within the comprehension of the people' (*C.M. Intelligencer*, September 1882, p. 546). (To be fair to Taylor, equally devastating criticism has been made of almost all pioneer translations into African languages, e.g. of Schön's Hausa translations.) The Englishman Dennis merely complained that Taylor's translations were too literal (and showed an inadequate grasp of *English* idiom!) (*C.M. Review*, 63, 1912, p. 227). Crowther made it clear that he was disappointed by Taylor's work, and thought it would have been better if he had paid more attention to Schön's advice (*C.M. Intelligencer*, September 1876, p. 536).

their first language, was inadequate when it came to understanding the literary English of the material they were *translating from*. Because they had spoken an African language at home in Freetown only as a second language (sometimes very irregularly), and the African languages in Freetown rapidly became mixed in dialect and corrupt, most of the Sierra Leoneans had an inadequate understanding of the language they were *translating into*. The gulf between Crowther and most of his assistants in these matters was concealed in the mission literature. Crowther had grown up in Yorubaland and he spoke Yoruba fluently: this gave him an advantage even in studying other African languages. Crowther had spoken English in England, and though it is true that his educational training had been little better than that of the majority of his assistants, he outranked them in sheer intellectual capacity.[88] Crowther was a native of Nigeria, and in Yorubaland was recognised as a son of the land; the agents of his Niger Mission were natives of Sierra Leone, not of the Niger. Their African-ness, lauded in mission literature of the time as in recent historical literature, made little or no impression on the nineteenth-century Niger, where they were regarded, with some reason, as 'black Europeans'. At Onitsha, Taylor seems to have made no attempt to seek out relatives in Iboland: and he reflected sadly in his journal that whereas one of his interpreters, an Ibo ex-slave who had returned home as a Christian after a few years away, made a great impression on the local people, a Freetown-born man who had never known traditional life was regarded as an outsider and intruder.[89] Thus, the Sierra Leoneans in the Niger Mission were doomed from the start to slide towards the tragic position in which they ultimately found themselves, disliked and even despised by both Europeans and Niger peoples as being neither fish nor fowl. Freetown's intermediary role between two cultures was vital to West African development, but on the Niger, the essentially temporary nature of the role showed up perhaps sooner than anywhere else. Worked out in linguistic terms – the early generation of Sierra Leoneans had a slight to moderate command of a Niger language when they reached the mission; the later generation had less than a slight command, and had therefore very little advantage over a European recruit. The mediocre quality of much of the linguistic work of the Niger Mission therefore stemmed from the fact that its agents were Sierra Leoneans, with inbuilt limitations. It was unfortunate, not least for these men, that the limitations were not publicly recognised: in linguistic as in other matters, they were unfairly expected to be all Crowthers.

It is only fair to add that one of the linguistic problems the Niger Mission faced was beyond even Crowther. We have seen that Schön met the problem of deep dialect divisions in Ibo as early as 1841. In 1857, Crowther selected for the first book in Ibo the so-called Isuama dialect, probably after consultation with Schön.[90] Twenty

---

[88] Crowther had also the advantage that he was a man of mature years before he took up language study: during his ten years or so in Freetown as a schoolteacher, he may have read widely in English. The best educated of Crowther's assistants were his son and Johnson, both of whom had had some education in England, and these men should be excepted from the general comments on the Sierra Leoneans.

[89] Crowther and Taylor, *op. cit.*, p. 312; cf. Ajayi, *op. cit.*, p. 43.

[90] It is of some interest that the term 'Isuama' apparently was used during slave-trade days: among the 'Carabali' in Cuba in the early eighteenth century were some 'Suamos' (Beltran, *op. cit.*, p. 135). Koelle in the *Polyglotta* unfortunately had little to say about 'Isoama' (p. 8). Today the name is applied to an interior section of the Southern Ibo, around Owerri (D. Forde and G. I. Jones, *The Ibo and Ibibio-speaking peoples of South-Eastern Nigeria*, 1950, p. 10 and map). It was noted in Freetown that the Ibo had no general name for themselves (Koelle, *op. cit.*, p. 7: on possible origins of the term 'Ibo', see Forde and Jones, *op. cit.*, p. 9).

years later he still hoped that Isuama would serve throughout Iboland, thinking no doubt of the way in which the dialect he himself had chosen for early Yoruba translations was rapidly being accepted as the standard literary form for that language. In 1875, when Crowther was able to turn again to Ibo studies, he called a conference at Onitsha of his Ibo-translators, to discuss problems relating to the language (a similar conference on Yoruba had just been held[91]). The first Rule which the conference enunciated was as follows: 'The standard and reading dialect of this language is strictly to be that of the Isuama, it being the one which all the other dialects will learn to speak, while the Isuama will yield to no other, hence translations in this dialect will be universally received by the nation.'[92] However, only a year later, Crowther was forced to admit that 'the chief difficulty [is] to know for certain which is the real Isuama'.[93] Isuama was supposed to be the dialect spoken by all the Ibos in Sierra Leone, whatever their individual origin, but Crowther began to realise that it was more a mixed than a central dialect, and that whereas a mixed dialect was inevitable in the small Ibo community in Freetown, and was possible because whole stretches of cultural vocabulary relating to traditional practices had been abandoned, it was not easily acceptable in Iboland.[94] In the 1880s, the mission gave up the attempt to use one dialect only, and translations were henceforth prepared at Onitsha and Bonny in separate dialects. The failure of the attempt to use the mixed dialect, Isuama, foreshadowed the failure in the early decades of the present century of the attempt to use another mixed dialect, 'Union Ibo', throughout Iboland.

The immediate practical value of all the publications discussed for the evangelical and educational work of the Niger Mission was limited. In general, they were used only by mission personnel and in mission schools, and their usefulness was no doubt reduced by the academic shortcomings mentioned. It is fairly clear that enthusiasm for the use of any particular linguistic publication was apt to be shortlived. Possibly the books were difficult to use, because of their errors; no doubt, at many schools the parents pressed for their children to learn to read in English not in the vernacular. But the impression remains that the mission, which devoted so much attention to the production of linguistic works, might reasonably have made more effort to see to it that the works produced were used. An inscription on the British Museum copies of the Igala and Igbira primers of 1866–7 tells its own story: they were presented to the Museum in the 1880s by the sympathetic Cust who noted on each – 'This book had been lost sight of. At a conference which I had with Bishop Crowther and Mr Schön they were sure of its existence and after much search it was produced.' In the 1860s, 1000 copies of each part of the Bible translated into Ibo were printed, but no further printing was called for before the 1880s. The single translation into Nupe of the early

---

[91] See J. F. A. Ajayi, 'How Yoruba was reduced to writing', *Odu*, 1961, pp. 49–58, on pp. 55–6.

[92] The remaining decisions of this conference were vague in the extreme: '2. One system of orthography must be pursued as near as possible for the present, to be improved upon at a subsequent revision. 3. The accents to be employed are acute, grave and circumflex, as will be hereafter laid down, to guide the tone and pronunciation as near as possible.' (C.M.S. Archives, G3/A3, 1880–1, paper 103 of 6.10.1881). The vacuity of these points contrasts very strongly with the decisions of the Yoruba conference (Ajayi, *op. cit.* (1961), pp. 55–6), where the majority of the participants were European missionaries, and it can only be concluded that the Niger Mission had decided intellectual limitations.

[93] *C.M. Intelligencer*, September 1876, p. 536.

[94] *C.M. Intelligencer*, March 1875, Crowther's report.

1860s was printed in 500 copies, and this sufficed until the 1880s.[95] It should not be assumed that even these small numbers of copies were circulated; boxes of copies were regularly lost in mission-house fires or when canoes overturned. The present writer was shown in 1952, at the C.M.S. headquarters at Onitsha, a shelf-ful of copies in mint condition of Crowther's Ibo primer, printed a century earlier and never opened.

The white missionaries who succeeded Crowther and most of his assistants on the Niger were young and excessively enthusiastic, much better educated than any of the Sierra Leoneans, perfervid in religion and in intellectual opinion. One of them, shortly after his arrival on the Niger in 1890, reported home – 'No grammar exists in print . . . Fancy, thirty years or more being allowed to slip by, without having drawn up an Ibo grammar or done any language work . . . As to translations into Ibo, there are very few indeed.'[96] The writer was H. H. Dobinson, who, after a period of weeks, was the only member of the original party to survive or continue on the Niger; he was therefore the only member able to recant his earlier ungracious and inaccurate opinions about the activity of Crowther's mission, which he did some time before his death on the river in 1897.[97] Though his 1890 statements about the previous work on Ibo were well wide of the mark, it is clear that he and his colleagues were misled by the relatively little use made by the Niger Mission of its own linguistic publications.

*   *   *

Understanding of the history of the Niger Mission has not been greatly helped by the current tendency to examine African history merely in order to extract from it simple morals concerning the wickedness of racialism or imperialism. Many factors other than racialism or imperialism contributed to the Niger débâcle, some of them relevant to the present discussion. It can be argued, for instance, that Crowther's enthusiasm for linguistic work was excessive from the point of view of rational mission strategy;[98] that, as bishop, he spent too much time on personal linguistic work, and too little on the close supervision of his assistants, whose suitability for recruitment or retention he was too apt to judge in terms of an optimistic appraisal of their linguistic potential or attainments rather than in terms of an episcopally severe view of their moral behaviour.

It can also be argued that enthusiasm for linguistic work contributed to the collapse of the mission in another way. We have noted that almost every literate agent tried his hand at linguistic work, and that much of what was written was published: consequently, many publications were of mediocre, or even more unsatisfactory, material. Precisely as Crowther's moral character surpassed that of his assistants – this in itself was little human condemnation of them, for his character approached saintliness – so his linguistic capacity outpaced theirs. But because of the aura attached to Crowther in mission circles, and because of the well-intentioned desire to demonstrate African

---

[95] *B.F.B.S. Annual Report*, 1860, 1861, 1864, 1865, 1867, 1868, 1880. Only 250 copies of the Ibo vocabulary were printed in 1883, but in 1884 500 Nupe reading books and 1000 Nupe catechisms were printed (*S.P.C.K. Report*, 1881, p. 28).

[96] Dobinson, *op. cit.*, pp. 45, 67.

[97] Ajayi, *op. cit.* (1965), p. 270.

[98] An obvious point is that the Niger Mission tackled too many languages at once. Of course, the existence of so many languages within its field of operations was the problem of the Mission par excellence, and the previous experience of the Yoruba Mission which had had to deal with a single tongue only, was no help at all. Again, once it had been decided that the mission should operate along a great river, it had been implicitly accepted that much of the work would be linguistic, or at least would involve problems of linguistic communication.

ability, the publications of the Niger Mission tended to be overrated – and some of them, if by Europeans, would almost certainly not have been published. By the 1880s, the pious fraud practised by the humanitarians and mission supporters in exaggerating the exploits of the Niger Mission in several fields brought nemesis. The European missionaries who came to the Niger noted the contrast between the published reports on linguistic publications and their real use in the field, between the flowery title-pages and expensive printing of the volumes and the linguistic poverty of their contents, between the linguistic pretensions of the Sierra Leoneans and their obvious limited intellectual capacity, and they were provoked into stupid and uncharitable reactions. The debasement of the Niger Mission was partly the inevitable sequel to its previous over-exaltation by well-meaning idealists.

Yet the linguistic work of the Niger Mission survived the downfall of the mission, and in any case should ultimately be judged in a wider context than that of the moral aims of the Niger Mission or its parent, the C.M.S. Let us begin by noting what happened to linguistic work on the Niger after the mission was 'reconstituted'. Henry Johnson was lost to the Niger, and Dandeson Crowther in the Delta, with a handful of assistants, was too busy first organising an independent pastorate, then returning on negotiated terms to the C.M.S. fold, to continue linguistic work: most of the other Sierra Leonean linguists (e.g. Paul, Buck, Carew, John) had been dismissed or down-graded. A few exceptional individuals continued work under the new regime. P. J. Williams was transferred from Lokoja to a C.M.S. Delta station, and here he worked on Ijaw: he translated the whole New Testament and printing began in London in 1896, but was suspended after part of one Gospel only had been printed, because of local criticism, and was never resumed.[99] It may be suspected that this episode demonstrates the growth of a feeling on the part of the Niger peoples that the work of the Sierra Leoneans in the linguistic field was now less needed. Williams, disappointed, returned to Sierra Leone, where he served faithfully in the church for many years, but did no more linguistic work. A Sierra Leonean who joined the Niger Mission just before Crowther's retirement and death, Julius H. Spencer, was probably the last link between Freetown and Ibo studies. At Onitsha, Spencer worked under Johnson and his successor Dobinson, and in 1892 he produced an elementary grammar of Ibo, which was re-issued with slight revisions in 1901: much revised and enlarged by the Englishman, T. J. Dennis, but with Spencer's name still on the title-page, the work reappeared in 1916 and again in 1927. Spencer also produced two reading books and a translation of Genesis in Ibo, all published anonymously around 1900.[100] A third Sierra Leonean, O. Thomas, a schoolteacher at Lokoja in the 1880s, later worked under European missionaries in Nupeland, and contributed to a translation of the Psalms in 1903.[101]

---

[99] T. H. Darlow and H. F. Moule, *B.F.B.S. catalogue*, 'Ijaw'. Williams had worked in Ijaw country earlier in his mission career, before he transferred to Lokoja and worked on Igbira.
[100] Spencer had a Yoruba father and an Ibo mother, and was a school-teacher in Freetown before he came to the Niger as a catechist in 1885 (*Niger and Yoruba Notes*, August 1901, p. 11; *Western Equatorial Africa Diocesan Magazine*, December 1907, p. 98). The 1916 edition of the Ibo grammar was reviewed by Northcote Thomas in *Man*, 1917, article 126, who wrote that Dennis's revision 'represents a great advance over Spencer's little work, but even now it is very far from complete'.
[101] Presumably a son of J. Thomas, a catechist for many years at Igbebe, who did some unpublished work on the Bunu dialect of Yoruba, spoken in that vicinity, Obadiah Thomas went to school at Lokoja and then taught in the school (C.M.S. Archives, CA 3/o 43, paper of 14.2.1879). His Nupe work is referred to in Darlow and Moule, *op. cit.*, 'Nupe'.

Up to about 1910, Sierra Leoneans continued to be recruited for missionary service on the Niger and in the Delta, though the total between 1890 and 1910 was probably under a score. The longest serving of these late arrivals retired from Nigeria only in the 1940s, and one of them returned to Nigeria in 1957 to attend the celebrations of the centenary of Christianity on the Niger. At least one of this last generation of Sierra Leonean missionaries in Nigeria did linguistic work: S. S. Williams compiled a primer of Ijaw which was published anonymously in 1913.[102] I know of no later work on/in lower Niger-Benue languages prepared by a Sierra Leonean.

Up to the early 1890s, the majority of works published in/on lower Niger-Benue languages were by Sierra Leoneans, but thereafter the Sierra Leonean contribution rapidly declined. While more and more works were published anonymously and translations increasingly were issued by committees, we know that the direction of the work, and even much of the actual translation done, was passing into the hands of white missionaries. For instance, translation of the Ibo Bible, begun by the Sierra Leoneans Taylor, Johnson and others, became the responsibility of the Englishmen Dobinson and Dennis; translation of the Nupe Bible, begun by Crowther and Johnson, was completed by the Englishman J. L. Macintyre and the Canadian A. W. Banfield. In academic linguistics, Europeans similarly took over: Macintyre and Banfield succeeded Crowther in Nupe studies, a series of European professional linguists followed up the Crowther/Schön work in Ibo. Linguistically, the later work was of course sounder and more complete than the pioneer studies. The publications by Crowther and his Sierra Leonean assistants in the Niger Mission were almost all superseded within twenty years of the end of the original Niger Mission: linguistically, the pace of supersession was all to the good.

Another tendency of the new period was for a greater contribution to linguistic work to be made by Nigerians. An interesting example of this is the Ijaw Bible: begun by Sierra Leoneans, the translation continued under European supervision but the main translator was Daniel O. Ockiya, an Ijaw, who triumphantly completed the work, after fifty years' labour, in 1956.[103] At Onitsha, Dobinson and Dennis were assisted in the translation of the Ibo Bible (completed 1906) by the Ibos J. O. Mba and T. D. Anyaegbunam, the former having earlier also helped Johnson; another Ibo, D. O. Pepple, had earlier helped the Sierra Leonean translators in the Delta.[104] Undoubtedly the emergence of a group of Nigerian translators, sons of the Niger homelands and true mother-tongue speakers of the languages, was a great step forward. Yet it is only fair to note that most of the individuals named were first engaged for translation work during the Sierra Leonean regime.

Between the Europeans and the Nigerians, there was eventually no room for the Sierra Leoneans on the Niger, and linguistically this was no great loss. But in terms of cultural history, there is surely something to regret in the changes of the 1890s, something more than mere sentiment at the passing of an age and the supersession of a social group. With all their defects and limitations, the African language publications of the

---

[102] After retirement from Nigeria, Canon Williams became pastor of the church at Regent village, Sierra Leone, from which post he has only recently retired. I had the pleasure in April 1963 of introducing linguists at the Third West African Languages Congress to Canon Williams in his church at Regent. This was exactly fifty years after the publication of his book, which marked the end of Sierra Leonean study of the lower Niger-Benue languages.
[103] G. E. Coldham, *African Scriptures*, 1966, 1, pp. 239–40.
[104] *Niger and Yoruba Notes*, August 1898, p. 14.

Niger Mission had been unique in Africa, in that they were produced, not by highly-educated Europeans, but by relatively poorly-educated Africans, sons of a 'developing' community in only its second or third generation of modernisation. Though on the Niger the Sierra Leoneans had seemed outsiders, in the panorama of Africa theirs was a modern African achievement, indicating what could be done elsewhere when conditions became favourable. Nowhere else in Africa in the nineteenth century – or for that matter, in the early decades of the twentieth century – was so much linguistic work done, so much under African control, as in the Niger Mission. The work was often brash and unsound, but the very casualness with which the Sierra Leoneans tackled unstudied and complex African languages encouraged other Africans to participate. The collapse of the Niger Mission threw a wet blanket over African enthusiasm for the study of African languages. Hereafter, such study seemed to call for academic qualifications which few Africans could possess, and African participation was further discouraged by unyielding European supervision and the chilly reward of anonymous publication. African linguistics grew more scientific but it lacked soul. And it may be doubted whether the exclusion of Africans from enthusiastic participation in the study was in the long run helpful to the development of African linguistics. A general disinterest in the study or even the literate use of vernaculars, noted in many parts of Africa by observers during the first half of the present century, can be explained in many ways. But it may be suggested that had the Niger Mission been graciously reformed rather than cruelly disbanded – had, for instance, Johnson succeeded Crowther at the head in the early 1880s, followed by limited and tactful European collaboration, and by a gradual replacement of Sierra Leonean by Nigerian agents – the linguistic work might have been improved, without any loss of enthusiasm, and the example of the expanding achievement of the mission might have infected other areas with the understanding that the renovation of African languages was both a duty and a responsibility of Africans themselves.

Apart from the example it afforded of African interest in African language development, the cultural achievement of the linguistic work of the Niger Mission lay in its bringing into the literate community of the modern world most of the lower Niger-Benue languages. Five were put into writing and given their earliest printed literature; thus raising them in the estimation, not only of their speakers, but of those in the outside world who had doubted whether the languages of this part of Africa were capable of being transferred to paper. Two languages, Ibo and Ijaw, received considerable attention. Of these five languages, three have not developed to date more than a very limited printed literature (though two, Igala and Nupe, have at least a complete Bible), and Ijaw and Ibo have only a small printed literature. In none of the languages, therefore, have printed literatures developed of the size and variety of those in Hausa and Yoruba. In the case of the smaller languages, this is perhaps understandable; in the case of Ibo, it is disappointing. Can it be that Ibo made a bad start in the hands of the Niger Mission?

But since the days of the Mission, Ibo has received a good deal of attention from Europeans, from missionaries and latterly from professional linguists, and this too has apparently not put matters right. Undoubtedly the slow progress of Ibo literature has something to do with the dialects that baffled Schön and Crowther. Yet there was a time when it seemed that a respectably vigorous Ibo literature was imminent. We have commented on the limited circulation of the Mission publications in Ibo. Nevertheless, some roots must have been firmly laid, for the Ibo catechism was being issued, by the late 1890s in printings of 10,000 copies, and by the 1910s in printings of 100,000 copies.[105] Elementary schoolbooks were similarly in great demand. Thus the Ibo experienced an upsurge of interest in literacy – but it was not a genuine and continuing interest in *vernacular* literacy. Ibo children, having been taught to read through vernacular primers, were hurried on by their parents to acquire, and to read, English, the language of opportunity; in this way the Ibo gained a position of power in the colonial and post-colonial social and administrative order in Nigeria, but the Ibo language was neglected. It would seem therefore that continuing Ibo disinterest in the Ibo language is due to the peculiar Ibo environment or psychology, as much as to the failure of generations of linguists to produce an acceptable solution to the dialect problem.

Perhaps, however, it was the success of the Niger Mission in putting Ibo into writing which convinced this people that the modern world was truly open to them, that its magic was but learnable devices, and that the art of reading was the surest gateway to an improved personal life and a great communal future. Among the schoolboys who learnt to read at the Onitsha station of the Mission was the father of the first President of the Republic of Nigeria. While the Ijaw, the Nupe, the Igala and the Igbira have not rushed into twentieth century life with quite the reckless impetus of the Ibo, all now contribute to Nigerian progress; and with these peoples, as with the Ibo, it was perhaps the reducing of their language to writing which proved the decisive first step into the modern world. Crowther and the other early linguists who toiled over these languages certainly hoped that one consequence of their activity would be the spread of new social principles, effecting the modernisation – or 'regeneration' as they termed it – of the peoples involved. As the most famous missionary in Africa of this period wrote concerning similar linguistic activity: 'The influence of the sacred scriptures in the true negro language will be immense. If we call the actual amount of conversion the direct results of missions, and the wide diffusion of better principles the indirect, I have no hesitation in asserting that the latter are of more importance than the former.'[106] The Sierra Leoneans have now retired from the Niger; in their own national territory, the sons of Christian Freetown are today a tiny, disorientated minority; but the historical influence of the Freetown community may surely still be discerned, not only in the advance of Christianity in Nigeria, but in the social and cultural progress of the Nigerian peoples.

---

[105] *S.P.C.K. Reports*, 1898, 1912. Many of the later Ibo publications of the Niger Mission were re-issued, after revision, in the 1890s and later, some being issued many times. Without comparing the various editions, it is impossible to say to what extent the first version was the basis of later ones, and there is as yet no bibliography of Ibo minor publications after 1893. In the bibliography that follows, I have therefore not attempted to note later editions if these were published after 1893. I have gained the impression that a mass of Ibo minor literature was published by C.M.S. workers between 1893 and 1914.

[106] D. Livingstone, *Missionary correspondence*, 1961, p. 299, letter of 12.10.1855.

BIBLIOGRAPHY OF NUPE, TO 1890

1828–54 [Early vocabularies are noted in the text.]

1860 Samuel Crowther, Nupe primer. / By the Rev. S.C., / native missionary / of the C.M.S. / , C.M.S., London

[2] Note on orthography; 3–22 words, phrases, lessons, Scripture verses, Decalogue, Lord's Prayer, in Nupe only.

1860 S. Crowther, The first seven chapters / of the / Gospel / according to / St. Matthew / in Nupe / translated by the / Rev. S.C., / native missionary of the C.M.S. / , B.F.B.S., London

1864 S. Crowther, A / grammar / and / vocabulary / of the / Nupe language, / compiled by the / Right Rev. Samuel Crowther, D.D., / Bishop of the Niger Territory / , C.M.S., London

Advertisement; pp. i–vi Introductory Remarks; [7]–31 An outline of the grammar; 31–5 Proverbs; 37–208 Vocabulary, English-Nupe, Nupe-English.

1867 Gerhard Rohlfs, 'Die Art der Begrüssung bei verschiedenen Neger-stämmen', *Petermann's Mitteilungen*, pp. 333–6

A few greetings in 'Nyfe'.

1877 S. Crowther, Labari wangi yan Yohanu / The Gospel according to St. John./ Translated into Nupe / by the / Right Rev. S.C., D.D. / Bishop of the Niger Territory / , C.M.S., London

1882 [Henry Johnson], A / Nupe reading book / for the use of schools / in the / Niger Mission / of the C.M.S. / , S.P.C.K., London

pp. 48; Preface signed H. J., Kipo Hill.

1883 H. Johnson, The catechism / of the / Church of England, / translated into the / Nupe language. / By the / Ven. H.J., / Archdeacon of the Upper Niger and missionary of the / C.M.S. / , S.P.C.K., London

pp. 12, Nupe only.

1883* [a broadside in Nupe], S.P.C.K., London

1886 H. Johnson and J. Christaller, Vocabularies / of the / Niger and Gold Coast, / West Africa. / By the / Ven. Archdeacon H.J., / of the Upper Niger and the / Reverend J.C., / Ashantiland. / , S.P.C.K., London

pp. iii–iv Preface by R. N. Cust; 1–34 vocabularies, about 250 words in each language (5–8 English-Nupe, 9–12 English-Kakanda [a Nupe dialect]).

1886 [H. Johnson and Charles Paul], Alikéwǫ wǒró / nyá / Isa Kristu / tšótšin to zàbòlúgo-yì / , B.F.B.S., London

Gospel of St. Matthew.

1886 [H. Johnson and C. Paul], Labǎri wáṅgi / nya / Marku, nimi Nupé / , B.F.B.S., London

Gospel of St. Mark.

1887 [H. Johnson and C. Paul], Labǎri wáṅgi / nya / Luka, nimi Nupé / , B.F.B.S. London

Gospel of St. Luke.

1887 [H. Johnson and C. Paul], Labǎri wáṅgi / nya / Yohanu, nimi Nupé / , B.F.B.S., London

Gospel of St. John.

BIBLIOGRAPHY OF IGALA, TO 1890

1848–57   [Early vocabularies are noted in the text.]

1867   Adam George Coomber, Igara primer / by the / Rev. A.G.C., / native missionary of the C.M.S. / , C.M.S., London

Note on orthography; pp. 1–8 Part First [letters, words, phrases, in a cursive script]; 9–26 letters, words, phrases, Scripture verses, Decalogue, Lord's Prayer, in italic script; all in Igala only.

1886   Johnson and Christaller, [see Nupe bibliography]

On pp. 17–20, about 250 words English-Igala.

BIBLIOGRAPHY OF IGBIRA, TO 1891

1848–54   [Early vocabularies are noted in the text.]

1866   [Adam George Coomber], Igbira otakerida, / or, / Igbira primer / C.M.S., London

Note on orthography; pp. 1–8 letters, words, phrases, in a cursive script, Igbira only; 9–14 letters, words, phrases, numbers, in italic script; 15–35 Igbira-English, English-Igbira vocabulary.

1883   [Pythias James Williams], Igbira otakida / agubọ odži kẹkẹ / kẹrọ / almadžiri Kristu / yi / ọnurāda Igbira / A reading book / in the / Igbira language, / for use in the / Day and Sunday schools / , S.P.C.K., London

[3] Explanatory Remarks [signed 'P.J.W., native catechist, Gbebe']; 5–30 words lessons.

1883*   [a broadside in Igbira], S.P.C.K., London

1886   Johnson and Christaller, [see Nupe bibliography]

On pp. 13–16, about 250 words English-Igbira.

1891   P. J. Williams, The / Gospel according to / Saint Matthew. / Translated into the / Igbira language by / P.J.W. /, B.F.B.S., London.

1777–1856 [Early vocabularies are noted in the text.]

1857   Samuel Crowther, Isoama-Ibo primer / by the Rev. S.C., / native mission-ary / of the C.M.S. / , C.M.S., London

pp. 17: words, sentences, Lord's Prayer, Decalogue and Scripture verses, in Ibo only. Reprinted 1859.

[1859]   [John Christopher Taylor], Isuama-Ibo Katekism. / Translated from / Dr Watts' / first catechism / , C.M.S., London

[3] Preface; [4] Lord's Prayer; 5–18 Isuama-Ibo Katekism [Ibo only]; Preface signed J. C. Taylor, New Brompton, Nov. 1859.

1860   J. C. Taylor, Óku ọ́mma nké owu Matia / The Gospel according to / St. Matthew / translated into the Ibo language / by the Rev. J.C.T., / native missionary of the C.M.S. / , C.M.S., London

[1860 or 1861]*   J. C. Taylor, Akwukwọ ekpére Isuama-Ibo, A selection from the Book of Common Prayer, translated into Ibo, London

Title from R. Lepsius, *Standard Alphabet*, 2nd edition, 1863, p. 5.

[1860 or 1861]*   S. Crowther and J. C. Taylor, Isuama-Ibo primer, revised and enlarged by Rev. J. C. T., London

Title in Lepsius.

[1860 or 1861]*   J. C. Taylor, Isuama-Ibo sermon, preached at Trinity Church, Kissy Road, Freetown, February 17th, 1859, London

Title in Lepsius.

1861   James Frederick / Jacob Friedrich Schön, Oku Ibo / Grammatical elements / of the / Ibo language. / By the Rev. J.F.S., / Chaplain of Melville Hospital, Chatham, / member of the German Oriental Society, / late missionary in West-Africa / , London

pp. 1–4 Preface; [1]–8 Contents; 1–86 Grammatical elements.

1864   J. C. Taylor, Okuomma nke Marki ma Luki. / The Gospels / according to / St. Mark and St. Luke. / Translated into the Ibo language / by the Rev J.C.T., / native missionary / , B.F.B.S., London

1865   J. C. Taylor, Óku ómma nke owu Yohanu. / The Gospel / according to / St. John. / Translated into the Ibo language / by the / Rev. J.C.T., / native missionary / , B.F.B.S., London

1866   J. C. Taylor, Ma ôru nke Apostili. / The Acts of the Apostles, / the Epistles of Paul to the / Corinthians, Galatians, / and / Ephesians. / Translated into the Ibo language / by the / Rev. J.C.T., / native missionary / , B.F.B.S., London

Though not mentioned on the title-page, the volume also contains a translation of the Epistle to the Philippians.

1870]   Frederick Weeks Smart, Ibo hymns. / By Mr F.W.S., / native catechist / , C.M.S., London

pp. 14.

[1870]   F. W. Smart, An / Ibo primer. / By Mr F.W.S., / native catechist / , C.M.S., London

pp. 19; words, sentences, list of Delta towns, Scripture verses, all in Ibo.

1871   J. C. Taylor, Akukwo ekpére Isúama-Ibo. / A selection / from the / Book of
Common Prayer, / according to the use of the / United Church of England
and Ireland. / Translated into Ibo, / for the use of the native Christians of
that nation. / Edited by / Rev. J.C.T., / native missionary of the C.M.S. / ,
C.M.S., London
pp. 91; Calendar, Morning and Evening Prayers, Litany, some Collects, Holy Communion, Baptism, Matrimony, Burial.

[1871?]   Isuama-Ibo hymns, [London?]
pp. 8.

[1872?]   [J. C. Taylor], [no title page], [on p. 1 –] Isuama-Ibo Church Katekism,
[on p. 8 –] The Order of Confirmation, [on p. 12 –] The thanksgiving of
women after childbirth, [London]
pp. 15, all Ibo except titles.

1877   F. Müller, Grundriss der Sprachwissenschaft, Wien, 1/2, pp. 115–25
'Die Ibo-Sprache', an analysis based on earlier sources.

1879*   Hymnal, Religious Tract Society, London
Listed in East [see Earlier bibliography]: annual reports of R.T.S. in the B.M. were
destroyed during the war.

1882   S. Crowther, Vocabulary / of the / Ibo language / by / the Right Rev.
Bishop C. / , S.P.C.K., London
pp. [v]–viii Preface; 1–109 Ibo-English.

1883   S. Crowther and J. F. Schön, Vocabulary / of the / Ibo language / by / the
Right Rev. Bishop Crowther. / Part II – English-Ibo. / Prepared by J.F.S. / ,
S.P.C.K., London
pp. 90.

1886   Johnson and Christaller, [see Nupe bibliography]
On pp. 21–3, about 250 words of English-Ibo.

1887   [no title page: on front paper –] Ibo / Common Prayer. / Printed at the
Lower Niger Mission Press, Bonny
pp. 1–60 portions of Prayer Book (Morning and Evening Prayers, Holy Communion,
Baptism, Burial, Litany); second pagination 1–19 Ibo hymns [Ibo only]: prepared by
a committee under D. C. Crowther. In the B.M. copy, a loose insert in different print
contains [4 pp] part of Holy Communion service.

1887   [on front paper –] Ibo translation / of the / Church Catechism. / Printed at
the Lower Niger Mission Press, Bonny
pp. 10, Ibo only.

1887   [on front paper –] Ibo translation / of / Simpson's Primer. / Printed at the
Lower Niger Mission Press, Bonny
pp. 1 Prefatory Notice [on orthography]; 2–22 words, lessons. Another edition, or
version, S.P.C.K., London, 1897.

1887   [on front paper –] Ibo translation / of / Dr Watts' / First Catechism. /
Printed at the Lower Niger Mission Press, Bonny
pp. 18.

1889*   Henry Johnson compiler, Ibo hymnbook, printed at the Upper Niger
Mission Press, Lokoja or Onitsha
See the text, p. 87, n. 72. Another edition, revised by H. H. Dobinson, Onitsha, 1891*.

1890?*   Watts' First Catechism in Ibo, printed at the Upper Niger Mission Press, Lokoja or Onitsha

        See the text, p. 87, n. 72.

1890?*   Portions of the Prayer Book in Ibo, printed at the Upper Niger Mission Press, Lokoja or Onitsha

        See the text, p. 87, n. 72. Another edition, revised by H. H. Dobinson, Onitsha, 1891*

1890?*   Simpson's Primer in Ibo, printed at the Upper Niger Mission Press, Lokoja or Onitsha

        See the text, p. 87, n. 72.

1892*   Julius Spencer, [An elementary grammar / of the / Ibo language / by / Rev. J.S. / C.M.S. missionary, Asaba, Southern Nigeria / , S.P.C.K., London]

        A second, enlarged edition (pp. vi, 52), 1901, has the above title; the first edition, referred to in the Preface, was probably printed at Onitsha. A third edition, enlarged and revised by T. J. Dennis, S.P.C.K., 1916; a fourth edition, Sheldon Press, London, 1927, retitled A new grammar of Ibo.

1892   [James Antoninus Pratt], [on front paper –] Ozi omma nke / St. John / Printed at the Delta Pastorate Press, Bonny

        Gospel of St. John. Revised by H. H. Dobinson, published B.F.B.S., 1896.

[1892 or 1893]   [no title page: on half page –] Akukwo Paul onye Apostle barala nde-Galatians

        Epistle to the Galatians: pp. 13. The copy seen in B.F.B.S. Library is badly printed and finished – a tentative print? Catalogued as from the Delta Pastorate Press, Bonny. Revised by H. H. Dobinson, published B.F.B.S., 1896.

[1892 or 1893]   [no title page: on half page –] Akukwo Paul onye Apostle barala nde-Filippians

        Epistle to the Philippians, chapter I only in the copy seen at B.F.B.S. Library: pp. 2; otherwise as previous item.

[1892 or 1893]   [no title page: on half page –] Akukwo Paul onye Apostle barala nde-Ephesians

        Epistle to the Ephesians: pp. 12; copy seen at B.F.B.S. Library; otherwise as previous items.

[1892 or 1893]   [no title page: on half page-] Ozi-omma Jisus Kreist otu St. Matthew bora

        Gospel of St. Matthew, eleven chapters only in the copy seen at B.F.B.S. Library; otherwise as the previous items.

1893   [H. Johnson and H. H. Dobinson], Ozioma / nke / Jesu Kristi, dinwenu ayi. / Dika / Matyu, Marku, Luka na Johanu / si deya / , B.F.B.S., London

        On the page before the title page – 'The Four Gospels in the Ibo language. Translated in the C.M.S.'s station at Onitsha, R. Niger, 1889 and 1891'. Matthew and Mark were translated by H. Johnson, Luke and John by H. H. Dobinson, who also revised the first two. The Gospels are paginated individually and were probably also issued thus.

1668–1854 [Early vocabularies are noted in the text.]

1862   John Christopher Taylor, Ijọ or Idšọ primer. / By the / Rev. J.C.T., / native missionary of the C.M.S. / , C.M.S., London

[ii] note on orthography; [iii]–iv Preface; 5–21 words, lessons, Lord's Prayer; 22–40 Vocabulary [Ijaw-English].

[1870]   Walter Ebenezer L. Carew, Portions of Scripture / translated into the / Ubani dialect / of the / Idzŏ language. / By Mr W.E.L.C., / native catechist / , C.M.S., London

pp. 20.

[1870]   W. E. L. Carew, A portion / of / Simpson's Primer, / translated by / Mr W.E.L.C., / native catechist / , C.M.S., London

pp. 2–12 Lessons [Ijaw only]; 12–17 hymns [Ijaw and English]; 18–21 First catechism by Isaac Watts [part only, in Ijaw].

[1870]   W. E. L. Carew, A primer / in the / Ubani dialect / of the / Idšọ language. / By Mr W.E.L.C., / native catechist / , C.M.S., London

p. 2 note on orthography; 3–26 words, lessons.

1885   [no title page: on front paper –] Dr Watts / First Catechism. / (Brass dialect.) / Printed at the Lower Niger Mission Press, Brass

pp. 8, Ijaw only.

1886   [no title page: on front cover-] Idzọ / Common Prayer. / (Brass dialect.) / Printed at the Lower Niger Mission Press, Brass

pp. 1–48 Morning and Evening Prayers, Litany, Holy Communion, Baptism, Burial; 49–57 Hymns; all in Ijaw. A translation by Thomas Johnson, revised by a committee at Brass.

1886   [no title page: on front paper –] Church Catechism. / (Brass dialect.) / Printed at the Lower Niger Mission Press, Brass

pp. 7, Ijaw only.

1886   [John David Garrick], [no title page: on front paper –] Ayiba egberi mi nghọ / St. John ye / (Idzọ, Brass dialect.) / Printed at the Lower Niger Mission Press, Brass

Gospel of St. John.

1896   Pythias James Williams, Matyu gẹ ebi egberimi / Tentative version of a portion of / St. Matthew's Gospel translated into the / Ijọ language (Brass dialect) / by / Rev. P.J.W. / Translated from the Revised Version of 1881 / , B.F.B.S., London

Up to chapter 25, verse 24.

EARLIER BIBLIOGRAPHIES
(of Hausa, Kanuri, Nupe, Igala, Igbira, Ibo, Ijaw)

1812   J. C. Adelung and J. S. Vater, Mithridates oder allgemeine Sprachenkunde ..., Berlin, vol. 3.

1826, 1837   J. C. Prichard, Researches into the physical history of mankind, London, 2nd edition, vol. 1: 3rd edition, vol. 2.

1845–6   R. G. Latham, 'Upon the philological ethnography of the countries around the Bight of Biafra', *Edinburgh New Philosophical Journal*, 40, pp. 327–9
Repeated in *Journal of the Ethnological Society of London*, 1, 1848, pp. 224–7.

1847   J. S. Vater revised B. Jülg, Litteratur der Grammatiken, Lexika und Wörtersammlungen aller Sprachen der Erde, Berlin

1848   R. G. Latham, 'On the present state and recent progress of ethnographical philology, Part 1, Africa', *Report of the 17th meeting of the British Association, 1847*, pp. 154–229

1858   W. H. I. Bleek, The Library of Sir George Grey: Philology, vol. 1, part 2, London and Leipzig
More detailed descriptions of the items listed than any later bibliography. Most of the items now in the South African Public Library.

1883   R. N. Cust, A sketch of the modern languages of Africa, London

1903–11   T. H. Darlow and H. F. Moule, Historical catalogue of the printed editions of the Holy Scriptures in the Library of B.F.B.S., 4 vols., London

1911–12   B. Struck, 'Linguistic bibliography of Northern Nigeria', *Journal of the African Society*, 11, pp. 47–61, 213–30
Accurate, detailed, and very full (including some though not all translations).

1926–7   D. Westermann, 'Westsudanische Studien', *Mitteilungen des Seminars für Orientalische Sprachen*, 29, pp. 1–31, 30, pp. 173–201

1941   R. M. East, A vernacular bibliography for the languages of Nigeria, Literature Bureau, Zaria
Incomplete and inadequately detailed.

1952   D. Westermann and M. A. Bryan, Handbook of African languages Part 2 / Languages of West Africa, International African Institute, London

1953   M. de Lavergne de Tressan, Inventaire linguistique de l'A.O.F. et du Togo, Mémoires de l'IFAN no. 30, Dakar

1956   A. N. Tucker and M. A. Bryan, Handbook of African languages Part 3 / The non-Bantu languages of North-Eastern Africa, International African Institute, London
The 'complete' bibliography of East Saharan languages, including Kanuri, on pp. 184–5 is full but not quite complete.

1958   R. Jones, Africa bibliography series / West Africa, International African Institute, London

1959   U. Hintze, Bibliographie der Kwa-Sprachen und der Sprachen der Togo-Restvölker, Deutsche Akademie der Wissenschaften zu Berlin Institut für Orientforschung, Veröffentlichung 42, Berlin
Excludes translations.

1966   G. E. Coldham, A bibliography of Scriptures in African languages, B.F.B.S. London
Revising and updating the relevant sections in Darlow/Moule. Privately circulated (to date).

INDEX

Authors of works cited in the bibliography or in the footnotes are not listed below unless the reference in the text is accompanied by comment. The following terms which appear throughout are not listed: Niger; Benue; Delta; Sahara; Sudan; Lake Chad; Freetown; Sierra Leone; London; England.